LIBERALISM
AND ITS
CRITICS

Edited by
MICHAEL SANDEL

359

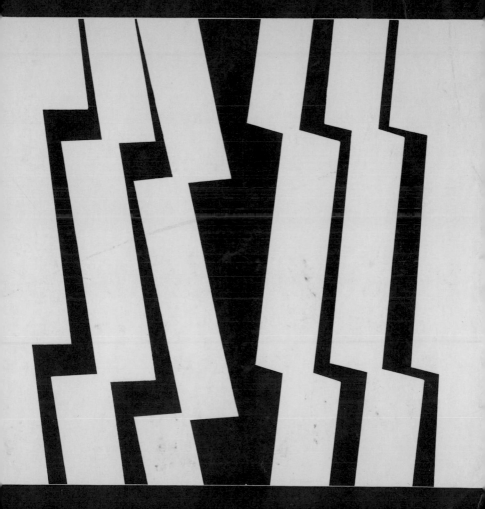

Liberalism and Its Critics

READINGS IN SOCIAL AND POLITICAL THEORY
Edited by William Connolly and Steven Lukes

Language and Politics *edited by Michael Shapiro*
Legitimacy and the State *edited by William Connolly*
Liberalism and Its Critics *edited by Michael J. Sandel*
Power *edited by Steven Lukes*
Rational Choice *edited by Jon Elster*

Liberalism and Its Critics

Edited by MICHAEL J. SANDEL

New York University Press
New York

© Michael J. Sandel, 1984

First published in 1984 in the U.S.A. by
New York University Press, Washington Square,
New York N.Y. 10003

Reprinted 1987

Library of Congress Cataloging in Publication Data

Main entry under title:
  Liberalism and its critics. — (Readings in social and political
  theory)
  Bibliography: p.
  Includes index.
  1. Liberalism — Addresses, essays, lectures.
  I. Sandel, Michael J.   II. Series
  JC571.L536   1984   302.5'1   84–16503

ISBN 0-8147-7840-2
ISBN 0-8147-7841-0 (pbk.)

p 10 9 8 7 6 5 4 3

Typeset by Katerprint Co. Ltd, Oxford
Printed and bound in Great Britain

Contents

Introduction

Liberals often take pride in defending what they oppose —
pornography, for example, or unpopular views. They say the state
should not impose a preferred way of life, but should leave its
citizens as free as possible to choose their own values and ends,
consistent with a similar liberty for others. This commitment to
freedom of choice requires liberals constantly to distinguish
between permission and praise, between allowing a practice and
endorsing it. It is one thing to allow pornography, they argue,
something else to affirm it.

Conservatives sometimes exploit this distinction by ignoring it.
They charge that those who would allow abortions favour abor-
tion, that opponents of school prayer oppose prayer, that those
who defend the rights of Communists sympathize with their cause.
And in a pattern of argument familiar in our politics, liberals reply
by invoking higher principles; it is not that they dislike, say,
pornography less, rather that they value toleration, or freedom of
choice, or fair procedures more.

But in contemporary debate, the liberal rejoinder seems
increasingly fragile, its moral basis increasingly unclear. Why
should toleration and freedom of choice prevail when other
important values are also at stake? Too often the answer implies
some version of moral relativism, the idea that it is wrong to
'legislate morality' because all morality is merely subjective. 'Who
is to say what is literature and what is filth? That is a value
judgement, and whose values should decide?'

Relativism usually appears less as a claim than as a question.
('Who is to judge?') But it is a question that can also be asked of the
values that liberals defend. Toleration and freedom and fairness
are values too, and they can hardly be defended by the claim that
no values can be defended. So it is a mistake to affirm liberal values
by arguing that all values are merely subjective. The relativist
defence of liberalism is no defence at all.

What, then, can be the moral basis of the higher principles the liberal invokes? Recent political philosophy has offered two main alternatives — one utilitarian, the other Kantian. The utilitarian view, following John Stuart Mill, defends liberal principles in the name of maximizing the general welfare. The state should not impose on its citizens a preferred way of life, even for their own good, because doing so will reduce the sum of human happiness, at least in the long run; better that people choose for themselves, even if, on occasion, they get it wrong. 'The only freedom which deserves the name', writes Mill, 'is that of pursuing our own good in our own way, so long as we do not attempt to deprive others of theirs, or impede their efforts to obtain it.' He adds that his argument does not depend on any notion of abstract right, only on the principle of the greatest good for the greatest number. 'I regard utility as the ultimate appeal on all ethical questions; but it must be utility in the largest sense, grounded on the permanent interests of man as a progressive being.'[1]

Many objections have been raised against utilitarianism as a general doctrine of moral philosophy. Some have questioned the concept of utility, and the assumption that all human goods are in principle commensurable. Others have objected that by reducing all values to preferences and desires, utilitarians are unable to admit qualitative distinctions of worth, unable to distinguish noble desires from base ones. But most recent debate has focused on whether utilitarianism offers a convincing basis for liberal principles, including respect for individual rights.

In one respect, utilitarianism would seem well-suited to liberal purposes. Maximizing utility does not require judging people's values, only aggregating them. And the willingness to aggregate preferences without judging them suggests a tolerant spirit, even a democratic one. When people go to the polls, we count their votes whatever they are.

But the utilitarian calculus is not always as liberal as it first appears. If enough cheering Romans pack the Colosseum to watch the lion devour the Christian, the collective pleasure of the Romans will surely outweigh the pain of the Christian, intense though it be. Or if a big majority abhors a small religion and wants it banned, the balance of preferences will favour suppression, not toleration. Utilitarians sometimes defend individual rights on the grounds that respecting them now will serve utility in the long run. But this calculation is precarious and contingent. It hardly secures the liberal promise not to impose on some the values of others. As the majority will is an inadequate instrument of liberal politics, so the utilitarian philosophy is an inadequate foundation for liberal principles. The case against utilitarianism was made most powerfully by Kant. He argued that empirical principles, such as utility, were unfit to serve as basis for the moral law. A wholly instrumental defence of freedom and rights not only leaves rights vulnerable, but fails to respect the inherent dignity of persons. The utilitarian calculus treats people as means to the happiness of others, not as ends in themselves, worthy of respect.[2]

Contemporary liberals extend Kant's argument with the claim that utilitarianism fails to take seriously the distinction between persons. In seeking above all to maximize the general welfare, the utilitarian treats society as a whole as if it were a single person; it conflates our many, diverse desires into a single system of desires, and tries to maximize. It is indifferent to the distribution of satisfactions among persons, except insofar as this may affect the overall sum. But this fails to respect our plurality and distinctness. It uses some as means to the happiness of all, and so fails to respect each as an end in himself.

Modern-day Kantians reject the utilitarian approach in favour of an ethic that takes rights more seriously. In their view, certain rights are so fundamental that even the general welfare cannot override them. As John Rawls writes: 'Each person possesses an inviolability founded on justice that even the welfare of society as a whole cannot override . . . the rights secured by justice are not subject to political bargaining or to the calculus of social interests.'[3]

So Kantian liberals need an account of rights that does not depend on utilitarian considerations. More than this, they need an account that does not depend on any particular conception of the good, that does not presuppose the superiority of one way of life over others. Only a justification neutral among ends could preserve the liberal resolve not to favour any particular ends, or to impose on its citizens a preferred way of life.

But what sort of justification could this be? How is it possible to affirm certain liberties and rights as fundamental without embracing some vision of the good life, without endorsing some ends over others? It would seem we are back to the relativist predicament – to affirm liberal principles without embracing any particular ends.

The solution proposed by Kantian liberals is to draw a distinction between the 'right' and the 'good' – between a framework of basic rights and liberties, and the conceptions of the good that people may choose to pursue within the framework. It is one thing for the state to support a fair framework, they argue, something else to affirm some particular ends. For example, it is one thing to defend the right to free speech so that people may be free to form their own opinions and choose their own ends, but something else to support it on the grounds that a life of political discussion is inherently worthier than a life unconcerned with public affairs, or on the grounds that free speech will increase the general welfare. Only the first defence is available on the Kantian view, resting as it does on the ideal of a neutral framework.

Now the commitment to a framework neutral among ends can be seen as a kind of value – in this sense the Kantian liberal is no relativist – but its value consists precisely in its refusal to affirm a preferred way of life or conception of the good. For Kantian liberals, then, the right is prior to the good, and in two senses. First, individual rights cannot be sacrificed for the sake of the general good, and second, the principles of justice that specify these rights cannot be premissed on any particular vision of the good life. What justifies the rights is not that they maximize the general welfare or otherwise promote the good, but rather that they comprise a fair framework within which individuals and groups can choose their own values and ends, consistent with a similar liberty for others.

Of course, proponents of the rights-based ethic notoriously disagree on what rights are fundamental, and on what political arrangements the ideal of the neutral framework requires. Egalitarian liberals support the welfare state, and favour a scheme of civil liberties together with certain social and economic rights – rights to welfare, education, health care, and so on. Libertarian liberals defend the market economy, and claim that redistributive policies violate people's rights; they favour a scheme of civil liberties combined with a strict regime of private property rights. But whether egalitarian or libertarian, rights-based liberalism begins with the claim that we are separate, individual persons, each with our own aims, interests, and conceptions of the good, and seeks a framework of rights that will enable us to realize our capacity as free moral agents, consistent with a similar liberty for others.

Within academic philosophy, the last decade or so has seen the ascendance of the rights-based ethic over the utilitarian one, due in large part to the powerful influence of John Rawls' *A Theory of Justice*. In the debate between utilitarian and rights-based theories, the rights-based ethic has come to prevail. The legal philosopher H. L. A. Hart recently described the shift from 'the old faith that some form of utilitarianism must capture the essence of political morality' to the new faith that 'the truth must lie with a doctrine of basic human rights, protecting specific basic liberties and interests of individuals. . . . Whereas not so long ago great energy and much ingenuity of many philosophers were devoted to making some form of utilitarianism work, latterly such energies and ingenuity have been devoted to the articulation of theories of basic rights.'[4]

But in philosophy as in life, the new faith becomes the old orthodoxy before long. Even as it has come to prevail over its utilitarian rival, the rights-based ethic has recently faced a growing challenge from a different direction, from a view that gives fuller expression to the claims of citizenship and community than the liberal vision allows. Recalling the arguments of Hegel against Kant, the communitarian critics of modern liberalism question the claim for the priority of the right over the good, and the picture of the freely-choosing individual it embodies. Following Aristotle, they argue that we cannot justify political arrangements without reference to common purposes and ends, and that we cannot conceive our personhood without reference to our role as citizens, and as participants in a common life.

This debate reflects two contrasting pictures of the self. The rights-based ethic, and the conception of the person it embodies, were shaped in large part in the encounter with utilitarianism. Where utilitarians conflate our many desires into a single system of desire, Kantians insist on the separateness of persons. Where the utilitarian self is simply defined as the sum of its desires, the Kantian self is a choosing self, independent of the desires and ends it may have at any moment. As Rawls writes: 'The self is prior to the ends which are affirmed by it; even a dominant end must be chosen from among numerous possibilities.'[5]

The priority of the self over its ends means I am never defined by my aims and attachments, but always capable of standing back to survey and assess and possibly to revise them. This is what is means to be a free and independent self, capable of choice. And this is the vision of the self that finds expression in the ideal of the state as a neutral framework. On the rights-based ethic, it is precisely because we are essentially separate, independent selves that we need a neutral framework, a framework of rights that refuses to choose among competing purposes and ends. If the self is prior to its ends, then the right must be prior to the good.

Communitarian critics of rights-based liberalism say we cannot conceive ourselves as independent in this way, as bearers of selves wholly detached from our aims and attachments. They say that certain of our roles are partly constitutive of the persons we are — as citizens of a country, or members of a movement, or partisans of a cause. But if we are partly defined by the communities we inhabit, then we must also be implicated in the purposes and ends characteristic of those communities. As Alasdair MacIntyre writes: 'what is good for me has to be the good for one who inhabits these roles.'[6] Open-ended though it be, the story of my life is always embedded in the story of those communities from which I derive my identity – whether family or city, tribe or nation, party or cause. On the communitarian view, these stories make a moral difference, not only a psychological one. They situate us in the world, and give our lives their moral particularity.

What is at stake for politics in the debate between unencumbered selves and situated ones? What are the practical differences between a politics of rights and a politics of the common good? On some issues, the two theories may produce different arguments for similar policies. For example, the civil rights movement of the 1960s might be justified by liberals in the name of human dignity and respect for persons, and by communitarians in the name of recognizing the full membership of fellow citizens wrongly excluded from the common life of the nation. And where liberals might support public education in hopes of equipping students to become autonomous individuals, capable of choosing their own ends and pursuing them effectively, communitarians might support public education in hopes of equipping students to become good citizens, capable of contributing meaningfully to public deliberations and pursuits.

On other issues, the two ethics might lead to different policies. Communitarians would be more likely than liberals to allow a town to ban pornographic bookstores, on the grounds that pornography offends its way of life and the values that sustain it. But a politics of civic virtue does not always part company with liberalism in favour of conservative policies. For example, communitarians would be more willing than some rights-oriented liberals to see states enact laws regulating plant closings, to protect their communities from the disruptive effects of capital mobility and sudden industrial change. More generally, where the liberal regards the expansion of individual rights and entitlements as unqualified moral and political progress, the communitarian is troubled by the tendency of liberal programmes to displace politics from smaller forms of association to more comprehensive ones. Where libertarian liberals defend the private economy and egalitarian liberals defend the welfare state, communitarians worry about the concentration of power in both the corporate economy and the bureaucratic state, and the erosion of those intermediate forms of community that have at times sustained a more vital public life.

Liberals often argue that a politics of the common good, and the moral particularity it affirms, open the way to prejudice and intolerance. The modern nation-state is not the Athenian *polis*, they point out; the scale and diversity of modern life have rendered the Aristotelian political ethic nostalgic at best and dangerous at worst. Any attempt to govern by a vision of the good is likely to lead to a slippery slope of totalitarian temptations.

Communitarians reply that intolerance flourishes most where forms of life are dislocated, roots unsettled, traditions undone. In our day, the totalitarian impulse has sprung less from the convictions of confidently situated selves than from the confusions of atomized, dislocated, frustrated selves, at sea in a world where common meanings have lost their force. As Hannah Arendt has written: 'What makes mass society so difficult to bear is not the number of people involved, or at least not primarily, but the fact that the world between them has lost its power to gather them together, to relate and to separate them.'[7] Insofar as our public life has withered, our sense of common involvement diminished, to that extent we lie vulnerable to the mass politics of totalitarian solutions. So responds the party of the common good to the party of rights. If the party of the common good is right, our most pressing moral and political project is to revitalize those civic republican possibilities implicit in our tradition but fading in our time.

The writings collected in this volume present leading statements of rights-based liberalism and some examples of the communitarian, or republican alternatives to that position. The principle of selection has been to shift the focus from the familiar debate between utilitarians and Kantian liberals – a debate now largely decided – in order to consider a more powerful challenge to the rights-based ethic, the one indebted, broadly speaking, to Aristotle, Hegel, and the civic republican tradition.

In 'Two Concepts of Liberty', perhaps the most influential essay of post-war political theory, Isaiah Berlin gives vigorous expression to a powerful strand of modern liberalism. It is the claim for the ultimate plurality of human values, and the impossibility ever finally of reconciling them.

The world that we encounter in ordinary experience is one in which we are faced with choices between ends equally ultimate, and claims equally absolute, the realization of some of which must inevitably involve the sacrifice of others. Indeed, it is because this is their situation that men place such immense value upon the freedom to choose; for if they had assurance that in some perfect state, realizable by men on earth, no ends pursued by them would ever be in conflict, the necessity and agony of choice would disappear, and with it the central importance of the freedom to choose.

In view of the ultimate plurality of ends, Berlin concludes, freedom of choice is 'a truer and more humane ideal' than the alternatives. And he quotes with approval the view of Joseph Schumpeter that 'to realise the relative validity of one's convictions, and yet stand for them unflinchingly, is what distinguishes a civilised man from a barbarian.' Although Berlin is not strictly speaking a relativist – he affirms the ideal of freedom of choice – his position comes perilously close to foundering on the relativist predicament. If one's convictions are only relatively valid, why stand for them unflinchingly? In a tragically-configured moral universe, such as Berlin assumes, is the ideal of freedom any *less* subject than competing ideals to the ultimate incommensurability of values? If so, in what can its privileged status consist? And if freedom has no morally privileged status, if it is just one value among many, then what can be said for liberalism?

John Rawls' *A Theory of Justice*, the major text of contemporary liberal political philosophy, proposes a way of acknowledging a plurality of ends while affirming nonetheless a regulative framework of liberties and rights. He would avoid the self-refuting tendency of liberal theories by deriving principles of justice in a way that does not presuppose any particular conception of the good. These principles specify basic rights and liberties, but, owing to the design of the 'original position', do not choose in advance among competing purposes and ends. The excerpts of his work presented here do not concern such widely-discussed topics as the original position and the difference principle, but focus instead on the structure of his theory, and in particular on his claim for the priority of the right over the good, and for the conception of the self that this entails. These are the aspects of his theory most characteristic of Kantian liberalism and most sharply opposed to the Aristotelian tradition and other teleological conceptions.

The selections by Ronald Dworkin, Friedrich Hayek, and Robert Nozick illustrate the similarities and differences within rights-based liberalism. Whereas Rawls and Dworkin advocate certain welfare rights that Hayek and Nozick oppose, all argue in the name of rights which do not rely on notions of moral merit or virtue, or an intrinsic human good. Dworkin, sympathetic to the welfare state, holds that 'government must be neutral' on the question of the good life, that political decisions must be 'independent of any particular conception of the good life, or of what gives value to life' (p. 64). And Nozick, arguing for a minimal state, holds that government must be 'scrupulously *neutral* between its citizens' (p. 105). Although Hayek and Nozick oppose the redistributive policies favoured by Rawls, all reject the idea that income and wealth should be distributed according to moral merit or desert. For Rawls, basing entitlements on merit or desert or virtue would put the good before the right; in order to preserve the priority of right, he bases entitlements on 'legitimate expectations' instead. For Hayek and Nozick, tying entitlements to merit or desert would undercut people's freedom to barter and trade as they choose, and to reap the benefits of their exchanges. All put primary emphasis on what Rawls calls 'the distinction between persons', and Nozick terms 'the fact of our separate existences'.

One reason liberals are reluctant to tie people's entitlements to their merit or desert or virtue is that, on the liberal conception of the person, the qualities that distinguish people as meritorious or deserving or virtuous are not essential constituents but only contingent attributes of the self. As Rawls argues, the endowments and opportunities that lead to good character and conscientious effort are 'arbitrary from a moral point of view' (p. 45). On the liberal view, the self is prior to its ends – this assures its capacity to *choose* its ends – and also prior to its roles and dispositions – this assures its independence from social conventions, and hence its separateness of person, its individuality.

The writings by Alasdair MacIntyre, Peter Berger, and Michael Sandel challenge the liberal view by calling into question the picture of the self that it implies. In contrast to the liberal's unencumbered self, MacIntyre proposes a narrative conception of the self, a self constituted in part by a life story with a certain *telos*, or point. As the *telos* is not fixed or fully identifiable in advance, the unity of a life is the unity of a narrative quest, a quest whose object is a fuller and more adequate grasp of a good only intimated at the outset. On the narrative view, my identity is not independent of my aims and attachments, but partly constituted by them; I am situated from the start, embedded in a history which locates me among others, and implicates my good in the good of the communities whose stories I share.

Berger offers an illuminating contrast between the concepts of honour and dignity, which corresponds to the contrast between situated selves and unencumbered ones. The concept of honour implies that identity is essentially linked to social roles, he points out, while the concept of dignity, more familiar in the liberal ethic, implies that identity is essentially independent of such roles. In the passage entitled 'Justice and the Good', I try to argue, along similar lines, that the unencumbered self presupposed by rights-based liberalism cannot adequately account for such notions as character, self-knowledge, and friendship.

The writings by Charles Taylor, Michael Walzer, and Michael Oakeshott illustrate the consequences for political discourse of assuming situated selves rather than unencumbered selves. In different ways, each sees political discourse as proceeding within the common meanings and traditions of a political community, not appealing to a critical standpoint wholly external to those meanings. Taylor identifies Hegel's critique of Kantian liberalism with Hegel's distinction between '*Sittlichkeit*' and '*Moralität*'. *Sittlichkeit*, or 'ethical life', refers to norms embodied in a community, and describes my obligation *qua* participant to realize moral possibilities already there, implicit in a way of life. *Moralität*, by contrast, refers to abstract principles as yet unrealized in a community, available to us *qua* individuals standing in radical opposition to community. As Taylor explains, Hegel runs counter to the moral instinct of liberalism by holding that not *Moralität* but *Sittlichkeit* is the highest moral aspiration; human freedom can only be achieved in a realized *Sittlichkeit*, an ethical political community that expresses the identity of its members.

Walzer, a democratic socialist, and Oakeshott, a traditional conservative, both conceive moral reasoning as an appeal to meanings internal to a political community, not an appeal to abstract principles. For Walzer, unlike Rawls, the case for the welfare state begins with a theory of membership, not rights.

Welfare rights are fixed only when a community adopts some program of mutual provision. There are strong arguments to be made that, under given historical conditions, such-and-such a program should be adopted. But these are not arguments about individual rights; they are arguments about the character of a particular political community (p. 204).

Similarly for Oakeshott, political traditions.

> compose a pattern and at the same time they intimate a sympathy for what does not fully appear. Political activity is the exploration of that sympathy; and consequently, relevant political reasoning will be the convincing exposure of a sympathy, present but not yet followed up, and the convincing demonstration that now is the appropriate moment for recognizing it. . . . In politics, then, every enterprise is a consequential enterprise, the pursuit, not of a dream, or of a general principle, but of an intimation (p. 229).

Finally, Hannah Arendt considers how the framers of the American constitution might have embodied freedom in what she regards as the only institution capable of sustaining it, the ward or council system. She concludes that the Western democracies have managed to represent interests but not to cultivate citizenship; they protect civil liberties but have not secured freedom in the republican sense of a shared public life.

NOTES

1 Mill, *On Liberty*, ch. I.
2 See Kant, *Groundwork of the Metaphysics of Morals* (1785); and 'On the Common Saying: "This May be True In Theory, But It Does Not Apply in Practice."' (1793).
3 Rawls, *A Theory of Justice* (Oxford: Oxford University Press, 1971), pp. 3–4.
4 Hart, 'Between Utility and Rights', in Alan Ryan (ed.) *The Idea of Freedom* (Oxford: Oxford University Press, 1979), p. 77.
5 Rawls, *A Theory of Justice*, p. 560.
6 MacIntyre, *After Virtue* (Notre Dame: University of Notre Dame Press, 1981), p. 205.
7 Arendt, *The Human Condition* (Chicago: University of Chicago Press, 1958), pp. 52–3.

PART I

1

Isaiah Berlin:
Two Concepts of Liberty*

I

To coerce a man is to deprive him of freedom — freedom from
what? Almost every moralist in human history has praised freedom.
Like happiness and goodness, like nature and reality, the meaning
of this term is so porous that there is little interpretation that it
seems able to resist. I do not propose to discuss either the history or
the more than two hundred senses of this protean word recorded by
historians of ideas. I propose to examine no more than two of the
senses — but those central ones, with a great deal of human history
behind them, and, I dare say, still to come. The first of these
political senses of freedom or liberty (I shall use both words to
mean the same), which (following much precedent) I shall call the
'negative' sense, is involved in the answer to the question 'What is
the area within which the subject — a person or group of persons —
is or should be left to do or be what he is able to do or be, without
interference by other persons?' The second, which I shall call the
positive sense, is involved in the answer to the question 'What, or
who, is the source of control or interference that can determine
someone to do, or be, this rather than that?' The two questions are
clearly different, even though the answers to them may overlap.

THE NOTION OF 'NEGATIVE' FREEDOM

I am normally said to be free to the degree to which no man or body
of men interferes with my activity. Political liberty in this sense is

*© Oxford University Press 1969. Reprinted from *Four Essays on
Liberty*, by Sir Isaiah Berlin (1969), by permission of Oxford University
Press.

simply the area within which a man can act unobstructed by others. If I am prevented by others from doing what I could otherwise do, I am to that degree unfree; and if this area is contracted by other men beyond a certain minimum, I can be described as being coerced, or, it may be, enslaved. Coercion is not, however, a term that covers every form of inability. If I say that I am unable to jump more than ten feet in the air, or cannot read because I am blind, or cannot understand the darker pages of Hegel, it would be eccentric to say that I am to that degree enslaved or coerced. Coercion implies the deliberate interference of other human beings within the area in which I could otherwise act. You lack political liberty or freedom only if you are prevented from attaining a goal by human beings.[1] Mere incapacity to attain a goal is not lack of political freedom.[2] This is brought out by the use of such modern expressions as 'economic freedom' and its counterpart, 'economic slavery'. It is argued, very plausibly, that if a man is too poor to afford something on which there is no legal ban – a loaf of bread, a journey round the world, recourse to the law courts – he is as little free to have it as he would be if it were forbidden him by law. If my poverty were a kind of disease, which prevented me from buying bread, or paying for the journey round the world or getting my case heard, as lameness prevents me from running, this inability would not naturally be described as a lack of freedom, least of all political freedom. It is only because I believe that my inability to get a given thing is due to the fact that other human beings have made arrangements whereby I am, whereas others are not, prevented from having enough money with which to pay for it, that I think myself a victim of coercion or slavery. In other words, this use of the term depends on a particular social and economic theory about the causes of my poverty or weakness. If my lack of material means is due to my lack of mental or physical capacity, then I begin to speak of being deprived of freedom (and not simply about poverty) only if I accept the theory.[3] If, in addition, I believe that I am being kept in want by a specific arrangement which I consider unjust or unfair, I speak of economic slavery or oppression. 'The nature of things does not madden us, only ill will does', said Rousseau. The criterion of oppression is the part that I believe to be played by other human beings, directly or indirectly, with or without the intention of doing so, in frustrating my wishes. By being free in this sense I mean not being interfered with by others. The wider the area of non-interference the wider my freedom.

This is what the classical English political philosophers meant when they used this word.[4] They disagreed about how wide the area could or should be. They supposed that it could not, as things were, be unlimited, because if it were, it would entail a state in which all men could boundlessly interfere with all other men; and this kind of 'natural' freedom would lead to social chaos in which men's minimum needs would not be satisfied; or else the liberties of the weak would be suppressed by the strong. Because they perceived that human purposes and activities do not automatically harmonize with one another, and because (whatever their official doctrines) they put high value on other goals, such as justice, or happiness, or culture, or security, or varying degrees of equality, they were prepared to curtail freedom in the interests of other values and, indeed, of freedom itself. For, without this, it was impossible to create the kind of association that they thought desirable. Consequently, it is assumed by these thinkers that the area of men's free action must be limited by law. But equally it is assumed, especially by such libertarians as Locke and Mill in England, and Constant and Tocqueville in France, that there ought to exist a certain minimum area of personal freedom which must on no account be violated; for if it is overstepped, the individual will find himself in an area too narrow for even that minimum development of his natural faculties which alone makes it possible to pursue, and even to conceive, the various ends which men hold good or right or sacred. It follows that a frontier must be drawn between the area of private life and that of public authority. Where it is to be drawn is a matter of argument, indeed of haggling. Men are largely interdependent, and no man's activity is so completely private as never to obstruct the lives of others in any way. 'Freedom for the pike is death for the minnows'; the liberty of some must depend on the restraint of others. 'Freedom for an Oxford don', others have been known to add, 'is a very different thing from freedom for an Egyptian peasant.'

This proposition derives its force from something that is both true and important, but the phrase itself remains a piece of political claptrap. It is true that to offer political rights, or safeguards against intervention by the state, to men who are half-naked, illiterate, underfed, and diseased is to mock their condition; they need medical help or education before they can understand, or make use of, an increase in their freedom. What is freedom to those who cannot make use of it? Without adequate conditions for the use of freedom, what is the value of freedom? First things come first: there are situations, as a nineteenth-century Russian radical writer declared, in which boots are superior to the works of Shakespeare; individual freedom is not everyone's primary need. For freedom is not the mere absence of frustration of whatever kind; this would inflate the meaning of the word until it meant too much or too little. The Egyptian peasant needs clothes or medicine before, and more than, personal liberty, but the minimum freedom that he needs today, and the greater degree of freedom that he may need tomorrow, is not some species of freedom peculiar to him, but identical with that of professors, artists, and millionaires.

What troubles the consciences of Western liberals is not, I think, the belief that the freedom that men seek differs according to their social or economic conditions, but that the minority who possess it have gained it by exploiting, or, at least, averting their gaze from, the vast majority who do not. They believe, with good reason, that if individual liberty is an ultimate end for human beings, none should be deprived of it by others; least of all that some should enjoy it at the expense of others. Equality of liberty; not to treat others as I should not wish them to treat me; repayment of my debt to those who alone have made possible my liberty or prosperity or enlightenment; justice, in its simplest and most universal sense – these are the foundations of liberal morality. Liberty is not the only goal of men. I can, like the Russian critic Belinsky, say that if others are to be deprived of it – if my brothers are to remain in poverty, squalor, and chains – then I do not want it for myself, I reject it with both hands and infinitely prefer to share their fate. But nothing is gained by a confusion of terms. To avoid glaring inequality or widespread misery I am ready to sacrifice some, or all, of my freedom: I may do so willingly and freely: but it is freedom that I am giving up for the sake of justice or equality or the love of my fellow men. I should be guilt-stricken, and rightly so, if I were not, in some circumstances, ready to make this sacrifice. But a sacrifice is not an increase in what is being sacrificed, namely freedom, however great the moral need or the compensation for it. Everything is what it is: liberty is liberty, not equality or fairness or justice or culture, or human happiness or a quiet conscience. If the liberty of myself or my class or nation depends on the misery of a number of other human beings, the system which promotes this is unjust and immoral. But if I curtail or lose my freedom, in order to lessen the shame of such inequality, and do not thereby materially increase the individual liberty of others, an absolute loss of liberty occurs. This may be compensated for by a gain in justice or in happiness or in peace, but the loss remains, and it is a confusion of values to say that although my 'liberal', individual freedom may go by the board, some other kind of freedom – 'social' or 'economic' – is increased. Yet it remains true that the freedom of some must at times be curtailed to secure the freedom of others. Upon what principle should this be done? If freedom is a sacred, untouchable value, there can be no such principle. One or other of these conflicting rules or principles must, at any rate in practice, yield: not always for reasons which can be clearly stated, let alone generalized into rules or universal maxims. Still, a practical compromise has to be found.

Philosophers with an optimistic view of human nature and a belief in the possibility of harmonizing human interests, such as Locke or Adam Smith and, in some moods, Mill, believed that social harmony and progress were compatible with reserving a large area for private life over which neither the state nor any other authority must be allowed to trespass. Hobbes, and those who agreed with him, especially conservative or reactionary thinkers, argued that if men were to be prevented from destroying one another and making social life a jungle or a wilderness, greater safeguards must be instituted to keep them in their places; he wished correspondingly to increase the area of centralized control and decrease that of the individual. But both sides agreed that some portion of human existence must remain independent of the sphere of social control. To invade that preserve, however small, would be despotism. The most eloquent of all defenders of freedom and privacy, Benjamin Constant, who had not forgotten the Jacobin dictatorship, declared that at the very least the liberty of religion, opinion, expression, property, must be guaranteed against arbitrary invasion. Jefferson, Burke, Paine, Mill, compiled different catalogues of individual liberties, but the argument for keeping authority at bay is always substantially the same. We must preserve a minimum area of personal freedom if we are not to 'degrade or deny our nature'. We cannot remain absolutely free, and must give up some of our liberty to preserve the rest. But total self-surrender is self-defeating. What then must be the minimum be? That which a man cannot give up without offending against the essence of his human nature. What is this essence? What are the standards which it entails? This has been, and perhaps always will be, a matter of infinite debate. But whatever the principle in terms of which the area of non-interference is to be drawn, whether it is that of natural law or natural rights, or of utility or the pronouncements of a categorical imperative, or the sanctity of the social contract, or any other concept with which men have sought to clarify and justify their convictions, liberty in this sense means liberty *from*; absence of interference beyond the shifting, but always recognizable, frontier. 'The only freedom which deserves the name is that of pursuing our own good in our own way', said the most celebrated of its champions. If this is so, is compulsion ever justified? Mill had no doubt that it was. Since justice demands that all individuals be entitled to a minimum of freedom, all other individuals were of necessity to be restrained, if need be by force, from depriving anyone of it. Indeed, the whole function of law was the prevention of just such collisions: the state was reduced to what Lassalle contemptuously described as the functions of a nightwatchman or traffic policeman.

What made the protection of individual liberty so sacred to Mill? In his famous essay he declares that, unless men are left to live as they wish 'in the path which merely concerns themselves', civilization cannot advance; the truth will not, for lack of a free market in ideas, come to light; there will be no scope for spontaneity, originality, genius, for mental energy, for moral courage. Society will be crushed by the weight of 'collective mediocrity'. Whatever is rich and diversified will be crushed by the weight of custom, by men's constant tendency to conformity, which breeds only 'withered capacities', 'pinched and hidebound', 'cramped and warped' human beings. 'Pagan self-assertion is as worthy as Christian self-denial'. 'All the errors which a man is likely to commit against advice and warning are far outweighed by the evil of allowing others to constrain him to what they deem is good.' The defence of liberty consists in the 'negative' goal of warding off interference. To threaten a man with persecution unless he submits to a life in which he exercises no choices of his goals; to block before him every door but one, no matter how noble the prospect upon which it opens, or how benevolent the motives of those who arrange this, is to sin against the truth that he is a man, a being with a life of his own to live. This is liberty as it has been conceived by liberals in the modern world from the days of Erasmus (some would say of Occam) to our own. Every plea for civil liberties and individual rights, every protest against exploitation and humiliation, against the encroachment of public authority, or the mass hypnosis of custom or organized propaganda, springs from this individualistic, and much disputed, conception of man.

Three facts about this position may be noted. In the first place Mill confuses two distinct notions. One is that all coercion is, in so far as it frustrates human desires, bad as such, although it may have to be applied to prevent other, greater evils; while non-interference, which is the opposite of coercion, is good as such, although it is not the only good. This is the 'negative' conception of liberty in its classical form. The other is that men should seek to discover the truth, or to develop a certain type of character of which Mill approved – critical, original, imaginative, independent, non-conforming to the point of eccentricity, and so on – and that truth can be found, and such character can be bred, only in conditions of freedom. Both these are liberal views, but they are not identical, and the connection between them is, at best, empirical. No one would argue that truth or freedom of self-expression could flourish where dogma crushes all thought. But the evidence of history tends to show (as, indeed, was argued by James Stephen in his formidable attack on Mill in his *Liberty, Equality, Fraternity*) that integrity, love of truth, and fiery individualism grow at least as often in severely disciplined communities among, for example, the puritan Calvinists of Scotland or New England, or under military discipline, as in more tolerant or indifferent societies; and if this is so, Mill's argument for liberty as a necessary condition for the growth of human genius falls to the ground. If his two goals proved incompatible, Mill would be faced with a cruel dilemma, quite apart from the futher difficulties created by the inconsistency of his doctrines with strict utilitarianism, even in his own humane version of it.[5]

In the second place, the doctrine is comparatively modern. There seems to be scarcely any discussion of individual liberty as a conscious political ideal (as opposed to its actual existence) in the ancient world. Condorcet had already remarked that the notion of individual rights was absent from the legal conceptions of the Romans and Greeks; this seems to hold equally of the Jewish, Chinese, and all other ancient civilizations that have since come to light.[6] The domination of this ideal has been the exception rather than the rule, even in the recent history of the West. Nor has liberty in this sense often formed a rallying cry for the great masses of mankind. The desire not to be impinged upon, to be left to oneself, has been a mark of high civilization both on the part of individuals and communities. The sense of privacy itself, of the area of personal relationships as something sacred in its own right, derives from a conception of freedom which, for all its religious roots, is scarcely older, in its developed state, than the Renaissance or the Reformation.[7] Yet its decline would mark the death of a civilization, of an entire moral outlook.

The third characteristic of this notion of liberty is of greater importance. It is that liberty in this sense is not incompatible with some kinds of autocracy, or at any rate with the absence of self-government. Liberty in this sense is principally concerned with the area of control, not with its source. Just as a democracy may, in fact, deprive the individual citizen of a great many liberties which he might have in some other form of society, so it is perfectly conceivable that a liberal-minded despot would allow his subjects a large measure of personal freedom. The despot who leaves his subjects a wide area of liberty may be unjust, or encourage the wildest inequalities, care little for order, or virtue, or knowledge; but provided he does not curb their liberty, or at least curbs it less than many other regimes, he meets with Mill's specification.[8] Freedom in this sense is not, at any rate logically, connected with democracy or self-government. Self-government may, on the whole, provide a better guarantee of the preservation of civil liberties than other regimes, and has been defended as such by libertarians. But there is no necessary connection between individual liberty and democratic rule. The answer to the question 'Who governs me?' is logically distinct from the question 'How far does government interfere with me?' It is in this difference that the great contrast between the two concepts of negative and positive liberty, in the end, consists.[9] For the 'positive' sense of liberty comes to light if we try to answer the question, not 'What am I free to do or be?', but 'By whom am I ruled?' or 'Who is to say what I am, and what I am not, to be or do?' the connection between democracy and individual liberty is a good deal more tenuous than it seemed to many advocates of both. The desire to be governed by myself, or at any rate to participate in the process by which my life is to be controlled, may be as deep a wish as that of a free area for action, and perhaps historically older. But it is not a desire for the same thing. So different is it, indeed, as to have led in the end to the great clash of ideologies that dominates our world. For it is this – the 'positive' conception of liberty: not freedom from, but freedom to – to lead one prescribed form of life – which the adherents of the 'negative' notion represent as being, at times, no better than a specious disguise for brutal tyranny.

II

THE NOTION OF POSITIVE FREEDOM

The 'positive' sense of the word 'liberty' derives from the wish on the part of the individual to be his own master. I wish my life and decisions to depend on myself, not on external forces of whatever kind. I wish to be the instrument of my own, not of other men's, acts of will. I wish to be a subject, not an object; to be moved by reasons, by conscious purposes, which are my own, not by causes which affect me, as it were, from outside. I wish to be somebody, not nobody; a doer — deciding, not being decided for, self-directed and not acted upon by external nature or by other men as if I were a thing, or an animal, or a slave incapable of playing a human role, that is, of conceiving goals and policies of my own and realizing them. This is at least part of what I mean when I say that I am rational, and that it is my reason that distinguishes me as a human being from the rest of the world. I wish, above all, to be conscious of myself as a thinking, willing, active being, bearing responsibility for my choices and able to explain them by references to my own ideas and purposes. I feel free to the degree that I believe this to be true, and enslaved to the degree that I am made to realize that it is not.

The freedom which consists in being one's own master, and the freedom which consists in not being prevented from choosing as I do by other men, may, on the face of it, seem concepts at no great logical distance from each other — no more than negative and positive ways of saying much the same thing. Yet the 'positive' and 'negative' notions of freedom historically developed in divergent directions not always by logically reputable steps, until, in the end, they came into direct conflict with each other.

One way of making this clear is in terms of the independent momentum which the, initially perhaps quite harmless, metaphor of self-mastery acquired. 'I am my own master'; 'I am slave to no man'; but may I not (as Platonists or Hegelians tend to say) be a slave to nature? Or to my own 'unbridled' passions? Are these not so many species of the identical genus 'slave' — some political or legal, others moral or spiritual? Have not men had the experience of liberating themselves from spiritual slavery, or slavery to nature, and do they not in the course of it become aware, on the one hand, of a self which dominates, and, on the other, of something in them which is brought to heel? This dominant self is then variously identified with reason, with my 'higher nature', with the self which calculates and aims at what will satisfy it in the long run, with my 'real', or 'ideal', or 'autonomous' self, or with my self 'at its best'; which is then contrasted with irrational impulse, uncontrolled desires, my 'lower' nature, the pursuit of immediate pleasures, my 'empirical' or 'heteronomous' self, swept by every gust of desire and passion, needing to be rigidly disciplined if it is ever to rise to the full height of its 'real' nature. Presently the two selves may be represented as divided by an even larger gap: the real self may be conceived as something wider than the individual (as the term is normally understood), as a social 'whole' of which the individual is an element or aspect: a tribe, a race, a church, a state, the great society of the living and the dead and the yet unborn. This entity is then identified as being the 'true' self which, by imposing its collective, or 'organic', single will upon its recalcitrant 'members', achieves its own, and therefore their, 'higher' freedom. The perils of using organic metaphors to justify the coercion of some men by others in order to raise them to a 'higher' level of freedom have often been pointed out. But what gives such plausibility as it has to this kind of language is that we recognize that it is possible, and at times justifiable, to coerce men in the name of some goal (let us say, justice or public health) which they would, if they were more enlightened, themselves pursue, but do not, because they are blind or ignorant or corrupt. This renders it easy for me to conceive of myself as coercing others for their own sake, in their, not my, interest. I am then claiming that I know what they truly need better than they know it themselves. What, at most, this entails is that they would not resist me if they were rational and as wise as I and understood their interests as I do. But I may go on to claim a good deal more than this. I may declare that they are actually aiming at what in their benighted state they consciously resist, because there exists within them an occult entity – their latent rational will, or their 'true' purpose – and that this entity, although it is belied by all that they overtly feel and do and say, is their 'real' self, of which the poor empirical self in space and time may know nothing or little; and that this inner spirit is the only self that deserves to have its wishes taken into account.[10] Once I take this view, I am in a position to ignore the actual wishes of men or societies, to bully, oppress, torture them in the name, and on behalf, of their 'real' selves, in the secure knowledge that whatever is the true goal of man (happiness, performance of duty, wisdom, a just society, self-fulfilment) must be identical with his freedom – the free choice of his 'true', albeit often submerged and inarticulate, self.

This paradox has been often exposed. It is one thing to say that I know what is good for X, while he himself does not; and even to ignore his wishes for its – and his – sake; and a very different one to say that he has *eo ipso* chosen it, not indeed consciously, not as he seems in everyday life, but in his role as a rational self which his empirical self may not know – the 'real' self which discerns the good, and cannot help choosing it once it is revealed. This monstrous impersonation, which consists in equating what X would choose if he were something he is not, or at least not yet, with what X actually seeks and chooses, is at the heart of all political theories of self-realization. It is one thing to say that I may be coerced for my own good which I am too blind to see: this may, on occasion, be for my benefit; indeed it may enlarge the scope of my liberty. It is another to say that if it is my good, then I am not being coerced, for I have willed it, whether I know this or not, and am free (or 'truly' free) even while my poor earthly body and foolish mind bitterly reject it, and struggle against those who seek however benevolently to impose it, with the greatest desperation.

This magical transformation, or sleight of hand (for which William James so justly mocked the Hegelians), can no doubt be perpetrated just as easily with the 'negative' concept of freedom, where the self that should not be interfered with is no longer the individual with his actual wishes and needs as they are normally conceived, but the 'real' man within, identified with the pursuit of some ideal purpose not dreamed of by his empirical self. And, as in the case of the 'positively' free self, this entity may be inflated into some super-personal entity – a state, a class, a nation, or the march of history itself, regarded as a more 'real' subject of attributes than the empirical self. But the 'positive' conception of freedom as self-mastery, with its suggestion of a man divided against himself, has, in fact, and as a matter of history, of doctrine and of practice, lent itself more easily to this splitting or personality into two: the transcendent, dominant controller, and the empirical bundle of desires and passions to be disciplined and brought to heel. It is this historical fact that has been influential. This demonstrates (if demonstration of so obvious a truth is needed) that conceptions of freedom directly derive from views of what constitutes a self, a person, a man. Enough manipulation with the definition of man, and freedom can be made to mean whatever the manipulator wishes. Recent history has made it only too clear that the issue is not merely academic.

The consequences of distinguishing between two selves will become even clearer if one considers the two major forms which the desire to be self-directed – directed by one's 'true' self – has historically taken: the first, that of self-abnegation in order to attain independence; the second, that of self-realization, or total self-identification with a specific principle or ideal in order to attain the selfsame end. . . .

III

LIBERTY AND SOVEREIGNTY

The French Revolution, like all great revolutions, was, at least in its Jacobin form, just such an eruption of the desire for 'positive' freedom of collective self-direction on the part of a large body of Frenchmen who felt liberated as a nation, even though the result was, for a good many of them, a severe restriction of individual freedoms. Rousseau had spoken exultantly of the fact that the laws of liberty might prove to be more austere than the yoke of tyranny. Tyranny is service to human masters. The law cannot be a tyrant. Rousseau does not mean by liberty the 'negative' freedom of the individual not to be interfered with within a defined area, but the possession by all, and not merely by some, of the fully qualified members of a society of a share in the public power which is entitled to interfere with every aspect of every citizen's life. The liberals of the first half of the nineteenth century correctly foresaw that liberty in this 'positive' sense could easily destroy too many of the 'negative' liberties that they held sacred. They pointed out that the sovereignty of the people could easily destroy that of individuals. Mill explained, patiently and unanswerably, that government by the people was not, in his sense, necessarily freedom at all. For those who govern are not necessarily the same 'people' as those who are governed, and democratic self-government is not the government 'of each by himself' but, at best, of 'each by the rest'. Mill and his disciples spoke of the tyranny of the majority and of the tyranny of 'the prevailing feeling and opinion', and saw no great difference between that and any other kind of tyranny which encroaches upon men's activities beyond the sacred frontiers of private life.

No one saw the conflict between the two types of liberty better, or expressed it more clearly, than Benjamin Constant. He pointed out that the transference by a successful rising of the unlimited authority, commonly called sovereignty, from one set of hands to another does not increase liberty, but merely shifts the burden of slavery. He reasonably asked why a man should deeply care whether he is crushed by a popular government or by a monarch, or even by a set of oppressive laws. He saw that the main problem for those who desire 'negative', individual freedom is not who wields this authority, but how much authority should be placed in any set of hands. For unlimited authority in anybody's grasp was bound, he believed, sooner or later, to destroy somebody. He maintained that usually men protested against this or that set of governors as oppressive, when the real cause of oppression lay in the mere fact of the accumulation of power itself, wherever it might happen to be, since liberty was endangered by the mere existence of absolute authority as such. 'It is not the arm that is unjust', he wrote, 'but the weapon that is too heavy – some weights are too heavy for the human hand.' Democracy may disarm a given oligarchy, a given privileged individual or set of individuals, but it can still crush individuals as mercilessly as any previous ruler. In an essay comparing the liberty of the moderns with that of the ancients he said that an equal right to oppress – or interfere – is not equivalent to liberty. Nor does universal consent to loss of liberty somehow miraculously preserve it merely by being universal, or by being consent. If I consent to be oppressed, or acquiesce in my condition with detachment or irony, am I the less oppressed? If I sell myself into slavery, am I the less a slave? If I commit suicide, am I the less dead because I have taken my own life freely? 'Popular government is a spasmodic tyranny, monarchy a more efficiently centralized despotism.' Constant saw in Rousseau the most dangerous enemy of individual liberty, because he had declared that 'by giving myself to all I give myself to none'. Constant could not see why, even though the sovereign is 'everybody', it should not oppress one of the 'members' of its indivisible self, if it so decided. I may, of course, prefer to be deprived of my liberties by an assembly, or a family, or a class, in which I am a minority. It may give me an opportunity one day of persuading the others to do for me that to which I feel I am entitled. But to be deprived of my liberty at the hands of my family or friends or fellow citizens is to be deprived of it just as effectively. Hobbes was at any rate more candid: he did not pretend that a sovereign does not enslave: he justified this slavery, but at least did not have the effrontery to call it freedom.

Throughout the nineteenth century liberal thinkers maintained that if liberty involved a limit upon the powers of any man to force me to do what I did not, or might not, wish to do, then, whatever the ideal in the name of which I was coerced, I was not free; that the doctrine of absolute sovereignty was a tyrannical doctrine in itself. If I wish to preserve my liberty, it is not enough to say that is must not be violated unless someone or other – the absolute ruler, or the popular assembly, or the King in Parliament, or the judges, or some combination of authorities, or the laws themselves – for the laws may be oppressive – authorizes its violation. I must establish a society in which there must be some frontiers of freedom which nobody should be permitted to cross. Different names or natures may be given to the rules that determine these frontiers: they may be called natural rights, or the word of God, or Natural Law, or the demands of utility or of the 'permanent interests of man'; I may believe them to be valid *a priori*, or assert them to be my own ultimate ends, or the ends of my society or culture. What these rules or commandments will have in common is that they are accepted so widely, and are grounded so deeply in the actual nature of men as they have developed through history, as to be, by now, an essential part of what we mean by being a normal human being. Genuine belief in the inviolability of a minimum extent of individual liberty entails some such absolute stand. For it is clear that it has little to hope for from the rule of majorities; democracy as such is logically uncommitted to it, and historically has at times failed to protect it, while remaining faithful to its own principles. Few governments, it has been observed, have found much difficulty in causing their subjects to generate any will that the government wanted. 'The triumph of despotism is to force the slaves to declare themselves free. It may need no force; the slaves may proclaim their freedom quite sincerely: but they are none the less slaves. Perhaps the chief value for liberals of political – 'positive' – rights, of participating in the government, is as a means for protecting what they hold to be an ultimate value, namely individual – 'negative' – liberty.

But if democracies can, without ceasing to be democratic, suppress freedom, at least as liberals have used the word, what would make a society truly free? For Constant, Mill, Tocqueville, and the liberal tradition to which they belong, no society is free unless it is governed by at any rate two interrelated principles: first, that no power, but only rights, can be regarded as absolute, so that all men, whatever power governs them, have an absolute right to refuse to behave inhumanly; and, second, that there are frontiers, not artificially drawn, within which men should be inviolable, these frontiers being defined in terms of rules so long and widely accepted that their observance has entered into the very conception of what it is to be a normal human being, and, therefore, also of what it is to act inhumanly or insanely; rules of which it would be absurd to say, for example, that they could be abrogated by some formal procedure on the part of some court or sovereign body. When I speak of a man as being normal, a part of what I mean is that he could not break these rules easily, without a qualm of revulsion. it is such rules as these that are broken when a man is declared guilty without trial, or punished under a retroactive law; when children

are ordered to denounce their parents, friends to betray one
another, soldiers to use methods of barbarism; when men are
tortured or murdered, or minorities are massacred because they
irritate a majority or a tyrant. Such acts, even if they are made legal
by the sovereign, cause horror even in these days, and this springs
from the recognition of the moral validity – irrespective of the laws
– of some absolute barriers to the imposition of one man's will on
another. The freedom of a society, or a class or a group, in this
sense of freedom, is measured by the strength of these barriers, and
the number and importance of the paths which they keep open for
their members – if not for all, for at any rate a great number of
them.[11]

This is almost at the opposite pole from the purposes of those
who believe in liberty in the 'positive' – self-directive – sense. The
former want to curb authority as such. The latter want it placed
in their own hands. That is a cardinal issue. These are not two
different interpretations of a single concept, but two profoundly
divergent and irreconcilable attitudes to the ends of life. It is as well
to recognize this, even if in practice it is often necessary to strike a
compromise between them. For each of them makes absolute
claims. These claims cannot both be fully satisfied. But it is a
profound lack of social and moral understanding not to recognize
that the satisfaction that each of them seeks is an ultimate value
which, both historically and morally, has an equal right to be
classed among the deepest interests of mankind.

IV

THE ONE AND THE MANY

One belief, more than any other, is responsible for the slaughter of
individuals on the altars of the great historical ideals – justice
or progress or the happiness of future generations, or the sacred
mission or emancipation of a nation or race or class, or even liberty
itself, which demands the sacrifice of individuals for the freedom of
society. This is the belief that somewhere, in the past or in the
future, in divine revelation or in the mind of an individual thinker,
in the pronouncements of history or science, or in the simple heart
of an uncorrupted good man, there is a final solution. This ancient
faith rests on the conviction that all the positive values in which

men have believed must, in the end, be compatible, and perhaps even entail one another. 'Nature binds truth, happiness, and virtue together as by an indissoluble chain', said one of the best men who ever lived, and spoke in similar terms of liberty, equality, and justice.[12] But is this true? It is a commonplace that neither political equality nor efficient organization nor social justice is compatible with more than a modicum of individual liberty, and certainly not with unrestricted *laissez-faire*; that justice and generosity, public and private loyalties, the demands of genius and the claims of society, can conflict violently with each other. And it is no great way from that to the generalization that not all good things are compatible, still less all the ideals of mankind. But somewhere, we shall be told, and in some way, it must be possible for all these values to live together, for unless this is so, the universe is not a cosmos, not a harmony; unless this is so, conflicts of values may be an intrinsic, irremovable element in human life. To admit that the fulfilment of some of our ideals may in principle make the fulfilment of others impossible is to say that the notion of total human fulfilment is a formal contradiction, a metaphysical chimera. For every rationalist metaphysician, from Plato to the last disciples of Hegel or Marx, this abandonment of the notion of a final harmony in which all riddles are solved, all contradictions reconciled, is a piece of crude empiricism, abdication before brute facts, intolerable bankruptcy of reason before things as they are, failure to explain and to justify, to reduce everything to a system, which 'reason' indignantly rejects. But if we are not armed with an *a priori* guarantee of the proposition that a total harmony of true values is somewhere to be found – perhaps in some ideal realm the characteristics of which we can, in our finite state, not so much as conceive – we must fall back on the ordinary resources of empirical observation and ordinary human knowledge. And these certainly give us no warrant for supposing (or even understanding what would be meant by saying) that all good things, or all bad things for that matter, are reconcilable with each other. The world that we encounter in ordinary experience is one in which we are faced with choices between ends equally ultimate, and claims equally absolute, the realization of some of which must inevitably involve the sacrifice of others. Indeed, it is because this is their situation that men place such immense value upon the freedom to choose; for if they had assurance that in some perfect state, realizable by men on earth, no ends pursued by them would ever be in conflict, the necessity and agony of choice would disappear, and with it the central importance of the freedom to choose. Any method of bringing this final state nearer would then seem fully justified, no matter how much freedom were sacrificed to forward its advance. It is, I have no doubt, some such dogmatic certainty that has been responsible for the deep, serene, unshakeable conviction in the minds of some of the most merciless tyrants and persecutors in history that what they did was fully justified by its purpose. I do not say that the ideal of self-perfection — whether for individuals or nations or churches or classes — is to be condemned in itself, or that the language which was used in its defence was in all cases the result of a confused or fraudulent use of words, or of moral or intellectual perversity. Indeed, I have tried to show that it is the notion of freedom in its 'positive' sense that is at the heart of the demands for national or social self-direction which animate the most powerful and morally just public movements of our time, and that not to recognize this is to misunderstand the most vital facts and ideas of our age. But equally it seems to me that the belief that some single formula can in principle be found whereby all the diverse ends of men can be harmoniously realized is demonstrably false. If, as I believe, the ends of men are many, and not all of them are in principle compatible with each other, then the possibility of conflict — and of tragedy — can never wholly be eliminated from human life, either personal or social. The necessity of choosing between absolute claims is then an inescapable characteristic of the human condition. This gives its value to freedom as Acton had conceived of it — as an end in itself, and not as a temporary need, arising out of our confused notions and irrational and disordered lives, a predicament which a panacea could one day put right.

I do not wish to say that individual freedom is, even in the most liberal societies, the sole, or even the dominant, criterion of social action. We compel children to be educated, and we forbid public executions. These are certainly curbs to freedom. We justify them on the grounds that ignorance, or a barbarian upbringing, or cruel pleasures and excitements are worse for us than the amount of restraint needed to repress them. This judgement in turn depends on how we determine good and evil, that is to say, on our moral, religious, intellectual, economic, and aesthetic values; which are, in their turn, bound up with our conception of man, and of the basic demands of his nature. In other words, our solution of such problems is based on our vision, by which we are consciously or unconsciously guided, of what constitutes a fulfilled human life, as contrasted with Mill's 'cramped and warped', 'pinched and hidebound' natures. To protest against the laws governing censorship or personal morals as intolerable infringements of personal liberty presupposes a belief that the activities which such laws forbid are fundamental needs of men as men, in a good (or, indeed, any) society. To defend such laws is to hold that these needs are not essential, or that they cannot be satisfied without sacrificing other values which come higher – satisfy deeper needs – than individual freedom, determined by some standard that is not merely subjective, a standard for which some objective status – empirical or *a priori* – is claimed.

The extent of a man's, or a people's, liberty to choose to live as they desire must be weighed against the claims of many other values, of which equality, or justice, or happiness, or security, or public order are perhaps the most obvious examples. For this reason, it cannot be unlimited. We are rightly reminded by R. H. Tawney that the liberty of the strong, whether their strength is physical or economic, must be restrained. This maxim claims respect, not as a consequence of some *a priori* rule, whereby the respect for the liberty of one man logically entails respect for the liberty of others like him; but simply because respect for the principles of justice, or shame at gross inequality of treatment, is as basic in men as the desire for liberty. That we cannot have everything is a necessary, not a contingent, truth. Burke's plea for the constant need to compensate, to reconcile, to balance; Mill's plea for novel 'experiments in living' with their permanent possibility of error, the knowledge that it is not merely in practice but in principle impossible to reach clear-cut and certain answers, even in an ideal world of wholly good and rational men and wholly clear ideas – may madden those who seek for final solutions and single, all-embracing systems, guaranteed to be eternal. Nevertheless, it is a conclusion that cannot be escaped by those who, with Kant, have learnt the truth that out of the crooked timber of humanity no straight thing was ever made.

There is little need to stress the fact that monism, and faith in a single criterion, has always proved a deep source of satisfaction both to the intellect and to the emotions. Whether the standard of judgement derives from the vision of some future perfection, as in the minds of the *philosophes* in the eighteenth century and their technocratic successors in our own day, or is rooted in the past – *la terre et les morts* – as maintained by German historicists or French theocrats, or neo-Conservatives in English-speaking countries, it is bound, provided it is inflexible enough, to encounter some unforeseen and unforeseeable human development, which it will not fit; and will then be used to justify the *a priori* barbarities of Procrustes – the vivisection of actual human societies into some fixed pattern dictated by our fallible understanding of a largely imaginary past or a wholly imaginary future. To preserve our absolute categories or ideals at the expense of human lives offends equally against the principles of science and of history; it is an attitude found in equal measure on the right and left wings in our days, and is not reconcilable with the principles accepted by those who respect the facts.

Pluralism, with the measure of 'negative' liberty that it entails, seems to me a truer and more human ideal than the goals of those who seek in the great, disciplined, authoritarian structures the ideal of 'positive' self-mastery by classes, or peoples, or the whole of mankind. It is truer, because it does, at least, recognize the fact that human goals are many, not all of them commensurable, and in perpetual rivalry with one another. To assume that all values can be graded on one scale, so that it is a mere matter of inspection to determine the highest, seems to me to falsify our knowledge that men are free agents, to represent moral decision as an operation which a slide-rule could, in principle, perform. To say that in some ultimate, all-reconciling, yet realizable synthesis, duty *is* interest, or individual freedom *is* pure democracy or an authoritarian state, is to throw a metaphysical blanket over either self-deceit or deliberate hypocrisy. It is more humane because it does not (as the system builders do) deprive men, in the name of some remote, or incoherent, ideal, of much that they have found to be indispensable to their life as unpredictably self-transforming human beings.[13] In the end, men choose between ultimate values; they choose as they do, because their life and thought are determined by fundamental moral categories and concepts that are, at any rate over large stretches of time and space, a part of their being and thought and sense of their own identity; part of what makes them human.

It may be that the ideal of freedom to choose ends without claiming eternal validity for them, and the pluralism of values connected with this, is only the late fruit of our declining capitalist civilization: an ideal which remote ages and primitive societies have not recognized, and one which posterity will regard with curiosity, even sympathy, but little comprehension. This may be so; but no sceptical conclusions seem to me to follow. Principles are not less sacred because their duration cannot be guaranteed. Indeed, the very desire for guarantees that our values are eternal and secure in some objective heaven is perhaps only a craving for the certainties of childhood or the absolute values of our primitive past. 'To realise the relative validity of one's convictions', said an admirable writer of our time, 'and yet stand for them unflinchingly, is what distinguishes a civilised man from a barbarian.' To demand more than this is perhaps a deep and incurable metaphysical need; but to allow it to determine one's practice is a symptom of an equally deep, and more dangerous, moral and political immaturity.

NOTES

[1] I do not, of course, mean to imply the truth of the converse.

[2] Helvétius made this point very clearly: 'The free man is the man who is not in irons, nor imprisoned in a gaol, nor terrorized like a slave by the fear of punishment . . . it is not lack of freedom not to fly like an eagle or swim like a whale.'

[3] The Marxist conception of social laws is, of course, the best-known version of this theory, but it forms a large element in some Christian and utilitarian, and all socialist, doctrines.

[4] 'A free man', said Hobbes, 'is he that . . . is not hindered to do what he hath the will to do.' Law is always a 'fetter', even if it protects you from being bound in chains that are heavier than those of the law, say, some more repressive law or custom, or arbitrary despotism or chaos. Bentham says much the same.

[5] This is but another illustration of the natural tendency of all but a very few thinkers to believe that all the things they hold good must be intimately connected, or at least compatible, with one another. The history of thought, like the history of nations, is strewn with examples of inconsistent, or at least disparate, elements artificially yoked together in a despotic system, or held together by the danger of some common enemy. In due course the danger passes, and conflicts between the allies arise, which often disrupt the system, sometimes to the great benefit of mankind.

[6] See the valuable discussion of this in Michel Villey, *Leçons d'histoire de la philosophie du droit*, who traces the embryo of the notion of subjective rights to Occam.

[7] Christian (and Jewish or Moslem) belief in the absolute authority of divine or natural laws, or in the equality of all men in the sight of God, is very different from belief in freedom to live as one prefers.

[8] Indeed, it is arguable that in the Prussia of Frederick the Great or in the Austria of Josef II men of imagination, originality, and creative genius, and, indeed, minorities of all kinds, were less persecuted and felt the pressure, both of institutions and custom, less heavy upon them than in many an earlier or later democracy.

[9] 'Negative liberty' is something the extent of which, in a given case, is difficult to estimate. It might, *prima facie*, seem to depend simply on the power to choose between at any rate two alternatives. Nevertheless, not all choices are equally free, or free at all. If in a totalitarian state I betray my friend under threat of torture, perhaps even if I act from

fear of losing my job, I can reasonably say that I did not act freely. Nevertheless, I did, of course, make a choice, and could, at any rate in theory, have chosen to be killed or tortured or imprisoned. The mere existence of alternatives is not, therefore, enough to make my action free (although it may be voluntary) in the normal sense of the word. The extent of my freedom seems to depend on (a) how many possibilities are open to me (although the method of counting these can never be more than impressionistic. Possibilities of action are not discrete entities like apples, which can be exhaustively enumerated); (b) how easy or difficult each of these possibilities is to actualize; (c) how important in my plan of life, given my character and circumstances, these possibilities are when compared with each other; (d) how far they are closed and opened by deliberate human acts; (e) what value not merely the agent, but the general sentiment of the society in which he lives, puts on the various possibilities. All these magnitudes must be 'integrated', and a conclusion, necessarily never precise, or indisputable, drawn from this process. It may well be that there are many incommensurable kinds and degrees of freedom, and that they cannot be drawn up on any single scale of magnitude. Moreover, in the case of societies, we are faced by such (logically absurd) questions as 'Would arrangement X increase the liberty of Mr A more than it would that of Messrs B, C, and D between them, added together?' The same difficulties arise in applying utilitarian criteria. Nevertheless, provided we do not demand precise measurement, we can give valid reasons for saying that the average subject of the King of Sweden is, on the whole, a good deal freer today than the average citizen of Spain or Albania. Total patterns of life must be compared directly as wholes, although the method by which we make the comparison, and the truth of the conclusions, are difficult or impossible to demonstrate. But the vagueness of the concepts, and the multiplicity of the criteria involved, is an attribute of the subject-matter itself, not of our imperfect methods of measurement, or incapacity for precise thought.

10 'The ideal of true freedom is the maximum of power for all the members of human society alike to make the best of themselves', said T. H. Green in 1881. Apart from the confusion of freedom with equality, this entails that if a man chose some immediate pleasure – which (in whose view?) would not enable him to make the best of himself (what self?) – what he was exercising was not 'true' freedom: and if deprived of it, would not lose anything that mattered. Green was a genuine liberal: but many a tyrant could use this formula to justify his worst acts of oppression.

11 In Great Britain such legal power is, of course, constitutionally vested in the absolute sovereign – the King in Parliament. What makes this country comparatively free, therefore, is the fact that this theoretically omnipotent entity is restrained by custom or opinion from behaving as such. It is clear that what matters is not the form of these restraints on power – whether they are legal, or moral, or constitutional – but their effectiveness.

[12] Condorcet, from whose *Esquisse* these words are quoted, declares that the task of social science is to show 'by what bonds Nature has united the progress of enlightenment with that of liberty, virtue, and respect for the natural rights of man; how these ideals, which alone are truly good, yet so often separated from each other that they are even believed to be incompatible, should, on the contrary, become inseparable, as soon as enlightenment has reached a certain level simultaneously among a large number of nations'. He goes on to say that: 'Men still preserve the errors of their childhood, of their country, and of their age long after having recognized all the truths needed for destroying them.' Ironically enough, his belief in the need and possibility of uniting all good things may well be precisely the kind of error he himself so well described.

[13] On this also Bentham seems to me to have spoken well: 'Individual interests are the only real interests . . . can it be conceived that there are men so absurd as to . . . prefer the man who is not to him who is; to torment the living, under pretence of promoting the happiness of them who are not born, and who may never be born?' This is one of the infrequent occasions when Burke agrees with Bentham; for this passage is at the heart of the empirical, as against the metaphysical, view of politics.

2
John Rawls: The Right and the Good Contrasted*

5. CLASSICAL UTILITARIANISM

... The striking feature of the utilitarian view of justice is that it does not matter, except indirectly, how this sum of satisfactions is distributed among individuals any more than it matters, except indirectly, how one man distributes his satisfactions over time. The correct distribution in either case is that which yields the maximum fulfillment. Society must allocate its means of satisfaction whatever these are, rights and duties, opportunities and privileges, and various forms of wealth, so as to achieve this maximum if it can. But in itself no distribution of satisfaction is better than another except that the more equal distribution is to be preferred to break ties.[1] It is true that certain common sense precepts of justice, particularly those which concern the protection of liberties and rights, or which express the claims of desert, seem to contradict this contention. But from a utilitarian standpoint the explanation of these precepts and of their seemingly stringent character is that they are those precepts which experience shows should be strictly respected and departed from only under exceptional circumstances if the sum of advantages is to be maximized.[2] Yet, as with all other precepts, those of justice are derivative from the one end of attaining the greatest balance of satisfaction. Thus there is no reason in principle why the greater gains of some should not compensate for the lesser losses of others; or more importantly, why the violation of the liberty of a few might not be made right by the greater good shared by many. It simply happens that under most conditions, at least in a reasonably advanced stage of civilization, the greatest sum of advantages is not attained in this

*Reprinted by permission of the publishers from A THEORY OF JUSTICE, by John Rawls, Cambridge, Mass: The Belknap Press of Harvard University Press, copyright © 1971 by the President and Fellows of Harvard College. Also in Great Britain by permission of Oxford University Press.

way. No doubt the strictness of common sense precepts of justice has a certain usefulness in limiting men's propensities to injustice and to socially injurious actions, but the utilitarian believes that to affirm this strictness as a first principle of morals is a mistake. For just as it is rational for one man to maximize the fulfillment of his system of desires, it is right for a society to maximize the net balance of satisfaction taken over all of its members.

The most natural way, then, of arriving at utilitarianism (although not, of course, the only way of doing so) is to adopt for society as a whole the principle of rational choice for one man. Once this is recognized, the place of the impartial spectator and the emphasis on sympathy in the history of utilitarian thought is readily understood. For it is by the conception of the impartial spectator and the use of sympathetic identification in guiding our imagination that the principle for one man is applied to society. It is this spectator who is conceived as carrying out the required organization of the desires of all persons into one coherent system of desire; it is by this construction that many persons are fused into one. Endowed with ideal powers of sympathy and imagination, the impartial spectator is the perfectly rational individual who identifies with and experiences the desires of others as if these desires were his own. In this way he ascertains the intensity of these desires and assigns them their appropriate weight in the one system of desire the satisfaction of which the ideal legislator then tries to maximize by adjusting the rules of the social system. On this conception of society separate individuals are thought of as so many different lines along which rights and duties are to be assigned and scarce means of satisfaction allocated in accordance with rules so as to give the greatest fulfillment of wants. The nature of the decision made by the ideal legislator is not, therefore, materially different from that of an entrepreneur deciding how to maximize his profit by producing this or that commodity, or that of a consumer deciding how to maximize his satisfaction by the purchase of this or that collection of goods. In each case there is a single person whose system of desires determines the best allocation of limited means. The correct decision is essentially a question of efficient administration. This view of social co-operation is the consequence of extending to society the principle of choice for one man, and then, to make this extension work, conflating all persons into one through the imaginative acts of the impartial sympathetic spectator. Utilitarianism does not take seriously the distinction between persons.

6. SOME RELATED CONTRASTS

It has seemed to many philosophers, and it appears to be supported by the convictions of common sense, that we distinguish as a matter of principle between the claims of liberty and right on the one hand and the desirability of increasing aggregate social welfare on the other; and that we give a certain priority, if not absolute weight, to the former. Each member of society is thought to have an inviolability founded on justice or, as some say, on natural right, which even the welfare of every one else cannot override. Justice denies that the loss of freedom for some is made right by a greater good shared by others. The reasoning which balances the gains and losses of different persons as if they were one person is excluded. Therefore in a just society the basic liberties are taken for granted and the rights secured by justice are not subject to political bargaining or to the calculus of social interests.

Justice as fairness attempts to account for these common sense convictions concerning the priority of justice by showing that they are the consequence of principles which would be chosen in the original position. These judgements reflect the rational preferences and the initial equality of the contracting parties. Although the utilitarian recognizes that, strictly speaking, his doctrine conflicts with these sentiments of justice, he maintains that common sense precepts of justice and notions of natural right have but a subordinate validity as secondary rules; they arise from the fact that under the conditions of civilized society there is great social utility in following them for the most part and in permitting violations only under exceptional circumstances. Even the excessive zeal with which we are apt to affirm these precepts and to appeal to these rights is itself granted a certain usefulness, since it counterbalances a natural human tendency to violate them in ways not sanctioned by utility. Once we understand this, the apparent disparity between the utilitarian principle and the strength of these persuasions of justice is no longer a philosophical difficulty. Thus while the contract doctrine accepts our convictions about the priority of justice as on the whole sound, utilitarianism seeks to account for them as a socially useful illusion.

A second contrast is that whereas the utilitarian extends to society the principle of choice for one man, justice as fairness, being a contract view, assumes that the principles of social choice, and so the principles of justice, are themselves the object of an original agreement. There is no reason to suppose that the principles which should regulate an association of men is simply an extension of the principle of choice for one man. On the contrary: if we assume that the correct regulative principle for anything depends on the nature of that thing, and that the plurality of distinct persons with separate systems of ends is an essential feature of human societies, we should not expect the principles of social choice to be utilitarian. To be sure, it has not been shown by anything said so far that the parties in the original position would not choose the principle of utility to define the terms of social co-operation. This is a difficult question which I shall examine later on. It is perfectly possible, from all that one knows at this point, that some form of the principle of utility would be adopted, and therefore that contract theory leads eventually to a deeper and more roundabout justification of utilitarianism. In fact a derivation of this kind is sometimes suggested by Bentham and Edgeworth, although it is not developed by them in any systematic way and to my knowledge it is not found in Sidgwick.[3] For the present I shall simply asssume that the persons in the original position would reject the utility principle and that they would adopt instead, for the kinds of reasons previously sketched, the two principles of justice already mentioned. In any case, from the standpoint of contract theory one cannot arrive at a principle of social choice merely by extending the principle of rational prudence to the system of desires constructed by the impartial spectator. To do this is not to take seriously the plurality and distinctness of individuals, nor to recognize as the basis of justice that to which men would consent. Here we may note a curious anomaly. It is customary to think of utilitarianism as individualistic, and certainly there are good reasons for this. The utilitarians were strong defenders of liberty and freedom of thought, and they held that the good of society is constituted by the advantages enjoyed by individuals. Yet utilitarianism is not individualistic, at least when arrived at by the more natural course of reflection, in that, by conflating all systems of desires, it applies to society the principle of choice for one man. And thus we see that the second contrast is related to the first, since it is this conflation, and the principle based upon it, which subjects the rights secured by justice to the calculus of social interests.

The last contrast that I shall mention now is that utilitarianism is a teleological theory whereas justice as fairness is not. By definition, then, the latter is a deontological theory, one that either does not specify the good independently from the right, or does not interpret the right as maximizing the good. (It should be noted that deontological theories are defined as non-teleological ones, not as views that characterize the rightness of institutions and acts independently from their consequences. All ethical doctrines worth our attention take consequences into account in judging rightness. One which did not would simply be irrational, crazy.) Justice as fairness is a deontological theory in the second way. For if it is assumed that the persons in the original position would choose a principle of equal liberty and restrict economic and social inequalities to those in everyone's interests, there is no reason to think that just institutions will maximize the good. (Here I suppose with utilitarianism that the good is defined as the satisfaction of rational desire.) Of course, it is not impossible that the most good is produced but it would be a coincidence. The question of attaining the greatest net balance of satisfaction never arises in justice as fairness; this maximum principle is not used at all.

There is a further point in this connection. In utilitarianism the satisfaction of any desire has some value in itself which must be taken into account in deciding what is right. In calculating the greatest balance of satisfaction it does not matter, except indirectly, what the desires are for.[4] We are to arrange institutions so as to obtain the greatest sum of satisfactions; we ask no questions about their source or quality but only how their satisfaction would affect the total of well-being. Social welfare depends directly and solely upon the levels of satisfaction or dissatisfaction of individuals. Thus if men take a certain pleasure in discriminating against one another, in subjecting others to a lesser liberty as a means of enhancing their self-respect, then the satisfaction of these desires must be weighed in our deliberations according to their intensity, or whatever, along with other desires. If society decides to deny them fulfillment, or to suppress them, it is because they tend to be socially destructive and a greater welfare can be achieved in other ways.

In justice as fairness, on the other hand, persons accept in advance a principle of equal liberty and they do this without a knowledge of their more particular ends. They implicitly agree, therefore, to conform their conceptions of their good to what the principles of justice require, or at least not to press claims which directly violate them. An individual who finds that he enjoys seeing others in positions of lesser liberty understands that he has no claim whatever to this enjoyment. The pleasure he takes in other's deprivations is wrong in itself: it is a satisfaction which requires the violation of a principle to which he would agree in the original position. The principles of right, and so of justice, put limits on which satisfactions have value; they impose restrictions on what are reasonable conceptions of one's good. In drawing up plans and in deciding on aspirations men are to take these constraints into account. Hence in justice as fairness one does not take men's propensities and inclinations as given, whatever they are, and then seek the best way to fulfill them. Rather, their desires and aspirations are restricted from the outset by the principles of justice which specify the boundaries that men's systems of ends must respect. We can express this by saying that in justice as fairness the concept of right is prior to that of the good. A just social system defines the scope within which develop their aims, and it provides a framework of rights and opportunities and the means of satisfaction within and by the use of which these ends may be equitably pursued. The priority of justice is accounted for, in part, by holding that the interests requiring the violation of justice have no value. Having no merit in the first place, they cannot override its claims.[5]

This priority of the right over the good in justice as fairness turns out to be a central feature of the conception. It imposes certain criteria on the design of the basic structure as a whole; these arrangements must not tend to generate propensities and attitudes contrary to the two principles of justice (that is, to certain principles which are given from the first a definite content) and they must ensure that just institutions are stable. Thus certain initial bounds are placed upon what is good and what forms of character are morally worthy, and so upon what kinds of persons men should be. Now any theory of justice will set up some limits of this kind, namely, those that are required if its first principles are to be satisfied given the circumstances. Utilitarianism excludes those desires and propensities which if encouraged or permitted would, in view of the situation, lead to a lesser net balance of satisfaction. But this restriction is largely formal, and in the absence of fairly detailed knowledge of the circumstances it does not give much indication of what these desires and propensities are. This is not, by itself, an objection to utilitarianism. It is simply a feature of utilitarian doctrine that it relies very heavily upon the natural facts and contingencies of human life in determining what forms of moral character are to be encouraged in a just society. The moral ideal of justice as fairness is more deeply embedded in the first principles of the ethical theory. This is characteristic of natural rights views (the contractarian tradition) in comparison with the theory of utility.

In setting forth these contrasts between justice as fairness and utilitarianism, I have had in mind only the classical doctrine. This is the view of Bentham and Sidgwick and of the utilitarian economists Edgeworth and Pigou. The kind of utilitarianism espoused by Hume would not serve my purpose; indeed, it is not strictly speaking utilitarian. In his well-known arguments against Locke's contract theory, for example, Hume maintains that the principles of fidelity and allegiance both have the same foundation in utility, and therefore that nothing is gained from basing political obligation on an original contract. Locke's doctrine represents, for Hume, an unnecessary shuffle: one might as well appeal directly to utility.[6] But all Hume seems to mean by utility is the general interests and necessities of society. The principles of fidelity and allegiance derive from utility in the sense that the maintenance of the social order is impossible unless these principles are generally respected. But then Hume assumes that each man stands to gain, as judged by his long-term advantage, when law and government conform to the precepts founded on utility. No mention is made of the gains of some outweighing the disadvantages of others. For Hume, then, utility seems to be identical with some form of the common good; institutions satisfy its demands when they are to everyone's interests, at least in the long run. Now if this interpretation of Hume is correct, there is offhand no conflict with the priority of justice and no incompatibility with Locke's contract doctrine. For the role of equal rights in Locke is precisely to ensure that the only permissible departures from the state of nature are those which respect these rights and serve the common interest. It is clear that all the transformations form the state of nature which Locke approves of satisfy this condition and are such that rational men concerned to advance their ends could consent to them in a state of equality. Hume nowhere disputes the propriety of these constraints. His critique of Locke's contract doctrine never denies, or even seems to recognize, its fundamental contention.

The merit of the classical view as formulated by Bentham, Edgeworth, and Sidgwick is that it clearly recognizes what is at stake, namely, the relative priority of the principles of justice and of the rights derived from these principles. The question is whether the imposition of disadvantages on a few can be outweighed by a greater sum of advantages enjoyed by others; or whether the weight of justice requires an equal liberty for all and permits only those economic and social inequalities which are to each person's interests. Implicit in the contrasts between classical utilitarianism and justice as fairness is a difference in the underlying conceptions of society. In the one we think of a well-ordered society as a scheme

of co-operation for reciprocal advantage regulated by principles
which persons would choose in an initial situation that is fair, in the
other as the efficient administration of social resources to maximize
the satisfaction of the system of desire constructed by the impartial
spectator from the many individual systems of desires accepted as
given. The comparison with classical utilitarianism in its more
natural derivation brings out this contrast.

48. LEGITIMATE EXPECTATIONS AND MORAL DESERT

There is a tendency for common sense to suppose that income and
wealth, and the good things in life generally, should be distributed
according to moral desert. Justice is happiness according to virtue.
While it is recognized that this ideal can never be fully carried
out, it is the appropriate conception of distributive justice, at least
as a *prima facie* principle, and society should try to realize it as
circumstances permit.[7] Now justice as fairness rejects this conception. Such a principle would not be chosen in the original position.
There seems to be no way of defining the requisite criterion in that
situation. Moreover, the notion of distribution according to virtue
fails to distinguish between moral desert and legitimate expectations. Thus it is true that as persons and groups take part in just
arrangements, they acquire claims on one another defined by the
publicly recognized rules. Having done various things encouraged
by the existing arrangements, they now have certain rights, and
just distributive shares honour these claims. A just scheme, then,
answers to what men are entitled to; it satisfies their legitimate
expectations as founded upon social institutions. But what they are
entitled to is not proportional to nor dependent upon their intrinsic
worth. The principles of justice that regulate the basic structure and
specify the duties and obligations of individuals do not mention
moral desert, and there is no tendency for distributive shares to
correspond to it.

This contention is borne out by the preceding account of
common sense precepts and their role in pure procedural justice.
For example, in determining wages a competitive economy gives
weight to the precept of contribution. But as we have seen, the
extent of one's contribution (estimated by one's marginal productivity) depends upon supply and demand. Surely a person's moral
worth does not vary according to how many offer similar skills, or
happen to want what he can produce. No one supposes that when

someone's abilities are less in demand or have deteriorated (as in the case of singers) his moral deservingness undergoes a similar shift. All of this is perfectly obvious and has long been agreed to.[8] It simply reflects the fact noted before that is one of the fixed points of our moral judgements that no one deserves his place in the distribution of natural assets any more than he deserves his initial starting place in society.

Moreover, none of the precepts of justice aims at rewarding virtue. The premiums earned by scarce natural talents, for example, are to cover the costs of training and to encourage the efforts of learning, as well as to direct ability to where it best furthers the common interest. The distributive shares that result do not correlate with moral worth, since the initial endowment of natural assets and the contingencies of their growth and nurture in early life are arbitrary from a moral point of view. The precept which seems intuitively to come closest to rewarding moral desert is that of distibution according to effort, or perhaps better, conscientious effort.[9] Once again, however, it seems clear that the effort a person is willing to make is influenced by his natural abilities and skills and the alternatives open to him. The better endowed are more likely, other things equal, to strive conscientiously, and there seems to be no way to discount for their greater good fortune. The idea of rewarding desert is impracticable. And certainly to the extent that the precept of need is emphasized, moral worth is ignored. Nor does the basic structure tend to balance the precepts of justice so as to achieve the requisite correspondence behind the scenes. It is regulated by the two principles of justice which define other aims entirely.

The same conclusion may be reached in another way. In the preceding remarks the notion of moral worth as distinct from a person's claims based upon his legitimate expectations has not been explained. Suppose, then, that we define this notion and show that it has no correlation with distributive shares. We have only to consider a well-ordered society, that is, a society in which institutions are just and this fact is publicly recognized. Its members also have a strong sense of justice, an effective desire to comply with the existing rules and to give one another that to which they are entitled. In this case we may assume that everyone is of equal moral worth. We have now defined this notion in terms of the sense of justice, the desire to act in accordance with the principles that would be chosen in the original position. But it is evident that understood in this way, the equal moral worth of persons does not entail that distributive shares are equal. Each is to receive what the principles of justice say he is entitled to, and these do not require equality.

The essential point is that the concept of moral worth does not provide a first principle of distributive justice. This is because it cannot be introduced until after the principles of justice and of natural duty and obligation have been acknowledged. Once these principles are on hand, moral worth can be defined as having a sense of justice; and as I shall discuss later, the virtues can be characterized as desires or tendencies to act upon the corresponding principles. Thus the concept of moral worth is secondary to those of right and justice, and it plays no role in the substantive definition of distributive shares. The case is analogous to the relation between the substantive rules of property and the law of robbery and theft. These offences and the demerits they entail presuppose the institution of property which is established for prior and independent social ends. For a society to organize itself with the aim of rewarding moral desert as a first principle would be like having the institution of property in order to punish thieves. The criterion to each according to his virtue would not, then, be chosen in the original position. Since the parties desire to advance their conceptions of the good, they have no reason for arranging their institutions so that distributive shares are determined by moral desert, even if they could find an antecedent standard for its definition.

In a well-ordered society individuals acquire claims to a share of the social product by doing certain things encouraged by the existing arrangements. The legitimate expectations that arise are the other side, so to speak, of the principle of fairness and the natural duty of justice. For in the way that one has a duty to uphold just arrangements, and an obligation to do one's part when one has accepted a position in them, so a person who has complied with the scheme and done his share has a right to be treated accordingly by others. They are bound to meet his legitimate expectations. Thus when just economic arrangements exist, the claims of individuals are properly settled by reference to the rules and precepts (with their respective weights) which these practices take as relevant. As we have seen, it is incorrect to say that just distributive shares reward individuals according to their moral worth. But what we can say is that, in the traditional phrase, a just scheme gives each person his due: that is, it allots to each what he is entitled to as defined by the scheme itself. The principles of justice for institutions and individuals establish that doing this is fair.

Now it should be noted that even though a person's claims are regulated by the existing rules, we can still make a distinction between being entitled to something and deserving it in a familar although non-moral sense.[10] To illustrate, after a game one often says that the losing side deserved to win. Here one does not mean that the victors are not entitled to claim the championship, or whatever spoils go to the winner. One means instead that the losing team displayed to a higher degree the skills and qualities that the game calls forth, and the exercise of which gives the sport its appeal. Therefore the losers truly deserved to win but lost out as a result of bad luck, or from other contingencies that caused the contest to miscarry. Similarly even the best economic arrangements will not always lead to the more preferred outcomes. The claims that individuals actually acquire inevitably deviate more or less widely from those that the scheme is designed to allow for. Some persons in favoured positions, for example, may not have to a higher degree than others the desired qualities and abilities. All this is evident enough. Its bearing here is that although we can indeed distinguish between the claims that existing arrangements require us to honour, given what individuals have done and how things have turned out, and the claims that would have resulted under more ideal circumstances, none of this implies that distributive shares should be in accordance with moral worth. Even when things happen in the best way, there is still no tendency for distribution and virtue to coincide.

No doubt some may still contend that distributive shares should match moral worth at least to the extent that this is feasible. They may believe that unless those who are better off have superior moral character, their having greater advantages is an affront to our sense of justice. Now this opinion may arise from thinking of distributive justice as somehow the opposite of retributive justice. It is true that in a reasonably well-ordered society those who are punished for violating just laws have normally done something wrong. This is because the purpose of the criminal law is to uphold basic natural duties, those which forbid us to injure other persons in their life and limb, or to deprive them of their liberty and property, and punishments are to serve this end. They are not simply a scheme of taxes and burdens designed to put a price on certain forms of conduct and in this way to guide men's conduct for mutual advantage. It would be far better if the acts proscribed by penal statutes were never done.[11] Thus a propensity to commit such acts is a mark of bad character, and in a just society legal punishments will only fall upon those who display these faults.

It is clear that the distribution of economic and social advantages is entirely different. These arrangements are not the converse, so to speak, of the criminal law, so that just as the one punishes certain offences, the other rewards moral worth.[12] The function of unequal distributive shares is to cover the costs of training and education, to attract individuals to places and associations where they are most needed from a social point to view, and so on. Assuming that everyone accepts the propriety of self- or group-interested motivation duly regulated by a sense of justice, each decides to do those things that best accord with his aims. Variations in wages and income and the perquisites of position are simply to influence these choices so that the end result accords with efficiency and justice. In a well-ordered society there would be no need for the penal law except insofar as the assurance problem made it necessary. The question of criminal justice belongs for the most part to partial compliance theory, whereas the account of distributive shares belongs to strict compliance theory and so to the consideration of the ideal scheme. To think of distributive and retributive justice as converses of one another is completely misleading and suggests a different justification for distributive shares than the one they in fact have.

68. SEVERAL CONTRASTS BETWEEN THE RIGHT AND THE GOOD

In order to bring out the structural features of the contract view, I shall now mention several contrasts between the concepts of the right and the good. Since these concepts enable us to explain moral worth, they are the two fundamental concepts of the theory. The structure of an ethical doctrine depends upon how it relates these two notions and defines their differences. The distinctive features of justice as fairness can be shown by noting these points.

One difference is that whereas the principles of justice (and the principles of right generally) are those that would be chosen in the original position, the principles of rational choice and the criteria of deliberative rationality are not chosen at all. The first task in the theory of justice is to define the initial situation so that the principles that result express the correct conception of justice from a philosophical point of view. This means that the typical features of this situation should represent reasonable constraints on arguments for accepting principles and that the principles agreed to should match our considered convictions of justice in reflective equilibrium. Now, the analogous problem for the theory of the good does not arise. There is, to begin with, no necessity for an agreement upon the principles of rational choice. Since each person is free to plan his life as he pleases (so long as is intentions are consistent with the principles of justice), unanimity concerning the standards of rationality is not required. All the theory of justice assumes is that, in the thin account of the good, the evident criteria of rational choice are sufficient to explain the preference for the primary goods, and that such variations as exist in conceptions of rationality do not affect the principles of justice adopted in the original position.

Nevertheless, I have assumed that human beings do recognize certain principles and that these standards may be taken by enumeration to replace the notion of rationality. We can, if we wish, allow certain variations in the list. Thus there is disagreement as to the best way to deal with uncertainty.[13] There is no reason, though, why individuals in making their plans should not be thought of as following their inclinations in this case. Therefore any principle of choice under uncertainty which seems plausible can be added to the list, so long as decisive arguments against it are not forthcoming. It is only in the thin theory of the good that we have to worry about these matters. Here the notion of rationality must be interpreted so that the general desire for the primary goods can be established and the choice of the principles of justice demonstrated. But even in this case, I have suggested that the conception of justice adopted is insensitive with respect to conflicting interpretations of rationality. But in any event, once the principles of justice are chosen, and we are working within the full theory, there is no need to set up the account of the good so as to force unanimity on all the standards of the rational choice. In fact, it would contradict the freedom of choice that justice as fairness assures to individuals and groups within the framework of just institutions.

A second contrast between the right and the good is that it is, in general, a good thing that individuals' conceptions of their good should differ in significant ways, whereas this is not so for conceptions of right. In a well-ordered society citizens hold the same principles of right and they try to reach the same judgement in particular cases. These principles are to establish a final ordering among the conflicting claims that persons make upon one another and it is essential that this ordering be identifiable from everyone's point of view, however difficult it may be in practice for everyone to accept it. On the other hand, individuals find their good in different ways, and many things may be good for one person that would not be good for another. Moreover, there is no urgency to reach publicly accepted judgement as to what is the good of particular individuals. The reasons that make such an agreement necessary in questions of justice do not obtain for judgements of value. Even when we take up another's point of view and attempt to estimate what would be to his advantage, we do so as an adviser, so to speak. We try to put ourselves in the other's place, and imagining that we have his aims and wants, we attempt to see things from his standpoint. Cases of paternalism aside, our judgement is offered when it is asked for, but there is no conflict of right if our advice is disputed and our opinion is not acted upon.

In a well-ordered society, then, the plans of life of individuals are different in the sense that these plans give prominence to different aims, and persons are left free to determine their good, the views of others being counted as merely advisory. Now this variety in conceptions of the good is itself a good thing, that is, it is rational for members of a well-ordered society to want their plans to be different. The reasons for this are obvious. Human beings have various talents and abilities the totality of which is unrealizable by any one person or group of persons. Thus we not only benefit from the complementary nature of our developed inclinations but we take pleasure in one another's activities. It is as if others were bringing forth a part of ourselves that we have not been able to cultivate. We have had to devote ourselves to other things, to only a small part of what we might have done. But the situation is quite otherwise with justice: here we require not only common principles but sufficiently similar ways of applying them in particular cases so that a final ordering of conflicting claims can be defined. Judgements of justice are advisory only in special circumstances.

The third difference is that many applications of the principles of justice are restricted by the veil of ignorance, whereas evaluations of a persons's good may rely upon a full knowledge of the facts. Thus, as we have seen, not only must the principles of justice be chosen in the absence of certain kinds of particular information, but when these principles are used in designing constitutions and basic social arrangements, and in deciding between laws and policies, we are subject to similar although not as strict limitations. The delegates to a constitutional convention, and ideal legislators and voters, are also required to take up a point of view in which they know only the appropriate general facts. An individual's conception of his good, on the other hand, is to be adjusted from the start to his particular situation. A rational plan of life takes into account our special abilities, interests, and circumstances, and therefore it quite properly depends upon our social position and natural assets. There is no objection to fitting rational plans to these contingencies, since the principles of justice have already been chosen and constrain the content of these plans, the ends that they encourage and the means that they use. But in judgements of justice, it is only at the judicial and administrative stage that all restrictions on information are dropped, and particular cases are to be decided in view of all the relevant facts.

In the light of these contrasts we may further clarify an important difference between the contract doctrine and utilitarianism. Since the principle of utility is to maximize the good understood as the satisfaction of rational desire, we are to take as given existing preferences and the possibilities of their continuation into the future, and then to strive for the greatest net balance of satisfaction. But as we have seen, the determination of rational plans is indeterminate in important ways. The more evident and easily applied principles of rational choice do not specify the best plan; a great deal remains to be decided. This indeterminacy is no difficulty for justice as fairness, since the details of plans do not affect in any way what is right or just. Our way of life, whatever our particular circumstances, must always conform to the principles of justice that are arrived at independently. Thus the arbitrary features of plans of life do not affect these principles, or how the basic structure is to be arranged. The indeterminacy in the notion of rationality does not translate itself into legitimate claims that men can impose on one another. The priority of the right prevents this.

The utilitarian, on the other hand, must concede the theoretical possibility that configurations of preferences allowed by this indeterminacy may lead to injustice as ordinarily understood. For example, assume that the larger part of society has an abhorrence for certain religious or sexual practices, and regards them as an abomination. This feeling is so intense that it is not enough that these practices be kept from the public view; the very thought that these things are going on is enough to arouse the majority to anger and hatred. Even when these attitudes are unsupportable on moral grounds, there appears to be no sure way to exclude them as irrational. Seeking the greatest satisfaction of desire may, then, justify harsh repressive measures against actions that cause no social injury. To defend individual liberty in this case the utilitarian has to show that given the circumstances the real balance of advantages in the long run still lies on the side of freedom; and this argument may or may not be successful.

In justice as fairness, however, this problem never arises. The intense convictions of the majority, if they are indeed mere preferences without any foundation in the principles of justice antecedently established, have no weight to begin with. The satisfaction of these feelings has no value that can be put in the scales against the claims of equal liberty. To have a complaint against the conduct and belief of others we must show that their actions injure us, or that the institutions that authorize what they do treat us unjustly. And this means that we must appeal to the principles that we would acknowledge in the original position. Against these principles neither the intensity of feeling nor its being shared by the majority counts for anything. On the contract view, then, the grounds of liberty are completely separate from existing preferences. Indeed, we may think of the principles of justice as an agreement not to take into account certain feelings when assessing the conduct of others. As I noted before, these points are familiar elements of the classical liberal doctrine. I have mentioned them again in order to show that the indeterminacy in the full theory of the good is no cause for objection. It may leave a person unsettled as to what to do, since it cannot provide him with instructions as to how to decide. But since the aim of justice is not to maximize the fulfilment of rational plans, the content of justice is not in any way affected. Of course, it cannot be denied that prevailing social attitudes tie the statesman's hands. The convictions and passions of the majority may make liberty impossible to maintain. But bowing to these practical necessities is a different thing from accepting the justification that if these feelings are strong enough and outweigh in intensity any feelings that might replace them, they should carry the decision. By contrast, the contract view requires that we move towards just institutions as speedily as the circumstances permit irrespective of existing sentiments. A definite scheme of ideal institutions is embedded in its principles of justice.

It is evident from these contrasts that in justice as fairness the concepts of the right and the good have markedly distinct features. These differences arise from the structure of contract theory and the priority of right and justice that results. I do not suggest, however, that the terms 'right' and 'good' (and their relatives) are normally used in ways that reflect these distinctions. Although our ordinary speech may tend to support the account of these concepts, this correspondence is not needed for the correctness of the contract doctrine. Rather, two things suffice. First, there is a way of mapping our considered judgements into the theory of justice such that in reflective equilibrium the counterparts of these convictions turn out to be true, to express judgements that we can accept. And second, once we understand the theory, we can acknowledge these interpretations as suitable renderings of what on reflection we now wish to maintain. Even though we would not normally use these replacements, perhaps because they are too cumbersome, or would be misunderstood, or whatever, we are prepared to grant that they cover in substance all that wants to be said. Certainly these substitutes may not mean the same as the ordinary judgements with which they are paired. How far this is the case is a question that I shall not examine. Moreover, the replacements may indicate a shift more or less drastic from our initial moral judgements as they existed prior to philosophical reflection. Some changes anyway are bound to have taken place as philosophical criticism and construction lead us to revise and extend our views. But what counts is whether the conception of justice as fairness, better than any other theory presently known to us, turns out to lead to true interpretations of our considered judgements, and provides a mode of expression for what we want to affirm.

84. HEDONISM AS A METHOD OF CHOICE

Traditionally hedonism is interpreted in one of two ways: either as the contention that the sole intrinsic good is pleasurable feeling, or as the psychological thesis that the only thing individuals strive for is pleasure. However I shall understand hedonism in a third way, namely, as trying to carry through the dominant-end conception of deliberation. It attempts to show how a rational choice is always possible, at least in principle. Although this effort fails, I shall examine it briefly for the light it throws upon the contrast between utilitarianism and the contract doctrine.

I imagine the hedonist to reason as follows. First he thinks that, if human life is to be guided by reason, there must exist a dominant end. There is no rational way to balance our competing aims against one another except as means to some higher end. Second, he interprets pleasure narrowly as agreeable feeling. Pleasantness as an attribute of feeling and sensation is thought to be the only plausible candidate for the role of the dominant end, and therefore it is the only thing good in itself. That, so conceived, pleasure alone is good is not postulated straightway as a first principle and then held to accord with our considered judgements of value. Rather pleasure is arrived at as the dominant end by a process of elimination. Granting that rational choices are possible, such an end must exist. At the same time this end cannot be happiness or any objective goal. To avoid the circularity of the one and the inhumanity and fanaticism of the other, the hedonist turns inwards. He finds the ultimate end in some definite quality of sensation or feeling identifiable by introspection. We can suppose, if we like, that pleasantness can be ostensively defined as that attribute which is common to the feelings and experiences towards which we have a favourable attitude and wish to prolong, other things equal. Thus, for purposes of illustration, one might say that pleasantness is that feature which is common to the experience of smelling roses, of tasting chocolate, of requited affection, and so on, and analogously for the opposite attribute of painfulness.[14]

The hedonist maintains, then, that a rational agent knows exactly how to proceed in determining his good: he is to ascertain which of the plans open to him promises the greatest net balance of pleasure over pain. This plan defines his rational choice, the best way to order his competing aims. The counting principles now apply trivially, since all good things are homogeneous and therefore comparable as means to the one end of pleasure. Of course these assessments are plagued by uncertainties and lack of information, and normally only the crudest estimates can be made. Yet for hedonism this is not a real difficulty: what counts is that the maximum of pleasure provides a clear idea of the good. We are now said to know the one thing the pursuit of which gives rational form to our life. Largely for these reasons Sidgwick thinks that pleasure must be the single rational end that is to guide deliberation.[15]

It is important to note two points. First, when pleasure is regarded as a special attribute of feeling and sensation, it is conceived as a definite measure on which calculations can be based. By reckoning in terms of the intensity and duration of pleasant experiences, the necessary computations can theoretically be made. The method of hedonism provides a first-person procedure of choice as the standard of happiness does not. Second, taking pleasure as the dominant end does not imply that we have any particular objective goals. We find pleasure in the most varied activities and in the quest for any number of things. Therefore aiming to maximize pleasurable feeling seems at least to avoid the appearance of fanaticism and inhumanity while still defining a rational method for first-person choice. Furthermore, the two traditional interpretations of hedonism are now easily accounted for. If pleasure is indeed the only end the pursuit of which enables us to identify rational plans, then surely pleasure would appear to be the sole intrinsic good, and so we would have arrived at the principle of hedonism by an argument from the conditions of rational deliberation. A variant of psychological hedonism also follows: for although it is going too far to say that rational conduct would always consciously aim at pleasure, it would in any case be regulated by a schedule of activities designed to maximize the net balance of pleasurable feeling. Since it leads to the more familiar interpretations, the thesis that the pursuit of pleasure provides the only rational method of deliberation seems to be the fundamental idea of hedonism.

It seems obvious that hedonism fails to define a reasonable dominant end. We need only note that once pleasure is conceived, as it must be, in a sufficiently definite way so that its intensity and duration can enter into the agent's calculations, then it is no longer plausible that it should be taken as the sole rational aim.[16] Surely the preference for a certain attribute of feeling or sensation above all else is as unbalanced and inhuman as an overriding desire to maximize one's power over others or one's material wealth. No doubt it is for this reason that Sidgwick is reluctant to grant that pleasantness is a particular quality of feeling; yet he must concede this if pleasure is to serve, as he wants it to, as the ultimate criterion to weigh ideal values such as knowledge, beauty, and friendship against one another.[17]

And then too there is the fact that there are different sorts of agreeable feelings themselves incomparable, as well as the quantitative dimensions of pleasure, intensity and duration. How are we to balance these when they conflict? Are we to choose a brief but intense pleasant experience of one kind of feeling over a less intense but longer pleasant experience of another? Aristotle says that the good man if necessary lays down his life for his friends, since he prefers a short period of intense pleasure to a long one of mild enjoyment, a twelvemonth of noble life to many years of humdrum existence.[18] But how does he decide this? Further, as Santayana observes, we must settle the relative worth of pleasure and pain. When Petrarch says that a thousand pleasures are not worth one pain, he adopts a standard for comparing them that is more basic than either. The person himself must make this decision, taking into account the full range of inclinations and desires, present and future. Clearly we have made no advance beyond deliberate rationality. The problem of a plurality of ends arises all over again within the class of subjective feelings.[19]

It may be objected that in economics and decision theory these problems are overcome. But this contention is based on a misunderstanding. In the theory of demand, for example, it is assumed that the consumer's preferences satisfy various postulates: they define a complete ordering over the set of alternatives and exhibit the properties of convexity and continuity, and the like. Given these assumptions, it can be shown that a utility function exists which matches these preferences in the sense that one alternative is chosen over another if and only if the value of the function for the selected alternative is greater. This function characterizes the individual's choices, what he in fact prefers, granted that his preferences meet certain stipulations. It asserts nothing at all about how a person arranges his decisions in such a coherent order to begin with, nor clearly can it claim to be a first-person procedure of choice that someone might reasonably follow, since it only records the outcome of his deliberations. At best the principles that economists have supposed the choices of rational individuals to satisfy can be presented as guidelines for us to consider when we make our decisions. But so understood, these criteria are just the principles of rational choice (or their analogues) and we are back once again with deliberative rationality.[20]

It seems indisputable, then, that there is no dominant end the pursuit of which accords with our considered judgements of value. The inclusive end of realizing a rational plan of life is an entirely different thing. But the failure of hedonism to provide a rational procedure of choice should occasion no surprise. Wittgenstein showed that it is a mistake to postulate certain special experiences to explain how we distinguish memories from imaginings, beliefs from suppositions, and so on for other mental acts. Similarly, it is antecedently unlikely that certain kinds of agreeable feeling can define a unit of account the use of which explains the possibility of rational deliberation. Neither pleasure nor any other determinate end can play the role that the hedonist would assign it.[21]

Now philosophers have supposed that characteristic experiences exist and guide our mental life for many different reasons. So while it seems a simple matter to show that hedonism gets us nowhere, the important thing is to see why one might be driven to resort to such a desperate expedient. I have already noted one possible reason: the desire to narrow down the scope of purely preferential choice in determining our good. In a teleological theory any vagueness or ambiguity in the conception of the good is transferred to that of the right. Hence if the good of individuals is something that, so to speak, is just up to them to decide as individuals, so likewise within certain limits is that which is right. But it is natural to think that what is right is not a matter of mere preference, and therefore one tries to find a definite conception of the good.

There is, however, another reason: a teleological theory needs a way to compare the diverse goods of different individuals so that the total good can be maximized. How can these assessments be made? Even if certain ends serve to organize the plans of individuals taken singly, they do not suffice to define a conception of right. It would appear, then, that the turn inwards to the standard of agreeable feeling is an attempt to find a common denominator among the plurality of persons, an interpersonal currency as it were, by means of which the social ordering can be specified. And this suggestion is all the more compelling if it is already maintained that this standard is the aim of each person to the extent that he is rational.

By way of conclusion, I should not say that a teleological doctrine is necessarily driven to some form of hedonism in order to define a coherent theory. Yet it does seem that the tendency in this direction has a certain naturalness. Hedonism is, one might say, the symptomatic drift of teleological theories insofar as they try to formulate a clear and applicable method of moral reasoning. The weakness of hedonism reflects the impossibility of defining an appropriate definite end to be maximized. And this suggests that the structure of teleological doctrines is radically misconceived: from the start they relate the right and the good in the wrong way. We should not attempt to give form to our life by first looking to the good independently defined. It is not our aims that primarily reveal our nature but rather the principles that we would acknowledge to govern the background conditions under which these aims are to be formed and the manner in which they are to be pursued. For the self is prior to the ends which are affirmed by it; even a dominant end must be chosen from among numerous possibilities. There is no way to get beyond deliberative rationality. We should therefore reverse the relation between the right and the good proposed by teleological doctrines and view the right as prior. The moral theory is then developed by working in the opposite direction.

NOTES

[1] On this point see Sidgwick, *The Methods of Ethics*, pp. 416 f.
[2] See J. S. Mill, *Utilitarianism*, ch. 5, last two paras.
[3] For Bentham see *The Principles of International Law*, Essay I, in *The Works of Jeremy Bentham*, ed. John Bowring (Edinburgh, 1838–43), vol. II, p. 537; for Edgeworth see *Mathematical Psychics*, pp. 52–6, and also the first pages of 'The Pure Theory of Taxation', *Economic Journal*, vol. 7 (1897), where the same argument is presented more briefly.
[4] Bentham, *The Principles of Morals and Legislation*, ch. I, sec. IV.

[5] The priority of right is a central feature of Kant's ethics. See, for example, *The Critique of Practical Reason*, ch. II, bk I of *pt I*, especially pp. 62–5 of vol. 5 of *Kants Gesammelte Schriften, Preussische Akademie der Wissenschaften* (Berlin, 1913). A clear statement is to be found in 'Theory and Practice' (to abbreviate the title), *Political Writings*, pp. 67 f.

[6] 'Of the Original Contract', *Essays: Moral, Political, and Literary*, ed. T. H. Green and T. H. Grose, vol. I (London, 1875), pp. 454 f.

[7] See, for example, W. D. Ross, *The Right and the Good* (Oxford, The Clarendon Press, 1930), pp. 21, 26–8, 35, 57 f. Similarly, Leibniz in 'On the Ultimate Origin of Things' (1697) speaks of the law of justice which 'declares that each one [each individual] participate in the perfection of the universe and in a happiness of his own in proportion to his own virtue and to the good will he entertains toward the common good.' *Leibniz*, ed. P. P. Wiener (New York, Charles Scribner's Sons, 1951), p. 353.

[8] See F. H. Knight, *The Ethics of Competition* (New York, Harper and Brothers, 1935), pp. 54–7.

[9] See Knight, ibid., p. 56 n.

[10] Here I borrow from Joel Feinberg, *Doing and Deserving* (Princeton, Princeton University Press, 1970), pp. 64 f.

[11] See H. L. A. Hart, *The Concept of Law* (Oxford, The Clarendon Press, 1961), p. 39; and Feinberg, *Doing and Deserving*, ch. 5.

[12] On this point, see Feinberg, ibid., pp. 62, 69 n.

[13] See the discussion in R. D. Luce and Howard Raiffa, *Games and Decisions* (New York, John Wiley and Sons, 1957), pp. 278–306.

[14] The illustration is from C. D. Broad, *Five Types of Ethical Theory* (London, Routledge and Kegan Paul, 1930), pp. 186 f.

[15] *The Methods of Ethics*, 7th edn (London, Macmillan, 1907), pp. 405–7, 479.

[16] As Broad observes in *Five Types of Ethical Theory*, p. 187.

[17] In *Methods of Ethics*, p. 127, Sidgwick denies that pleasure is a measurable quality of feeling independent of its relation from volition. This is the view of some writers, he says, but one he cannot accept. He defines pleasure 'as a feeling which, when experienced by intelligent beings, is at least apprehended as desirable or – in cases of comparison – preferable'. It would seem that the view he here rejects is the one he relies upon later as the final criterion to introduce coherence among ends. See pp. 405–7, 479. Otherwise the hedonist method of choice no longer provides instructions that can be followed.

[18] *Nicomachean Ethics*, 1169a17–26.

[19] *The Life of Reason in Common Sense* (New York, Charles Scribner's, Sons 1905), pp. 237 f.

[20] Thus to the objection that price theory must fail because it seeks to predict the unpredictable, the decisions of persons with free will, Walras says: 'Actually, we have never attempted to predict decisions made under conditions of perfect freedom; we have only tried to express the

effects of such decisions in terms of mathematics. In our theory each trader may be assumed to determine his utility or want curves as he pleases.' *Elements of Pure Economics*, trans. William Jaffé (Homewood, Ill., Richard D. Irwin, 1954), p. 256. See also P. A. Samuelson, *Foundations of Economic Analysis* (Cambridge, Harvard University Press, 1947), the remarks pp. 90–2, 97 f; and R.D. Luce and Howard Raiffa, *Games and Decisions* (New York, John Wiley and Sons, 1957), pp. 16, 21–4, 38.

21 See the *Philosophical Investigations* (Oxford, Basil Blackwell, 1953). The argument against postulating special experiences is made throughout for many different cases. For the application to pleasure, see the remarks of G. E. M. Anscombe, *Intention* (Oxford, Basil Blackwell, 1957). Anscombe says: 'We might adapt a remark of Wittgenstein's about meaning and say "Pleasure cannot be an impression; for no impression could have the consequences of pleasure." They [the British Empiricists] were saying that something which they thought of as like a particular tickle or itch was quite obviously the point of doing anything whatsoever' (p. 77). See also Gilbert Ryle, 'Pleasure', *Proceedings of the Aristotelian Society*, supp. vol. 28 (1954), and *Dilemmas* (Cambridge, The University Press, 1954), ch. 4; Anthony Kenny, *Action, Emotion and Will* (London, Routledge and Kegan Paul, 1963), ch. 6; and C. C. W. Taylor, 'Pleasure', *Analysis*, supp. vol. (1963). These studies present what seems to be the more correct view. In the text I try to explain the motivation from the standpoint of moral philosophy of the so-called British Empiricist conception of pleasure. That it is fallacious I pretty much take for granted, as the writers mentioned have, I believe, shown.

3

Ronald Dworkin: Liberalism*

I

... Is there a thread of principle that runs through the core liberal positions, and that distinguishes these from the corresponding conservative positions? There is a familiar answer to this question that is mistaken, but mistaken in an illuminating way. The politics of democracies, according to this answer, recognizes several independent constitutive political ideals, the most important of which are the ideals of liberty and equality. Unfortunately, liberty and equality often conflict: sometimes the only effective means to promote equality require some limitation of liberty, and sometimes the consequences of promoting liberty are detrimental to equality. In these cases, good government consists in the best compromise between the competing ideals, but different politicians and citizens will make that compromise differently. Liberals tend relatively to favour equality more and liberty less than conservatives do, and the core set of liberal positions I described is the result of striking the balance that way.

This account offers a theory about what liberalism is. Liberalism shares the same constitutive principles with many other political theories, including conservatism, but is distinguished from these by attaching different relative importance to different principles. The theory therefore leaves room, on the spectrum it describes, for the radical who cares even more for equality and less for liberty than the liberal, and therefore stands even further away from the extreme conservative. The liberal becomes the man in the middle, which explains why liberalism is so often now considered wish-washy, an untenable compromise between two more forthright positions.

No doubt this description of American politics could be made

* Reprinted from *Liberalism* by Ronald Dworkin, in *Public and Private Morality* by Stuart Hampshire (ed.), 1978, by permission of Cambridge University Press.

more sophisticated. It might make room for other independent constitutive ideals shared by liberalism and its opponents, like stability or security, so that the compromises involved in particular decisions are made out to be more complex. But if the nerve of the theory remains the competition between liberty and equality as constitutive ideals, then the theory cannot succeed. . . . It seems to apply, at best, to only a limited number of the political controversies it tries to explain. It is designed for economic controversies, but is either irrelevant or misleading in the case of censorship and pornography, and indeed, in the criminal law generally.

But there is a much more important defect in this explanation. It assumes that liberty is measurable so that, if two political decisions each invades the liberty of a citizen, we can sensibly say that one decision takes more liberty away from him than the other. That assumption is necessary, because otherwise the postulate, that liberty is a constitutive ideal of both the liberal and conservative political structures, cannot be maintained. Even firm conservatives are content that their liberty to drive as they wish (for example to drive uptown on Lexington Avenue) may be invaded for the sake, not of some important competing political ideal, but only for marginal gains in convenience or orderly traffic patterns. But since traffic regulation plainly involves some loss of liberty, the conservative cannot be said to value liberty as such unless he is able to show that, for some reason, less liberty is lost by traffic regulation than by restrictions on, for example, free speech, or the liberty to sell for prices others are willing to pay, or whatever other liberty he takes to be fundamental.

But that is precisely what he cannot show, because we do not have a concept of liberty that is quantifiable in the way that demonstration would require. He cannot say, for example, that traffic regulations interfere less with what most men and women want to do than would a law forbidding them to speak out in favour of Communism, or a law requiring them not to fix their prices as they think best. Most people care more about driving than speaking for Communism, and have no occasion to fix prices even if they want to. I do not mean that we can make no sense of the idea of fundamental liberties, like freedom of speech. But we cannot argue in their favour by showing that they protect more liberty, taken to be an even roughly measurable commodity, than does the right to drive as we wish; the fundamental liberties are important because we value something else that they protect. But if that is so, then we cannot explain the difference between liberal and conservative political positions by supposing that the latter protect the commodity of liberty, valued for its own sake, more effectively than the former.[1]

It might now be said, however, that the other half of the liberty–equality explanation may be salvaged. Even if we cannot say that conservatives value liberty, as such, more than liberals, we can still say that they value equality less, and that the different political positions may be explained in that way. Conservatives tend to discount the importance of equality when set beside other goals, like general prosperity or even security; while liberals, in contrast, value equality relatively more, and radicals more still. Once again, it is apparent that this explanation is tailored to the economic controversies, and fits poorly with the non-economic controversies. Once again, however, its defects are more general and more important. We must identify more clearly the sense in which equality could be a constitutive ideal for either liberals or conservatives. Once we do so we shall see that it is misleading to say that the conservative values equality, in that sense, less than the liberal. We shall want to say, instead, that he has a different conception of what equality requires.

We must distinguish between two different principles that take equality to be a political ideal.[2] The first requires that the government treat all those in its charge *as equals*, that is, as entitled to its equal concern and respect. That is not an empty requirement: most of us do not suppose that we must, as individuals, treat our neighbour's children with the same concern as our own, or treat everyone we meet with the same respect. It is nevertheless plausible to think that any government should treat all its citizens as equals in that way. The second principle requires that the government treat all those in its charge *equally* in the distribution of some resource of opportunity, or at least work to secure the state of affairs in which they all are equal or more nearly equal in that respect. It is, of course, conceded by everyone that the government cannot make everyone equal in every respect, but people do disagree about how far government should try to secure equality in some particular resource; for example, in monetary wealth.

If we look only at the economic–political controversies, then we might well be justified in saying that liberals want more equality in the sense of the second principle than conservatives do. But it would be a mistake to conclude that they value equality in the sense of the first and more fundamental principle any more highly. I say that the first principle is more fundamental because I assume that, for both liberals and conservatives, the first is constitutive and the second derivative. Sometimes treating people equally is the only way to treat them as equals; but sometimes not. Suppose a limited amount of emergency relief is available for two equally populous areas injured by floods; treating the citizens of both areas as equals requires giving more aid to the more seriously devastated area rather than splitting the available funds equally. The conservative believes that in many other, less apparent, cases treating citizens equally amounts to not treating them as equals. He might concede, for example, that positive discrimination in university admissions will work to make the two races more nearly equal in wealth, but nevertheless maintain that such programmes do not treat black and white university applicants as equals. If he is a utilitarian he will have a similar, though much more general, argument against any redistribution of wealth that reduces economic efficiency. He will say that the only way to treat people as equals is to maximize the average welfare of all members of community, counting gains and losses to all in the same scales, and that a free market is the only, or best, instrument for achieving that goal. This is not (I think) a good argument, but if the conservative who makes it is sincere he cannot be said to have discounted the importance of treating all citizens as equals.

So we must reject the simple idea that liberalism consists in a distinctive weighting between constitutive principles of equality and liberty. But our discussion of the idea of equality suggests a more fruitful line. I assume (as I said) that there is broad agreement within modern politics that the government must treat all its citizens with equal concern and respect. I do not mean to deny the great power of prejudice in, for example, American politics. But few citizens, and even fewer politicians, would now admit to political convictions that contradict the abstract principle of equal concern and respect. Different people hold, however, as our discussion made plain, very different conceptions of what that abstract principle requires in particular cases.

II

What does it mean for the government to treat its citizens as equals? That is, I think, the same question as the question of what it means for the government to treat all its citizens as free, or as independent, or with equal dignity. In any case, it is a question that has been central to political theory at least since Kant.

It may be answered in two fundamentally different ways. The

first supposes that government must be neutral on what might be called the question of the good life. The second supposes that government cannot be neutral on that question, because it cannot treat its citizens as equal human beings without a theory of what human beings ought to be. I must explain that distinction further. Each person follows a more-or-less articulate conception of what gives value to life. The scholar who values a life of contemplation has such a conception; so does the television-watching, beer-drinking citizen who is fond of saying 'This is the life', though of course he has thought less about the issue and is less able to describe or defend his conception.

The first theory of equality supposes that political decisions must be, so far as is possible, independent of any particular conception of the good life, or of what gives value to life. Since the citizens of a society differ in their conceptions, the government does not treat them as equals if it prefers one conception to another, either because the officials believe that one is intrinsically superior, or because one is held by the more numerous or more powerful group. The second theory argues, on the contrary, that the content of equal treatment cannot be independent of some theory about the good for man or the good of life, because treating a person as an equal means treating him the way the good or truly wise person would wish to be treated. Good government consists in fostering or at least recognizing good lives; treatment as an equal consists in treating each person as if he were desirous of leading the life that is in fact good, at least so far as this is possible.

This distinction is very abstract, but it is also very important. I shall now argue that liberalism takes, as its constitutive political morality, the first conception of equality. I shall try to support that claim in this way. In the next section of this essay I shall show how it is plausible, and even likely, that a thoughtful person who accepted the first conception of equality would, given the economic and political circumstances of America in the last several decades, reach the positions I identified as the familiar core of liberal positions. If so, then the hypothesis satisfies the second of the conditions I described for a successful theory. In the following section I shall try to satisfy the third condition by showing how it is plausible and even likely that someone who held a particular version of the second theory of equality would reach what are normally regarded as the core of American conservative positions. I say 'a particular version of' because American conservatism does not follow automatically from rejecting the liberal theory of equality. The second (or non-liberal) theory of equality holds merely that the treatment government owes citizens is at least partly determined by some conception of the good life. Many political theories share that thesis, including theories as far apart as, for example, American conservatism and various forms of socialism or Marxism, though these will of course differ in the conception of the good life they adopt, and hence in the political institutions and decisions they endorse. In this respect, liberalism is decidedly not some compromise or half-way house between more forceful positions, but stands on one side of an important line that distinguishes it from all competitors taken as a group.

I shall not provide arguments in this essay that my theory of liberalism meets the first condition I described – that the theory must provide a political morality that it makes sense to suppose people in our culture hold – though I think it plain that the theory does meet this condition. The fourth condition requires that a theory be as abstract and general as the first three conditions allow. I doubt there will be objections to my theory on that account.

III

I now define a liberal as someone who holds the first, or liberal, theory of what equality requires. Suppose that a liberal is asked to found a new state. He is required to dictate its constitution and fundamental institutions. He must propose a general theory of political distribution, that is, a theory of how whatever the community has to assign, by way of goods or resources or opportunities, should be assigned. He will arrive initially at something like this principle of rough equality: resources and opportunities should be distributed, so far as possible, equally, so that roughly the same share of whatever is available is devoted to satisfying the ambitions of each. Any other general aim of distribution will assume either that the fate of some people should be of greater concern than that of others, or that the ambitions or talents of some are more worthy, and should be supported more generously on that account.

Someone may object that this principle of rough equality is unfair because it ignores the fact that people have different tastes, and that some of these are more expensive to satisfy than others, so that, for example, the man who prefers champagne will need more funds if he is not to be frustrated than the man satisfied with beer. But the liberal may reply that tastes as to which people differ are, by and large, not afflictions, like diseases, but are rather cultivated, in accordance with each person's theory of what his life should be like.³ The most effective neutrality, therefore, requires that the same share be devoted to each, so that the choice between expensive and less expensive tastes can be made by each person for himself, with no sense that his overall share will be enlarged by choosing a more expensive life, or that, whatever he chooses, his choice will subsidize those who have chosen more expensively.⁴

But what does the principle of rough equality of distribution require in practice? If all resources were distributed directly by the government through grants of food, housing, and so forth; if every opportunity citizens have were provided directly by the government through the provisions of civil and criminal law; if every citizen had exactly the same talents; if every citizen started his life with no more than what any other citizen had at the start; and if every citizen had exactly the same theory of the good life and hence exactly the same scheme of preferences as every other citizen, including preferences between productive activity of different forms and leisure, then the principle of rough equality of treatment could be satisfied simply by equal distributions of everything to be distributed and by civil and criminal laws of universal application. Government would arrange for production that maximized the mix of goods, including jobs and leisure, that everyone favoured, distributing the product equally.

Of course, none of these conditions of similarity holds. But the moral relevance of different sorts of diversity are very different, as may be shown by the following exercise. Suppose all the conditions of similarity I mentioned did hold except the last: citizens have different theories of the good and hence different preferences. They therefore disagree about what product the raw materials and labour and savings of the community should be used to produce, and about which activities should be prohibited or regulated so as to make others possible or easier. The liberal, as lawgiver, now needs mechanisms to satisfy the principles of equal treatment in spite of these disagreements. He will decide that there are no better mechanisms available, as general political institutions, than the two main institutions of our own political economy: the economic market, for decisions about what goods shall be produced and how they shall be distributed, and representative democracy, for collective decisions about what conduct shall be prohibited or regulated so that other conduct might be made possible or convenient. Each of these familiar institutions may be expected to provide a more egalitarian division than any other general arrangement. The market, if it can be made to function efficiently, will determine for each product a price that reflects the cost in resources of material, labour and capital that might have been applied to produce something different that someone else wants. That cost determines, for anyone who consumes that product, how much his account should be charged in computing the egalitarian division of social resources. It provides a measure of how much more his account should be charged for a house than a book, and for one book rather than another. The market will also provide, for the labourer, a measure of how much should be credited to his account for his choice of productive activity over leisure, and for one activity rather than another. It will tell us, through the price it puts on his labour, how much he would gain or lose by his decision to pursue one career rather than another. These measurements make a citizen's own distribution a function of the personal preferences of others as well as of his own, and it is the sum of these personal preferences that fixes the true cost to the community of meeting his own preferences for goods and activities. The egalitarian distribution, which requires that the cost of satisfying one person's preferences should as far as is possible be equal to the cost of satisfying another's, cannot be enforced unless those measurements are made.

We are familiar with the anti-egalitarian consequences of free enterprise in practice; it may therefore seem paradoxical that the liberal as lawgiver should choose a market economy for reasons of equality rather than efficiency. But, under the special condition that people differ only in preferences for goods and activities, the market is more egalitarian than any alternative of comparable generality. The most plausible alternative would be to allow decisions of production, investment, price and wage to be made by elected officials in a socialist economy. But what principles should officials use in making those decisions? The liberal might tell them to mimic the decisions that a market would make if it was working efficiently under proper competition and full knowledge. This mimicry would be, in practice, much less efficient than an actual market would be. In any case, unless the liberal had reason to think it would be much more efficient, he would have good reason to reject it. Any minimally efficient mimicking of a hypothetical market would require invasions of privacy to determine what decisions individuals would make if forced actually to pay for their investment, consumption and employment decisions at market rates, and this information gathering would be, in many other ways, much more expensive than an actual market. Inevitably, moreover, the assumptions officials make about how people would behave in a hypothetical market reflect the officials' own beliefs about how people should behave. So there would be, for the liberal, little to gain and much to lose in a socialist economy in which officials were asked to mimic a hypothetical market.

But any other instructions would be a direct violation of the liberal theory of what equality requires, because if a decision is made to produce and sell goods at a price below the price a market would fix, then those who prefer those goods are, *pro tanto*, receiving more than an equal share of the resources of the community at the expense of those who would prefer some other use of the resources. Suppose the limited demand for books, matched against the demand for competing uses for wood-pulp, would fix the price of books at a point higher than the socialist managers of the economy will charge; those who want books are having less charged to their account than the egalitarian principle would require. It might be said that in a socialist economy books are simply valued more, because they are inherently more worthy uses of social resources, quite apart from the popular demand for books. But the liberal theory of equality rules out that appeal to the inherent value of one theory of what is good in life.

In a society in which people differed only in preferences, then, a market would be favoured for its egalitarian consequences. Inequality of monetary wealth would be the consequence only of the fact that some preferences are more expensive than others, including the preference for leisure time rather than the most lucrative productive activity. But we must now return to the real world. In the actual society for which the liberal must construct political institutions, there are all the other differences. Talents are not distributed equally, so the decision of one person to work in a factory rather than a law firm, or not to work at all, will be governed in large part by his abilities rather than his preferences for work or between work and leisure. The institutions of wealth, which allow people to dispose of what they receive by gift, mean that children of the successful will start with more wealth than the children of the unsuccessful. Some people have special needs, because they are handicapped; their handicap will not only disable them from the most productive and lucrative employment, but will incapacitate them from using the proceeds of whatever employment they find as efficiently, so that they will need more than those who are not handicapped to satisfy identical ambitions.

These inequalities will have great, often catastrophic, effects on the distribution that a market economy will provide. But, unlike differences in preferences, the differences these inequalities make are indefensible according to the liberal conception of equality. It is obviously obnoxious to the liberal conception, for example, that someone should have more of what the community as a whole has to distribute because he or his father had superior skill or luck. The liberal lawgiver therefore faces a difficult task. His conception of equality requires an economic system that produces certain inequalities (those that reflect the true differential costs of goods and opportunities) but not others (those that follow from differences in ability, inheritance, etc.). The market produces both the required and the forbidden inequalities, and there is no alternative system that can be relied upon to produce the former without the latter.

The liberal must be tempted, therefore, to a reform of the market through a scheme of redistribution that leaves its pricing system relatively intact but sharply limits, at least, the inequalities in welfare that his initial principle prohibits. No solution will seem perfect. The liberal may find the best answer in a scheme of welfare rights financed through redistributive income and inheritance taxes of the conventional sort, which redistributes just to the Rawlsian point, that is, to the point at which the worst-off group would be harmed rather than benefited by further transfers. In that case, he will remain a reluctant capitalist, believing that a market economy so reformed is superior, from the standpoint of his conception of equality, to any practical socialist alternative. Or he may believe that the redistribution that is possible in a capitalist economy will be so inadequate, or will be purchased at the cost of such inefficiency, that it is better to proceed in a more radical way, by substituting socialist for market decisions over a large part of the economy, and then relying on the political process to insure that prices are set in a manner at least roughly consistent with his conception of equality. In that case he will be a reluctant socialist, who acknowledges the egalitarian defects of socialism but counts them as less severe than the practical alternatives. In either case, he chooses a mixed economic system — either redistributive capitalism or limited socialism — not in order to compromise antagonistic ideals of efficiency and equality, but to achieve the best practical realization of the demands of equality itself.

Let us assume that in this manner the liberal either refines or partially retracts his original selection of a market economy. He must now consider the second of the two familiar institutions he first selected, which is representative democracy. Democracy is justified because it enforces the right of each person to respect and concern as an individual; but in practice the decisions of a democratic majority may often violate that right, according to the liberal theory of what the right requires. Suppose a legislature elected by a majority decides to make criminal some act (like speaking in favour of an unpopular political position, or participating in eccentric sexual practices) not because the act deprives others of opportunities they want, but because the majority disapproves of those views or that sexual morality. The political decision, in other words, reflects not simply some accommodation of the *personal* preferences of everyone, in such a way as to make the opportunities of all as nearly equal as may be, but the domination of one set of *external* preferences, that is, preferences people have about what others shall do or have.[5] The decision invades rather than enforces the right of citizens to be treated as equals.

How can the liberal protect citizens against that sort of violation of their fundamental right? It will not do for the liberal simply to instruct legislators, in some constitutional exhortation, to disregard the external preferences of their constituents. Citizens will vote these preferences in electing their representatives, and a legislator who chooses to ignore them will not survive. In any case, it is sometimes impossible to distinguish, even by introspection, the external and personal components of a political position: this is the case, for example, with associational preferences, which are the preferences some people have for opportunities, like the opportunity to attend public schools, but only with others of the same 'background'.

The liberal, therefore, needs a scheme of civil rights, whose effect will be to determine those political decisions that are antecedently likely to reflect strong external preferences, and to remove those decisions from majoritarian political institutions altogether. Of course, the scheme of rights necessary to do this will depend on general facts about the prejudices and other external preferences of the majority at any given time, and different liberals will disagree about what is needed at any particular time.[6] But the rights encoded in the Bill of Rights of the United States Constitution, as interpreted (on the whole) by the Supreme Court, are those that a substantial number of liberals would think reasonably well suited to what the United States now requires (though most would think that the protection of the individual in certain important areas, including sexual publication and practice, are much too weak).

The main parts of the criminal law, however, present a special problem not easily met by a scheme of civil rights that disable the legislature from taking certain political decisions. The liberal knows that many of the most important decisions required by an effective criminal law are not made by legislators at all, but by prosecutors deciding whom to prosecute for what crime, and by juries and judges deciding whom to convict and what sentences to impose. He also knows that these decisions are antecedently very likely to be corrupted by the external preferences of those who make these decisions because those they judge, typically, have attitudes and ways of life very different from their own. The liberal does not have available, as protection against these decisions, any strategy comparable to the strategy of civil rights that simply remove a decision from an institution. Decisions to prosecute, convict and sentence must be made by someone. But he has available, in the notion of procedural rights, a different device to protect equality in a different way. He will insist that criminal procedure be structured to achieve a margin of safety in decisions, so that the process is biased strongly against the conviction of the innocent. It would be a mistake to suppose that the liberal thinks that these procedural rights will improve the *accuracy* of the criminal process, that is, the probability that any particular decision about guilt or innocence will be the right one. Procedural rights intervene in the process, even at the cost of inaccuracy, to compensate in a rough way for the antecedent risk that a criminal process, especially if it is largely administered by one class against another, will be corrupted by the impact of external preferences that cannot be eliminated directly. This is, of course, only the briefest sketch of how various substantive and procedural civil rights follow from the liberal's initial conception of equality; it is meant to suggest, rather than demonstrate, the more precise argument that would be available for more particular rights.

So the liberal, drawn to the economic market and to political democracy for distinctly egalitarian reasons, finds that these institutions will produce inegalitarian results unless he adds to his scheme different sorts of individual rights. These rights will function as trump cards held by individuals; they will enable individuals to resist particular decisions in spite of the fact that these decisions are or would be reached through the normal workings of general institutions that are not themselves challenged. The ultimate justification for these rights is that they are necessary to protect equal concern and respect; but they are not to be understood as representing equality in contrast to some other goal or principle served by democracy or the economic market. The familiar idea, for example, that rights of redistribution are justified by an ideal of equality that overrides the efficiency ideals of the market in certain cases, has no place in liberal theory. For the liberal, rights are justified, not by some principle in competition with an independent justification of the political and economic institutions they qualify, but in order to make more perfect the only justification on which these other institutions may themselves rely. If the liberal arguments for a particular right are sound, then the right is an unqualified improvement in political morality, not a necessary but regrettable compromise of some other independent goal, like economic efficiency.

IV

I said that the conservative holds one among a number of possible alternatives to the liberal conception of equality. Each of these alternatives shares the opinion that treating a person with respect requires treating him as the good man would wish to be treated. The conservative supposes that the good man would wish to be treated in accordance with the principles of a special sort of society, which I shall call the virtuous society. A virtuous society has these general features. Its members share a sound conception of virtue, that is, of the qualities and dispositions people should strive to have and exhibit. They share this conception in virtue not only privately, as individuals, but publicly: they believe their community, in its social and political activity, exhibits virtues, and that they have a responsibility, as citizens, to promote these virtues. In that sense they treat the lives of other members of their community as part of their own lives. The conservative position is not the only position that relies on this ideal of the virtuous society (some forms of socialism rely on it as well). But the conservative is distinct in believing that his own society, with its present institutions, is a virtuous society for the special reason that its history and common experience are better guides to sound virtue than any non-historical and therefore abstract deduction of virtue from first principles could provide.

Suppose a conservative is asked to draft a constitution for a society generally like ours, which he believes to be virtuous. Like the liberal, he will see great merit in the familiar institutions of political democracy and an economic market. The appeal of these institutions will be very different for the conservative, however. The economic market, in practice, assigns greater rewards to those who, because they have the virtues of talent and industry, supply more of what is wanted by the other members of the virtuous society; and that is, for the conservative, the paradigm of fairness in distribution. Political democracy distributes opportunities, through the provisions of civil and criminal law, as the citizens of a virtuous society wish it to be distributed, and that process will provide more scope for virtuous activity and less for vice than any less democratic technique. Democracy has a further advantage, moreover, that no other technique could have. It allows the community to use the processes of legislation to reaffirm, as a community, its public conception of virtue.

The appeal of the familiar institutions to the conservative is, therefore, very different from their appeal to the liberal. Since the conservative and the liberal both find the familiar institutions useful, though for different reasons, the existence of these institutions, as institutions, will not necessarily be a point of controversy between them. But they will disagree sharply over which corrective devices, in the form of individual rights, are necessary in order to maintain justice, and the disagreement will not be a matter of degree. The liberal, as I said, finds the market defective principally because it allows morally irrelevant differences, like differences in talent, to affect distribution, and he therefore considers that those who have less talent, as the market judges talent, have a right to some form of redistribution in the name of justice. But the conservative prizes just the feature of the market that puts a premium on talents prized in the community, because these are, in a virtuous community, virtues. So he will find no genuine merit, but only expediency, in the idea of redistribution. He will allow room, of course, for the virtue of charity, for it is a virtue that is part of the public catalogue; but he will prefer private charity to public, because it is a purer expression of that virtue. He may accept public charity as well, particularly when it seems necessary to retain the political allegiance of those who would otherwise suffer too much to tolerate a capitalist society at all. But public charity, justified either on grounds of virtue or expediency, will seem to the conservative a compromise with a primary justification of the market, rather than, as redistribution seems to the liberal, an improvement in that primary justification.

Nor will the conservative find the same defects in representative democracy that the liberal finds there. The conservative will not aim to exclude moralistic or other external preferences from the democratic process by any scheme of civil rights; on the contrary, it is the pride of democracy, for him, that external preferences are legislated into a public morality. But the conservative will find different defects in democracy, and he will contemplate a different scheme of rights to diminish the injustice they work.

The economic market distributes rewards for talents valued in the virtuous society, but since these talents are unequally distributed, wealth will be concentrated, and the wealthy will be at the mercy of an envious political majority anxious to take by law what it cannot take by talent. Justice requires some protection for the successful. The conservative will be (as historically he has been) anxious to hold some line against extensions of the vote to those groups most likely to be envious, but there is an apparent conflict between the ideals of abstract equality, even in the conservative conception, and disenfranchisement of large parts of the population. In any case, if conservatism is to be politically powerful, it must not threaten to exclude from political power those who would be asked to consent, formally or tacitly, to their own exclusion. The conservative will find more appeal in the different, and politically much more feasible, idea of rights to property.

These rights have the same force, though of course radically different content, as the liberal's civil rights. The liberal will, for his own purposes, accept some right to property, because he will count some sovereignty over a range of personal possessions essential to dignity. But the conservative will strive for rights to property of a very different order; he will want rights that protect, not some minimum dominion over a range of possessions independently shown to be desirable, but an unlimited dominion over whatever has been acquired through an institution that defines and rewards talent.

The conservative will not, of course, follow the liberal in the latter's concern for procedural rights in the criminal process. He will accept the basic institutions of criminal legislation and trial as proper; but he will see, in the possible acquittal of the guilty, not simply an inefficiency in the strategy of deterrence, but an affront to the basic principle that the censure of vice is indispensable to the honour of virtue. He will believe, therefore, that just criminal procedures are those that improve the antecedent probability that particular decisions of guilt or innocence will be accurate. He will support rights against interrogation or self-incrimination, for example, when such rights seem necessary to protect against torture or other means likely to elicit a confession from the innocent; but he will lose his concern for such rights when non-coercion can be guaranteed in other ways.

The fair-minded conservative will be concerned about racial discrimination, but his concern will differ from the concern of the liberal, and the remedies he will countenance will also be different. The distinction between equality of opportunity and equality of result is crucial to the conservative: the institutions of the economic market and representative democracy cannot achieve what he supposes they do unless each citizen has an equal opportunity to capitalize on his genuine talents and other virtues in the contest these institutions provide. But since the conservative knows that these virtues are unequally distributed, he also knows that equality of opportunity must have been denied if the outcome of the contest is equality of result.

The fair conservative must, therefore, attend to the charge that prejudice denies equality of opportunity between members of different races, and he must accept the justice of remedies designed to reinstate that equality, so far as this may be possible. But he will steadily oppose any form of 'affirmative action' that offers special opportunities, like places in medical school or jobs, on criteria other than some proper conception of the virtue appropriate to the reward.

The issue of gun control, which I have thus far not mentioned, is an excellent illustration of the power of the conservative's constitutive political morality. He favours strict control of sexual publication and practice, but he opposes parallel control of the ownership or use of guns, though of course guns are more dangerous than sex. President Ford, in the second Carter–Ford debate, put the conservative position of gun control especially clearly. Sensible conservatives do not dispute that private and uncontrolled ownership of guns leads to violence, because it puts guns in circulation that bad men may use badly. But (President Ford said) if we meet that problem by not allowing good men to have guns, we are punishing the wrong people. It is, of course, distinctive to the conservative's position to regard regulation as condemnation and hence as punishment. But he must regard regulation that way, because he believes that opportunities should be distributed, in a virtuous society, so as to promote virtuous acts at the expense of vicious ones.

V

In place of a conclusion, I shall say something, though not much, about two of the many important questions raised by what I have said. The first is the question posed in the first section of the essay. Does the theory of liberalism I described answer the sceptical thesis? Does it explain our present uncertainty about what liberalism now requires, and whether it is a genuine and tenable political theory? A great part of that uncertainty can be traced, as I said, to doubts about the connections between liberalism and the suddenly unfashionable idea of economic growth. The opinion is popular that some form of utilitarianism, which does take growth to be a value in itself, is constitutive of liberalism; but my arguments, if successful, show that this opinion is a mistake. Economic growth, as conventionally measured, was a derivative element in New Deal liberalism. It seemed to play a useful role in achieving the complex egalitarian distribution of resources that liberalism requires. If it now appears that economic growth injures more than it aids the liberal conception of equality, then the liberal is free to reject or curtail growth as a strategy. If the effect of growth is debatable, as I believe it is, then liberals will be uncertain, and appear to straddle the issue.

But the matter is more complicated than that analysis makes it seem, because economic growth may be deplored for many different reasons, some of which are plainly not available to the liberal. There is a powerful sentiment that a simpler way of life is better, in itself, than the life of consumption most Americans have recently preferred; this simpler life requires living in harmony with nature, and is therefore disturbed when, for example, a beautiful mountainside is spoiled by strip mining for the coal that lies within it. Should the mountainside be saved, in order to protect a way of life that depends upon it, either by regulation that prohibits mining, or by acquisition with taxpayers' money of a national park? May a liberal support such policies, consistently with his constitutive political morality? If he believes that government intervention is necessary to achieve a fair distribution of resources, on the ground that the market does not fairly reflect the preferences of those who want a park against those who want what the coal will produce, then he has a standard, egalitarian reason for supporting intervention. But suppose he does not believe that, but rather believes that those who want the park have a superior conception of what a truly worthwhile life is. A non-liberal may support conservation on that theory; but a liberal may not.

Suppose, however, that the liberal holds a different, more complex, belief about the importance of preserving natural resources. He believes that the conquest of unspoilt terrain by the consumer economy is self-fuelling and irreversible, and that this process will make a way of life that has been desired and found satisfying in the past unavailable to future generations, and indeed to the future of those who now seem unaware of its appeal. He fears that this way of life will become unknown, so that the process is not neutral amongst competing ideas of the good life, but in fact destructive of the very possibility of some of these. In that case the liberal has reasons for a programme of conservation that are not only consistent with his constitutive morality, but in fact sponsored by it.

I raise these possible lines of argument, not to provide the liberal with an easier path to a popular political position, but to illustrate the complexity of the issues that the new politics has provided. Liberalism seems precise and powerful when it is relatively clear what practical political positions are derivative from its fundamental constitutive morality; on these occasions politics allows what I called a liberal settlement of political positions. But such a settlement is fragile, and when it dissolves liberals must regroup, first through study and analysis, which will encourage a fresh and deeper understanding of what liberalism is, and then through the formation of a new and contemporary programme for liberals. The study and theory are not yet in progress, and the new programme is not yet in sight.

The second question I wish to mention, finally, is a question I have not touched at all. What is to be said in favour of liberalism? I do not suppose that I have made liberalism more attractive by arguing that its constitutive morality is a theory of equality that requires official neutrality amongst theories of what is valuable in life. The argument will provoke a variety of objections. It might be said that liberalism so conceived rests on scepticism about theories of the good, or that it is based on a mean view of human nature that assumes that human beings are atoms who can exist and find self-fulfilment apart from political community, or that it is self-contradictory because liberalism must itself be a theory of the good, or that it denies to political society its highest function and ultimate justification, which is that society must help its members to achieve what is in fact good. The first three of these objections need not concern us for long, because they are based on philosophical mistakes which I can quickly name if not refute. Liberalism cannot be based on scepticism. Its constitutive morality provides that human beings must be treated as equals by their government, not because there is no right and wrong in political morality, but because that is what is right. Liberalism does not rest on any special theory of personality, nor does it deny that most human beings will think that what is good for them is that they be active in society. Liberalism is not self-contradictory: the liberal conception of equality is a principle of political organization that is required by justice, not a way of life for individuals, and liberals, as such, are indifferent as to whether people choose to speak out on political matters, or to lead eccentric lives, or otherwise to behave as liberals are supposed to prefer.

But the fourth objection cannot so easily be set aside. There is no easy way to demonstrate the proper role in institutions that have a monopoly of power over the lives of others; reasonable and moral men will disagree. The issue is at bottom the issue I identified: what is the content of the respect that is necessary to dignity and independence?

That raises problems in moral philosophy and in the philosophy of mind that are fundamental for political theory though not discussed here; but this essay does bear on one issue sometimes thought to be relevant. It is sometimes said that liberalism must be wrong because it assumes that the opinions people have about the sort of lives they want are self-generated, whereas these opinions are in fact the products of the economic system or other aspects of the society in which they live. That would be an objection to liberalism if liberalism were based on some form of preference-utilitarianism which argued that justice in distribution consists in maximizing the extent to which people have what they happen to want. It is useful to point out, against that preference-utilitarianism, that since the preferences people have are formed by the system of distribution already in place, these preferences will tend to support that system, which is both circular and unfair. But liberalism, as I have described it, does not make the content of preferences the test of fairness in distribution. On the contrary, it is anxious to protect individuals whose needs are special or whose ambitions are eccentric from the fact that more popular preferences are institutionally and socially reinforced, for that is the effect and justification of the liberal's scheme of economic and political rights. Liberalism responds to the claim, that preferences are caused by systems of distribution, with the sensible answer that in that case it is all the more important that distribution be fair in itself, not as tested by the preferences it produces.

NOTES

[1] See Dworkin, *Taking Rights Seriously*, ch. 12.
[2] See *Taking Rights Seriously*, p. 227.
[3] See Scanlon, 'Preference and Urgency', *J. Phil.*, LXXII, p. 655.
[4] A very different objection calls attention to the fact that some people are afflicted with incapacities like blindness or mental disease, so that they require more resources to satisfy the *same* scheme of preferences. That

is a more appealing objection to my principle of rough equality of treatment, but it calls, not for choosing a different basic principle of distribution, but for corrections in the application of the principle like those I considered later.

5 Dworkin, *Taking Rights Seriously*, pp. 234 ff, 275.
6 See Dworkin, 'Social Sciences and Constitutional Rights', *The Educational Forum*, XLI (March, 1977), p. 271.

4

Friedrich A. Hayek: Equality, Value, and Merit*

*I have no respect for the passion for equality,
which seems to me merely idealizing envy.*

Oliver Wendell Holmes, Jr.

(1) The great aim of the struggle for liberty has been equality before the law. This equality under the rules which the state enforces may be supplemented by a similar equality of the rules that men voluntarily obey in their relations with one another. This extension of the principle of equality to the rules of moral and social conduct is the chief expression of what is commonly called the democratic spirit – and probably that aspect of it that does most to make inoffensive the inequalities that liberty necessarily produces.

Equality of the general rules of law and conduct, however, is the only kind of equality conductive to liberty and the only equality which we can secure without destroying liberty. Not only has liberty nothing to do with any other sort of equality, but it is even bound to produce inequality in many respects. This is the necessary result and part of the justification of individual liberty: if the result of individual liberty did not demonstrate that some manners of living are more successful than others, much of the case for it would vanish.

It is neither because it assumes that people are in fact equal nor because it attempts to make them equal that the argument for liberty demands that government treat them equally. This argument

*Reprinted from Friedrich Hayek, *The Constitution of Liberty* by permission of Chicago University Press. © 1960 by The University of Chicago. In Great Britain, published by permission of Routledge and Kegan Paul Ltd.

not only recognizes that individuals are very different but in a great measure rests on that assumption. It insists that these individual differences provide no justification for government to treat them differently. And it objects to the differences in treatment by the state that would be necessary if persons who are in fact very different were to be assured equal positions in life.

Modern advocates of a more far-reaching material equality usually deny that their demands are based on any assumption of the factual equality of all men.[1] It is nevertheless still widely believed that this is the main justification for such demands. Nothing, however, is more damaging to the demand for equal treatment than to base it on so obviously untrue an assumption as that of the factual equality of all men. To rest the case for equal treatment of national or racial minorities on the assertion that they do not differ from other men is implicitly to admit that factual inequality would justify unequal treatment; and the proof that some differences do, in fact, exist would not be long in forthcoming. It is of the essence of the demand for equality before the law that people should be treated alike in spite of the fact that they are different.

(2) The boundless variety of human nature – the wide range of differences in individual capacities and potentialities – is one of the most distinctive facts about the human species. Its evolution has made it probably the most variable among all kinds of creatures. It has been well said that

> biology, with variability as its cornerstone, confers on every human individual a unique set of attributes which give him a dignity he could not otherwise possess. Every newborn baby is an unknown quantity so far as potentialities are concerned because there are many thousands of unknown interrelated genes and gene-patterns which contribute to his make-up. As a result of nature and nurture the newborn infant may become one of the greatest of men or women ever to have lived. In every case he or she has the making of a distinctive individual. . . . If the differences are not very important, then freedom is not very important and the idea of individual worth is not very important.[2]

The writer justly adds that the widely held uniformity theory of human nature, 'which on the surface appears to accord with democracy . . . would in time undermine the very basic ideals of freedom and individual worth and render life as we know it meaningless.'[3]

It has been the fashion in modern times to minimize the importance of congenital differences between men and to ascribe all the important differences to the influence of environment.[4] However important the latter may be, we must not overlook the fact that individuals are very different from the outset. The importance of individual differences would hardly be less if all people were brought up in very similar environments. As a statement of fact, it just is not true that 'all men are born equal'. We may continue to use this hallowed phrase to express the ideal that legally and morally all men ought to be treated alike. But if we want to understand what this ideal of equality can or should mean, the first requirement is that we free ourselves from the belief in factual equality.

From the fact that people are very different it follows that, if we treat them equally, the result must be inequality in their actual position,[5] and that the only way to place them in an equal position would be to treat them differently. Equality before the law and material equality are therefore not only different but are in conflict with each other; and we can achieve either the one or the other, but not both at the same time. The equality before the law which freedom requires leads to material inequality. Our argument will be that, though where the state must use coercion for other reasons, it should treat all people alike, the desire of making people more alike in their condition cannot be accepted in a free society as a justification for further and discriminatory coercion.

We do not object to equality as such. It merely happens to be the case that a demand for equality is the professed motive of most of those who desire to impose upon society a preconceived pattern of distribution. Our objection is against all attempts to impress upon society a deliberately chosen pattern of distribution, whether it be an order of equality or of inequality. We shall indeed see that many of those who demand an extension of equality do not really demand equality but a distribution that conforms more closely to human conceptions of individual merit and that their desires are as irreconcilable with freedom as the more strictly egalitarian demands.

If one objects to the use of coercion in order to bring about a more even or a more just distribution, this does not mean that one does not regard these as desirable. But if we wish to preserve a free society, it is essential that we recognize that the desirability of a particular object is not sufficient justification for the use of coercion. One may well feel attracted to a community in which there are no extreme contrasts between rich and poor and may welcome the fact that the general increase in wealth seems gradually to reduce those differences. I fully share these feelings and certainly regard the degree of social equality that the United States has achieved as wholly admirable.

There also seems no reason why these widely felt preferences should not guide policy in some respects. Wherever there is a legitimate need for government action and we have to choose between different methods of satisfying such a need, those that incidentally also reduce inequality may well be preferable. If, for example, in the law of intestate succession one kind of provision will be more conducive to equality than another, this may be a strong argument in its favour. It is a different matter, however, if it is demanded that, in order to produce substantive equality, we should abandon the basic postulate of a free society, namely, the limitation of all coercion by equal law. Against this we shall hold that economic inequality is not one of the evils which justify our resorting to discriminatory coercion or privilege as a remedy.

(3) Our contention rests on two basic propositions which probably need only be stated to win fairly general assent. The first of them is an expression of the belief in a certain similarity of all human beings: it is the proposition that no man or group of men possesses the capacity to determine conclusively the potentialities of other human beings and that we should certainly never trust anyone invariably to exercise such a capacity. However great the differences between men may be, we have no ground for believing that they will ever be so great as to enable one man's mind in a particular instance to comprehend fully all that another responsible man's mind is capable of.

The second basic proposition is that the acquisition by any member of the community of additional capacities to do things which may be valuable must always be regarded as a gain for that community. It is true that particular people may be worse off because of the superior ability of some new competitor in their field; but any such additional ability in the community is likely to benefit the majority. This implies that the desirability of increasing the abilities and opportunities of any individual does not depend on whether the same can also be done for the others – provided, of course, that others are not thereby deprived of the opportunity of acquiring the same or other abilities which might have been accessible to them had they not been secured by that individual.

Egalitarians generally regard differently those differences in individual capacities which are inborn and those which are due to the influences of environment, or those which are the result of 'nature' and those which are the result of 'nurture'. Neither, be it said at once, has anything to do with moral merit.[6] Though either may greatly affect the value which an individual has for his fellows, no more credit belongs to him for having been born with desirable qualities than for having grown up under favourable circumstances. The distinction between the two is important only because the former advantages are due to circumstances clearly beyond human control, while the latter are due to factors which we might be able to alter. The important question is whether there is a case for so changing our institutions as to eliminate as much as possible those advantages due to environment. Are we to agree that 'all inequalities that rest on birth and inherited property ought to be abolished and none remain unless it is an effect of superior talent and industry'?[7]

The fact that certain advantages rest on human arrangements does not necessarily mean that we could provide the same advantages for all or that, if they are given to some, somebody else is thereby deprived of them. The most important factors to be considered in this connection are the family, inheritance, and education, and it is against the inequality which they produce that criticism is mainly directed. They are, however, not the only important factors of environment. Geographic conditions such as climate and landscape, not to speak of local and sectional differences in cultural and moral traditions, are scarcely less important. We can, however, consider here only the three factors whose effects are most commonly impugned.

So far as the family is concerned, there exists a curious contrast between the esteem most people profess for the institution and their dislike of the fact that being born into a particular family should confer on a person special advantages. It seems to be widely believed that, while useful qualities which a person acquires because of his native gifts under conditions which are the same for all are socially beneficial, the same qualities become somehow undesirable if they are the result of environmental advantages not available to others. Yet it is difficult to see why the same useful quality which is welcomed when it is the result of a person's natural endowment should be less valuable when it is the product of such circumstances as intelligent parents or a good home.

The value which most people attach to the institution of the family rests on the belief that, as a rule, parents can do more to prepare their children for a satisfactory life than anyone else. This means not only that the benefits which particular people derive from their family environment will be different but also that these benefits may operate cumulatively through several generations. What reason can there be for believing that a desirable quality in a person is less valuable to society if it has been the result of family background than if it has not? There is, indeed, good reason to think that there are some socially valuable qualities which will be rarely acquired in a single generation but which will generally be formed only by the continuous efforts of two or three. This means simply that there are parts of the cultural heritage of a society that are more effectively transmitted through the family. Granted this, it would be unreasonable to deny that a society is likely to get a better elite if ascent is not limited to one generation, if individuals are not deliberately made to start from the same level, and if children are not deprived of the chance to benefit from the better education and material environment which their parents may be able to provide. To admit this is merely to recognize that belonging to a particular family is part of the individual personality, that society is made up as much of families as of individuals, and that the transmission of the heritage of civilization within the family is as important a tool in man's striving towards better things as is the heredity of beneficial physical attributes.

(4) Many people who agree that the family is desirable as an instrument for the transmission of morals, tastes, and knowledge, still question the desirability of the transmission of material property. Yet there can be little doubt that, in order that the former may be possible, some continuity of standards, of the external forms of life, is essential, and that this will be achieved only if it is possible to transmit not only immaterial but also material advantages. There is, of course, neither greater merit nor any greater injustice involved in some people being born to wealthy parents than there is in others being born to kind or intelligent parents. The fact is that it is no less of an advantage to the community if at least some children can start with the advantages which at any given time only wealthy homes can offer than if some children inherit great intelligence or are taught better morals at home.

We are not concerned here with the chief argument for private inheritance, namely, that it seems essential as a means to preserve the dispersal in the control of capital and as an inducement for its accumulation. Rather, our concern here is whether the fact that it confers unmerited benefits on some is a valid argument against the institution. It is unquestionably one of the institutional causes of inequality. In the present context we need not enquire whether liberty demands unlimited freedom of bequest. Our problem here is merely whether people ought to be free to pass on to children or others such material possessions as will cause substantial inequality.

Once we agree that it is desirable to harness the natural instincts of parents to equip the new generation as well as they can, there seems no sensible ground for limiting this to non-material benefits. The family's function of passing on standards and traditions is closely tied up with the possibility of transmitting material goods. And it is difficult to see how it would serve the true interest of society to limit the gain in material conditions to one generation.

There is also another consideration which, though it may appear somewhat cynical, strongly suggests that if we wish to make the best use of the natural partiality of parents for their children, we ought not to preclude the transmission of property. It seems certain that among the many ways in which those who have gained power and influence might provide for their children, the bequest of a fortune is socially by far the cheapest. Without this outlet, these men would look for other ways of providing for their children, such as placing them in positions which might bring them the income and the prestige that a fortune would have done; and this would cause a waste of resources and an injustice much greater than is caused by the inheritance of property. Such is the case with all societies in which inheritance of property does not exist, including the communist. Those who dislike the inequalities caused by inheritance should therefore recognize that, men being what they are, it is the least of evils, even from their point of view.

(5) Though inheritance used to be the most widely criticized source of inequality, it is today probably no longer so. Egalitarian agitation now tends to concentrate on the unequal advantages due to differences in education. There is a growing tendency to express the desire to secure equality of conditions in the claim that the best education we have learned to provide for some should be made gratuitously available for all and that, if this is not possible, one should not be allowed to get a better education than the rest merely because one's parents are able to pay for it, but only those and all those who can pass a uniform test of ability should be admitted to the benefits of the limited resources of higher education.

The problem of educational policy raises too many issues to allow of their being discussed incidentally under the general heading of equality. For the present we shall only point out that enforced equality in this field can hardly avoid preventing some from getting the education they otherwise might. Whatever we might do, there is no way of preventing those advantages which only some can have, and which it is desirable that some should have, from going to people who neither individually merit them nor will make as good a use of them as some other person might have done. Such a problem cannot be satisfactorily solved by the exclusive and coercive powers of the state.

It is instructive at this point to glance briefly at the change that the ideal of equality has undergone in this field in modern times. A hundred years ago, at the height of the classical liberal movement, the demand was generally expressed by the phrase *la carrière ouverte aux talents*. It was a demand that all man-made obstacles to the rise of some should be removed, that all privileges of individuals should be abolished, and that what the state contributed to the chance of improving one's conditions should be the same for all. That so long as people were different and grew up in different families this could not assure an equal start was fairly generally accepted. It was understood that the duty of government was not to ensure that everybody had the same prospect of reaching a given position but merely to make available to all on equal terms those facilities which in their nature depended on government action. That the results were bound to be different, not only because the individuals were different, but also because only a small part of the relevant circumstances depended on government action, was taken for granted.

This conception that all should be allowed to try has been largely replaced by the altogether different conception that all must be assured an equal start and the same prospects. This means little less than that the government, instead of providing the same circum stances for all, should aim at controlling all conditions relevant to a particular individual's prospects and so adjust them to his capacities as to assure him of the same prospects as everybody else. Such deliberate adaptation of opportunities to individual aims and capacities would, of course, be the opposite of freedom. Nor could it be justified as a means of making the best use of all available knowledge except on the assumption that government knows best how individual capacities can be used.

When we enquire into the justification of these demands, we find that they rest on the discontent that the success of some people often produces in those that are less successful, or, to put it bluntly, on envy. The modern tendency to gratify this passion and to disguise it in the respectable garment of social justice is developing into a serious threat to freedom. Recently an attempt was made to base these demands on the argument that it ought to be the aim of politics to remove all sources of discontent.[8] This would, of course, necessarily mean that it is the responsibility of government to see that nobody is healthier or possesses a happier temperament, a better-suited spouse or more prospering children, than anybody else. If really all unfulfilled desires have a claim on the community, individual responsibility is at an end. However human, envy is certainly not one of the sources of discontent that a free society can eliminate. It is probably one of the essential conditions for the preservation of such a society that we do not countenance envy, not sanction its demands by camouflaging it as social justice, but treat it, in the words of John Stuart Mill, as 'the most anti-social and evil of all passions'.[9]

(6) While most of the strictly egalitarian demands are based on nothing better than envy, we must recognize that much that on the surface appears as a demand for greater equality is in fact a demand for a juster distribution of the good things of this world and springs therefore from much more creditable motives. Most people will object not to the bare fact of inequality but to the fact that the differences in reward do not correspond to any recognizable differences in the merits of those who receive them. The answer commonly given to this is that a free society on the whole achieves this kind of justice.[10] This, however, is an indefensible contention if by justice is meant proportionality of reward to moral merit. Any attempt to found the case for freedom on this argument is very damaging to it, since it concedes that material rewards ought to be made to correspond to recognizable merit and then opposes the conclusion that most people will draw from this by an assertion which is untrue. The proper answer is that in a free system it is neither desirable nor practicable that material rewards should be made generally to correspond to what men recognize as merit and that it is an essential characteristic of a free society that an individual's position should not necessarily depend on the views that his fellows hold about the merit he has acquired.

This contention may appear at first so strange and even shocking that I will ask the reader to suspend judgement until I have further explained the distinction between value and merit.[11] The difficulty in making the point clear is due to the fact that the term 'merit', which is the only one available to describe what I mean, is also used in a wider and vaguer sense. It will be used here exclusively to describe the attributes of conduct that make it deserving of praise, that is, the moral character of the action and not the value of the achievement.[12]

As we have seen throughout our discussion, the value that the performance or capacity of a person has to his fellows has no neccessary connection with its ascertainable merit in this sense. The inborn as well as the acquired gifts of a person clearly have a value to his fellows which does not depend on any credit due to him for possessing them. There is little a man can do to alter the fact that his special talents are very common or exceedingly rare. A good mind or a fine voice, a beautiful face or a skilful hand, and a ready wit or an attractive personality are in a large measure as independent of a person's efforts as the opportunities or the experiences he has had. In all these instances the value which a person's capacities or services have for us and for which he is recompensed has little relation to anything that we can call moral merit or deserts. Our problem is whether it is desirable that people should enjoy advantages in proportion to the benefits which their fellows derive from their activities or whether the distribution of these advantages should be based on other men's views of their merits.

Reward according to merit must in practice mean reward according to assessable merit, merit that other people can recognize and agree upon and not merit merely in the sight of some higher power. Assessable merit in this sense presupposes that we can ascertain that a man has done what some accepted rule of conduct demanded of him and that this has cost him some pain and effort. Whether this has been the case cannot be judged by the result: merit is not a matter of the objective outcome but of subjective effort. The attempt to achieve a valuable result may be highly meritorious but a complete failure, and full success may be entirely the result of accident and thus without merit. If we know that a man has done his best we will often wish to see him rewarded irrespective of the result; and if we know that a most valuable achievement is almost entirely due to luck or favourable circumstances, we will give little credit to the author.

We may wish that we were able to draw this distinction in every instance. In fact, we can do so only rarely with any degree of assurance. It is possible only where we possess all the knowledge which was at the disposal of the acting person, including a knowledge of his skill and confidence, his state of mind and his feelings, his capacity for attention, his energy and persistence, etc. The possibility of a true judgement of merit thus depends on the presence of precisely those conditions whose general absence is the main argument for liberty. It is because we want people to use knowledge which we do not possess that we let them decide for themselves. But insofar as we want them to be free to use capacities and knowledge of facts which we do not have, we are not in a position to judge the merit of their achievements. To decide on merit presupposes that we can judge whether people have made such use of their opportunities as they ought to have made and how much effort of will or self-denial this has cost them; it presupposes also that we can distinguish between that part of their achievement which is due to circumstances within their control and that part which is not.

(7) The incompatibility of reward according to merit with freedom to choose one's pursuit is most evident in those areas where the uncertainty of the outcome is particularly great and our individual estimates of the changes of various kinds of effort very different.[13] In those speculative efforts which we call 'research' or 'exploration', or in economic activities which we commonly describe as 'speculation', we cannot expect to attract those best qualified for them unless we give the successful ones all the credit or gain, though many others may have striven as meritoriously. For the same reason that nobody can know beforehand who will be the successful ones, nobody can say who has earned greater merit. It would clearly not serve our purpose if we let all who have honestly striven share in the prize. Moreover, to do so would make it necessary that somebody have the right to decide who is to be allowed to strive for it. If in their pursuit of uncertain goals people are to use their own knowledge and capacities, they must be guided, not by what other people think they ought to do, but by the value others attach to the result at which they aim.

What is so obviously true about those undertakings which we commonly regard as risky is scarcely less true of any chosen object we decide to pursue. Any such decision is beset with uncertainty, and if the choice is to be as wise as it is humanly possible to make it, the alternative results anticipated must be labelled according to their value. If the remuneration did not correspond to the value that the product of a man's efforts has for his fellows, he would have no basis for deciding whether the pursuit of a given object is worth the effort and risk. He would necessarily have to be told what to do, and some other person's estimate of what was the best use of his capacities would have to determine both his duties and his remuneration.[14]

The fact is, of course, that we do not wish people to earn a maximum of merit but to achieve a maximum of usefulness at a minimum of pain and sacrifice and therefore a minimum of merit. Not only would it be impossible for us to reward all merit justly, but it would not even be desirable that people should aim chiefly at earning a maximum of merit. Any attempt to induce them to do this would necessarily result in people being rewarded differently for the same service. And it is only the value of the result that we can judge with any degree of confidence, not the different degrees of effort and care that it has cost different people to achieve it.

The prizes that a free society offers for the result serve to tell those who strive for them how much effort they are worth. However, the same prizes will go to all those who produce the same result, regardless of effort. What is true here of the remuneration for the same services rendered by different people is even more true of the relative remuneration for different services requiring different gifts and capacities: they will have little relation to merit. The market will generally offer for services of any kind the value they will have for those who benefit from them; but it will rarely be known whether it was necessary to offer so much in order to obtain these services, and often, no doubt, the community could have had them for much less. The pianist who was reported not long ago to have said that he would perform even if he had to pay for the privilege probably described the position of many who earn large incomes from activities which are also their chief pleasure.

(8) Though most people regard as very natural the claim that nobody should be rewarded more than he deserves for his pain and effort, it is nevertheless based on a colossal presumption. It presumes that we are able to judge in every individual instance how well people use the different opportunities and talents given to them and how meritorious their achievements are in the light of all the circumstances which have them possible. It presumes that some human beings are in a position to determine conclusively what a person is worth and are entitled to determine what he may achieve. It presumes, then, what the argument for liberty specifically rejects: that we can and do know all that guides a person's action.

A society in which the position of the individuals was made to correspond to human ideas of moral merit would therefore be the exact opposite of a free society. It would be a society in which people were rewarded for duty performed instead of for success, in which every move of every individual was guided by what other people thought he ought to do, and in which the individual was thus relieved of the responsibility and the risk of decision. But if nobody's knowledge is sufficient to guide all human action, there is also no human being who is competent to reward all efforts according to merit.

In our individual conduct we generally act on the assumption that it is the value of a person's performance and not his merit that determines our obligation to him. Whatever may be true in more intimate relations, in the ordinary business of life we do not feel that, because a man has rendered us a service at a great sacrifice, our debt to him is determined by this, so long as we could have had the same service provided with ease by somebody else. In our dealings with other men we feel tht we are doing justice if we recompense value rendered with equal value, without enquiring what it might have cost the particular individual to supply us with these services. What determines our responsibility is the advantage we derive from what others offer us, not their merit in providing it.

We also expect in our dealings with others to be remunerated not according to our subjective merit but according to what our services are worth to them. Indeed, so long as we think in terms of our relations to particular people, we are generally quite aware that the mark of the free man is to be dependent for his livelihood not on other people's views of his merit but solely on what he has to offer them. It is only when we think of our position or our income as determined by 'society' as a whole that we demand reward according to merit.

Though moral value or merit is a species of value, not all value is moral value, and most of our judgements of value are not moral judgements. That this must be so in a free society is a point of cardinal importance; and the failure to distinguish between value and merit has been the source of serious confusion. We do not necessarily admire all activities whose product we value; and in most instances where we value what we get, we are in no position to assess the merit of those who have provided it for us. If a man's ability in a given field is more valuable after thirty years' work than it was earlier, this is independent of whether these thirty years were most profitable and enjoyable or whether they were a time of unceasing sacrifice and worry. If the pursuit of a hobby produces a special skill or an accidental invention turns out to be extremely useful to others, the fact that there is little merit in it does make it any less valuable than if the result had been produced by painful effort.

This difference between value and merit is not peculiar to any one type of society – it would exist anywhere. We might, of course, attempt to make rewards correspond to merit instead of value, but we are not likely to succeed in this. In attempting it, we would destroy the incentives which enable people to decide for themselves what they should do. Moreover, it is more than doubtful whether even a fairly successful attempt to make rewards correspond to merit would produce a more attractive or even a tolerable social order. A society in which it was generally presumed that a high income was proof of merit and a low income of the lack of it, in which it was universally believed that position and remuneration corresponded to merit, in which there was no other road to success than the approval of one's conduct by the majority of one's fellows, would probably be much more unbearable to the unsuccessful ones than one in which it was frankly recognized that there was no necessary connection between merit and success.[15]

It would probably contribute more to human happiness if, instead of trying to make remuneration correspond to merit, we made clearer how uncertain is the connection between value and merit. We are probably all much too ready to ascribe personal merit where there is, in fact, only superior value. The possession by an individual or a group of a superior civilization or education certainly represents an important value and constitutes as asset for the community to which they belong; but it usually constitutes little merit. Popularity and esteem do not depend more on merit than does financial success. It is, in fact, largely because we are so used to assuming an often non-existent merit wherever we find value that we balk when, in particular instances, the discrepancy is too large to be ignored.

There is every reason why we ought to endeavour to honour special merit where it has gone without adequate reward. But the problem of rewarding action of outstanding merit which we wish to be widely known as an example is different from that of the incentives on which the ordinary functioning of society rests. A free society produces institutions in which, for those who prefer it, a man's advancement depends on the judgement of some superior or of the majority of his fellows. Indeed, as organizations grow larger and more complex, the task of ascertaining the individual's contribution will become more difficult; and it will become increasingly necessary that, for many, merit in the eyes of the managers rather than the ascertainable value of the contribution should determine the rewards. So long as this does not produce a situation in which a single comprehensive scale of merit is imposed upon the whole society, so long as a multiplicity of organizations compete with one another in offering different prospects, this is not merely compatible with freedom but extends the range of choice open to the individual.

(9) Justice, like liberty and coercion, is a concept which, for the sake of clarity, ought to be confined to the deliberate treatment of men by other men. It is an aspect of the intentional determination of those conditions of people's lives that are subject to such control. Insofar as we want the efforts of individuals to be guided by their own views about prospects and chances, the results of the individual's efforts are necessarily unpredictable, and the question as to whether the resulting distribution of incomes is just has no meaning.[16] Justice does require that those conditions of people's lives that are determined by government be provided equally for all. But equality of those conditions must lead to inequality of results. Neither the equal provision of particular public facilities nor the equal treatment of different partners in our voluntary dealings with one another will secure reward that is proportional to merit. Reward for merit is reward for obeying the wishes of others in what we do, not compensation for the benefits we have conferred upon them by doing what we thought best.

It is, in fact, one of the objections against attempts by government to fix income scales that the state must attempt to be just in all it does. Once the principle of reward according to merit is accepted as the just foundation for the distribution of incomes, justice would require that all who desire it should be rewarded according to that principle. Soon it would also be demanded that the same principle be applied to all and that incomes not in proportion to recognizable merit not be tolerated. Even an attempt merely to distinguish between those incomes or gains which are 'earned' and those which are not will set up a principle which the state will have to try to apply but cannot in fact apply generally.[17] And every such attempt at deliberate control of some remunerations is bound to create further demands for new controls. The principle of distributive justice, once introduced, would not be fulfilled until the whole of society was organized in accordance with it. This would produce a kind of society which in all essential respects would be the opposite of a free society — a society in which authority decided what the individual was to do and how he was to do it.

(10) In conclusion we must briefly look at another argument on which the demands for a more equal distribution are frequently based, though it is rarely explicitly stated. This is the contention

that membership in a particular community or nation entitles the individual to a particular material standard that is determined by the general wealth of the group to which he belongs. This demand is in curious conflict with the desire to base distribution on personal merit. There is clearly no merit in being born into a particular community, and no argument of justice can be based on the accident of a particular individual's being born in one place rather than another. A relatively wealthy community in fact regularly confers advantages on its poorest members unknown to those born in poor communities. In a wealthy community the only justification its members can have for insisting on further advantages is that there is much private wealth that the government can confiscate and redistribute and that men who constantly see such wealth being enjoyed by others will have a stronger desire for it than those who know of it only abstractly, if at all.

There is no obvious reason why the joint efforts of the members of any group to ensure the maintenance of law and order and to organize the provision of certain services should give the members a claim to a particular share in the wealth of this group. Such claims would be especially difficult to defend where those who advanced them were unwilling to concede the same rights to those who did not belong to the same nation or community. The recognition of such claims on a national scale would in fact only create a new kind of collective (but not less exclusive) property right in the resources of the nation that could not be justified on the same grounds as individual property. Few people would be prepared to recognize the justice of these demands on a world scale. And the bare fact that within a given nation the majority had the actual power to enforce such demands, while in the world as a whole it did not yet have it, would hardly make them more just.

There are good reasons why we should endeavour to use whatever political organization we have at our disposal to make provision for the weak or infirm or for the victims of unforeseeable disaster. It may well be true that the most effective method of providing against certain risks common to all citizens of a state is to give every citizen protection against those risks. The level on which such provisions against common risks can be made will necessarily depend on the general wealth of the community.

It is an entirely different matter, however, to suggest that those who are poor, merely in the sense that there are those in the same community who are richer, are entitled to a share in the wealth of the latter or that being born into a group that has reached a particular level of civilization and comfort confers a title to a share in all its benefits. The fact that all citizens have an interest in the common provision of some services is no justification for anyone's claiming as a right a share in all the benefits. It may set a standard for what some ought to be willing to give, but not for what anyone can demand.

National groups will become more and more exclusive as the acceptance of this view that we have been contending against spreads. Rather than admit people to the advantages that living in their country offers, a nation will prefer to keep them out altogether; for, once admitted, they will soon claim as a right a particular share in its wealth. The conception that citizenship or even residence in a country confers a claim to a particular standard of living is becoming a serious source of international friction. And since the only justification for applying the principle within a given country is that its government has the power to enforce it, we must not be surprised if we find the same principle being applied by force on an international scale. Once the right of the majority to the benefits that minorities enjoy is recognized on a national scale, there is no reason why this should stop at the boundaries of the existing states.

NOTES

The quotation at the head of the chapter is taken from *The Holmes–Laski Letters: The Correspondence of Mr Justice Holmes and Harold J. Laski, 1916–35* (Cambridge: Harvard University Press, 1953), II, p. 942. A German translation of an earlier version of this chapter has appeared in *Ordo*, vol. x (1958).

[1] See, e.g., R. H. Tawney, *Equality* (London, 1931), p. 47.
[2] Roger J. Williams, *Free and Unequal: The Biological Basis of Individual Liberty* (Austin: University of Texas Press, 1953), pp. 23 and 70; cf. also J. B. S. Haldane, *The Inequality of Man* (London, 1932), and P. B. Medawar, *The Uniqueness of the Individual* (London, 1957).
[3] Williams, *Free and Unequal*, p. 152.
[4] See the description of this fashionable view in H. M. Kallen's article 'Behaviorism', *ESS*, II, p. 498: 'At birth human infants, regardless of their heredity, are as equal as Fords.'
[5] Cf. Plato *Laws* vi. 757A: 'To unequals equals become unequal.'
[6] Cf. F. H. Knight, *Freedom and Reform* (New York, 1947), p. 151: 'There is no visible reason why anyone is more or less entitled to the earnings of inherited personal capacities than to those of inherited property in any other form'; and the discussion in W. Roepke, *Mass und Mitte* (Erlenbach and Zurich, 1950), pp. 65–75.

[7] This is the position of R. H. Tawney as summarized by J. P. Plamenatz, 'Equality of Opportunity', in *Aspects of Human Equality*, ed. L. Bryson and others (New York, 1956), p. 100.

[8] C. A. R. Crosland, *The Future of Socialism* (London, 1956), p. 205.

[9] J. S. Mill, *On Liberty*, ed. R. B. McCallum (Oxford, 1946), p. 70.

[10] Cf. W. B. Gallie, 'Liberal Morality and Socialist Morality', in *Philosophy, Politics, and Society*, ed. P. Laslett (Oxford, 1956), pp. 123–5. The author represents it as the essence of 'liberal morality' that it claims that rewards are equal to merit in a free society. This was the position of some nineteenth-century liberals which often weakened their argument. A characteristic example is W. G. Sumner, who argued (*What Social Classes Owe to Each Other*, reprinted in *Freeman*, VI (Los Angeles, n.d.), 141) that if all 'have equal chances so far as chances are provided or limited by society', this will 'produce unequal results – that is results which shall be proportioned to the merits of individuals.' This is true only if 'merit' is used in the sense in which we have used 'value', without any moral connotations, but certainly not if it is meant to suggest proportionality to any endeavour to do the good or right thing, or to any subjective effort to conform to an ideal standard.

But, as we shall presently see, Mr Gallie is right that, in the Aristotelian terms he uses, liberalism aims at commutative justice and socialism at distributive justice. But, like most socialists, he does not see that distributive justice is irreconcilable with freedom in the choice of one's activities: it is the justice of a hierarchic organization, not of a free society.

[11] Although I believe that this distinction between merit and value is the same as that which Aristotle and Thomas Aquinas had in mind when they distinguished 'distributive justice' from 'commutative justice', I prefer not to tie up the discussion with all the difficulties and confusions which in the course of time have become associated with these traditional concepts. That what we call here 'reward according to merit' corresponds to the Aristotelian distributive justice seems clear. The difficult concept is that of 'commutative justice', and to speak of justice in this sense seems always to cause a little confusion. Cf. M. Solomon, *Der Begriff der Gerechtigkeit bei Aristoteles* (Leiden, 1937); and for a survey of the extensive literature G. del Vecchio, *Die Gerechtigkeit* (2nd ed.: Basel, 1950).

[12] The terminological difficulties arise from the fact that we use the word merit also in an objective sense and will speak of the 'merit' of an idea, a book, or a picture, irrespective of the merit acquired by the person who has created them. Sometimes the word is also used to describe what we regard as the 'true' value of some achievement as distinguished from its market value. Yet even a human achievement which has the greatest value or merit in this sense is not necessarily proof of moral merit on the part of him to whom it is due. It seems that our use has the sanction of philosophical tradition. Cf., for instance, D. Hume, *Treatise*, II, p. 252: 'The external performance has no merit. We must look within to find

the moral quality. . . . The ultimate object of our praise and approbation is the motive, that produc'd them.'

13 Cf. the important essay by A. A. Alchian, 'Uncertainty, Evolution, and Economic Theory', *JPE*, LVIII (1950), especially pp. 213–14, Sec, II, headed 'Success Is Based on Results, Not Motivation'. It probably is also no accident that the American economist who has done most to advance our understanding of a free society, F. H. Knight, began his professional career with a study of *Risk, Uncertainty, and Profit*. Cf. also B. de Jouvenel, *Power* (London, 1948), p. 298.

14 It is often maintained that justice requires that remuneration be proportional to the unpleasantness of the job and that for this reason the street cleaner or the sewage worker ought to be paid more than the doctor or office worker. This, indeed, would seem to be the consequence of the principle of remuneration according to merit (or 'distributive justice'). In a market such a result would come about only if all people were equally skilful in all jobs so that those who could earn as much as others in the more pleasant occupations would have to be paid more to undertake the distasteful ones. In the actual world those unpleasant jobs provide those whose usefulness in the more attractive jobs is small an opportunity to earn more than they could elsewhere. That persons who have little to offer their fellows should be able to earn an income similar to that of the rest only at a much greater sacrifice is inevitable in any arrangement under which the individual is allowed to choose his own sphere of usefulness.

15 Cf. Crosland, *The Future of Socialism*, p. 235: 'Even if all the failures could be convinced that they had an equal chance, their discontent would still not be assuaged; indeed it might actually be intensified. When opportunities are known to be unequal, and the selection clearly biased towards wealth or lineage, people can comfort themselves for failure by saying that they never had a proper chance – the system was unfair, the scales too heavily weighted against them. But if the selection is obviously by merit, this source of comfort disappears, and failure induces a total sense of inferiority, with no excuse or consolation; and this, by a natural quirk of human nature, actually increases the envy and resentment at the success of others.' Cf. also ch. 24, at n. 8. I have not yet seen Michael Young, *The Rise of the Meritocracy* (London, 1958), which, judging from reviews, appears to bring out these problems very clearly.

16 See the interesting discussion in R. G. Collingwood, 'Economics as a Philosophical Science', *Ethics*, vol. XXXVI (1926), who concludes (p. 174): 'A just price, a just wage, a just rate of interest, is a contradiction in terms. The question what a person ought to get in return for his goods and labor is a question absolutely devoid of meaning. The only valid questions are what he *can* get in return for his goods or labor, and whether he ought to sell them at all.'

17 It is, of course, possible to give the distinction between 'earned' and 'unearned' incomes, gains, or increments a fairly precise legal meaning,

but it then rapidly ceases to correspond to the moral distinction which provides its justification. Any serious attempt to apply the moral distinction in practice soon meets the same insuperable difficulties as any attempt to assess subjective merit. How little these difficulties are generally understood by philosophers (except in rare instances, as that quoted in the preceding note) is well illustrated by a discussion in L. S. Stebbing, *Thinking to Some Purpose* (Pelican Books: London, 1939), p. 184, in which, as an illustration of a distinction which is clear but not sharp, she chooses that between 'legitimate' and 'excess' profits and asserts: 'The distinction is clear between "excess profits" (or "profiteering") and "legitimate profits", although it is not a sharp distinction.'

5

Robert Nozick: Moral Constraints and Distributive Justice*

I

THE MINIMAL STATE AND THE ULTRAMINIMAL STATE

The night-watchman state of classical liberal theory, limited to the functions of protecting all its citizens against violence, theft, and fraud, and to the enforcement of contracts, and so on, appears to be redistributive.[1] We can imagine at least one social arrangement intermediate between the scheme of private protective associations and the night-watchman state. Since the night-watchman state is often called a minimal state, we shall call this other arrangement the *ultraminimal state*. An ultraminimal state maintains a monopoly over all use of force except that necessary in immediate self-defence, and so excludes private (or agency) retaliation for wrong and exaction of compensation; but it provides protection and enforcement services *only* to those who purchase its protection and enforcement policies. People who don't buy a protection contract from the monopoly don't get protected. The minimal (night-watchman) state is equivalent to the ultraminimal state conjoined with a (clearly redistributive) Friedmanesque voucher plan, financed from tax revenues.[2] Under this plan all people, or some (for example, those in need), are given tax-funded vouchers that can be used only for their purchase of a protection policy from the ultraminimal state.

Since the night-watchman state appears redistributive to the extent that it compels some people to pay for the protection of others, its proponents must explain why this redistributive function

---

* From *Anarchy, State and Utopia*, by Robert Nozick © 1974 by Basic Books, Inc., Publishers. Reprinted by permission of the publisher.

of the state is unique. If some redistribution is legitimate in order to protect everyone, why is redistribution not legitimate for other attractive and desirable purposes as well? What rationale specifically selects protective services as the sole subject of legitimate redistributive activities? A rationale, once found, may show that this provision of protective service is *not* redistributive. More precisely, the term 'redistributive' applies to types of *reasons* for an arrangement, rather than to an arrangement itself. We might elliptically call an arrangement 'redistributive' if its major (only possible) supporting reasons are themselves redistributive. ('Paternalistic' functions similarly.) Finding compelling non-redistributive reasons would cause us to drop this label. Whether we say an institution that takes money from some and gives it to others is redistributive will depend upon *why* we think it does so. Returning stolen money or compensating for violations of rights are *not* redistributive reasons. I have spoken until now of the night-watchman state's *appearing* to be redistributive, to leave open the possibility that non-redistributive types of reasons might be found to justify the provision of protective services for some by others.

A proponent of the ultraminimal state may seem to occupy an inconsistent position, even though he avoids the question of what makes protection uniquely suitable for redistributive provision. Greatly concerned to protect rights against violation, he makes this the sole function of the state; and he protests that all other functions are illegitimate because they themselves involve the violation of rights. Since he accords paramount place to the protection and non-violation of rights, how can he support the ultraminimal state, which would seem to leave some person's rights unprotected or ill-protected? How can he support this *in the name of* the non-violation of rights?

MORAL CONSTRAINTS AND MORAL GOALS

This question assumes that a moral concern can function only as a moral *goal*, as an end state for some activities to achieve as their result. It may, indeed, seem to be a necessary truth that 'right', 'ought', 'should', and so on, are to be explained in terms of what is, or is intended to be, productive of the greatest good, with all goals built into the good.[3] Thus it is often thought that what is wrong with utilitarianism (which *is* of this form) is its too narrow conception of good. Utilitarianism doesn't, it is said, properly take rights and their non-violation into account; it instead leaves them a derivative status. Many of the counter-example cases to utilitarianism fit under this objection, for example, punishing an innocent man to save a neighbourhood from a vengeful rampage. But a theory may include in a primary way the non-violation of rights, yet include it in the wrong place and the wrong manner. For suppose some condition about minimizing the total (weighted) amount of violations of rights is built into the desirable end state to be achieved. We then would have something like a 'utilitarianism of rights'; violations of rights (to be *minimized*) merely would replace the total happiness as the relevant end state in the utilitarian structure. (Note that we do not hold the non-violation of our rights as our sole greatest good or even rank it first lexicographically to exclude trade-offs, if there is some desirable society we would choose to inhabit even though in it some rights of ours sometimes are violated, rather than move to a desert island where we could survive alone.) This still would require us to violate someone's rights when doing so minimizes the total (weighted) amount of violation of rights in the society. For example, violating someone's rights might deflect others from *their* intended action of gravely violating rights, or might remove their motive for doing so, or might divert their attention, and so on. A mob rampaging through a part of town killing and burning *will* violate the rights of those living there. Therefore, someone might try to justify his punishing another *he* knows to be innocent of a crime that enraged a mob, on the grounds that punishing this innocent person would help to avoid even greater violations of rights by others, and so would lead to a minimum weighted score of rights violations in the society.

In contrast to incorporating rights into the end state to be achieved, one might place them as side constraints upon the actions to be done: don't violate constraints C. The rights of others determine the constraints upon your actions. (A *goal-directed* view with constraints added would be: among those acts available to you that don't violate constraints C, act so as to maximize goal G. Here, the rights of others would constrain your goal-directed behaviour. I do not mean to imply that the correct moral view includes mandatory goals that must be pursued, even within the constraints.) This view differs from one that tries to build the side constraints C *into* the goal G. The side-constraint view forbids you to violate these moral constraints in the pursuit of your goals; whereas the view whose objective is too minimize the violation of these rights allows you to violate the rights (the constraints) in order to lessen their total violation in the society.[4]

The claim that the proponent of the ultraminimal state is

inconsistent, we now can see, assumes that he is a 'utilitarian of rights'. It assumes that his goal is, for example, to minimize the weighted amount of the violation of rights in the society, and that he should pursue this goal even through means that themselves violate people's rights. Instead, he may place the non-violation of rights as a constraint upon action, rather than (or in addition to) building it into the end state to be realized. The position held by this proponent of the ultraminimal state will be a consistent one if his conception of rights holds that your being *forced* to contribute to another's welfare violates your rights, whereas someone else's not providing you with things you need greatly, including things essential to the protection of your rights, does not *itself* violate your rights, even though it avoids making it more difficult for someone else to violate them. (That conception will be consistent provided it does not construe the monopoly element of the ultraminimal state as itself a violation of rights.) That it is a consistent position does not, of course, show that it is an acceptable one.

WHY SIDE CONSTRAINTS?

Isn't it *irrational* to accept a side constraint C, rather than a view that directs minimizing the violations of C? (The latter view treats C as a condition rather than a constraint.) If non-violation of C is so important, shouldn't that be the goal? How can a concern for the non-violation of C lead to the refusal to violate C even when this would prevent other more extensive violations of C? What is the rationale for placing the non-violation of rights as a side constraint upon action instead of including it solely as a goal of one's actions?

Side constraints upon action reflect the underlying Kantian principle that individuals are ends and not merely means; they may not be sacrificed or used for the achieving of other ends without their consent. Individuals are inviolable. More should be said to illuminate this talk of ends and means. Consider a prime example of a means, a tool. There is no side constraint on how we may use a tool, other than the moral constraints on how we may use it upon others. There are procedures to be followed to preserve it for future use ('don't leave it out in the rain'), and there are more and less efficient ways of using it. But there is no limit on what we may do to it to best achieve our goals. Now imagine that there was an overrideable constraint C on some tool's use. For example, the tool might have been lent to you only on the condition that C not be violated unless the gain from doing so was above a certain specified amount, or unless it was necessary to achieve a certain specified goal. Here the object is not *completely* your tool, for use according to your wish or whim. But it is a tool nevertheless, even with regard to the overrideable constraint. If we add constraints on its use that may not be overridden, then the object may not be used as a tool *in those ways*. *In those respects*, it is not a tool at all. Can one add enough constraints so that an object cannot be used as a tool at all, in *any* respect?

Can behaviour towards a person be constrained so that he is not to be used for any end except as he chooses? This is an impossibly stringent condition if it requires everyone who provides us with a good to approve positively of every use to which we wish to put it. Even the requirement that he merely should not object to any use we plan would seriously curtail bilateral exchange, not to mention sequences of such exchanges. It is sufficient that the other party stands to gain enough from the exchange so that he is willing to go through with it, even though he objects to one or more of the uses to which you shall put the good. Under such conditions, the other party is not being used solely as a means, in that respect. Another party, however, who would not choose to interact with you if he knew of the uses to which you *intend* to put his actions or good, *is* being used as a means, even if he receives enough to choose (in his ignorance) to interact with you. ('All along, you were just *using* me' can be said by someone who chose to interact only because he was ignorant of another's goals and of the uses to which he himself would be put.) Is it morally incumbent upon someone to reveal his intended uses of an interaction if he has good reason to believe the other would refuse to interact if he knew? Is he *using* the other person, if he does not reveal this? And what of the cases where the other does not choose to be of use at all? In getting pleasure from seeing an attractive person go by, does one use the other solely as a means?[5] Does someone so use an object of sexual fantasies? These and related questions raise very interesting issues for moral philosophy; but not, I think, for political philosophy.

Political philosophy is concerned only with *certain* ways that persons may not use others; primarily, physically aggressing against them. A specific side constraint upon action towards others expresses the fact that others may not be used in the specific ways the side constraint excludes. Side constraints express the inviolability of others, in the ways they specify. These modes of inviolability are expressed by the following injunction: 'Don't use people in specified ways.' An end-state view, on the other hand, would express the view that people are ends and not merely means (if it chooses to express this view at all), by a different injunction: 'Minimize the use in specified ways of persons as means.' Following this precept itself may involve using someone as a means in one of the ways specified. Had Kant held this view, he would have given the second formula of the categorical imperative as, 'So act as to minimize the use of humanity simply as a means', rather than the one he actually used: 'Act in such a way that you always treat humanity, whether in your own person or in the person of any other, never simply as a means, but always at the same time as an end.'[6]

Side constraints express the inviolability of other persons. But why may not one violate persons for the greater social good? Individually, we each sometimes choose to undergo some pain or sacrifice for a greater benefit or to avoid a greater harm: we go to the dentist to avoid worse suffering later; we do some unpleasant work for its results; some persons diet to improve their health or looks; some save money to support themselves when they are older. In each case, some cost is borne for the sake of the greater overall good. Why not, *similarly*, hold that some persons have to bear some costs that benefit other persons more, for the sake of the overall social good? But there is no *social entity* with a good that undergoes some sacrifice for its own good. There are only individual people, different individual people, with their own individual lives. Using one of these people for the benefit of others, uses him and benefits the others. Nothing more. What happens is that something is done to him for the sake of others. Talk of an overall social good covers this up. (Intentionally?) To use a person in this way does not sufficiently respect and take account of the fact that he is a separate person,[7] that his is the only life he has. He does not get some overbalancing good from his sacrifice, and no one is entitled to force this upon him – least of all a state or government that claims his allegiance (as other individuals do not) and that therefore scrupulously must be *neutral* between its citizens.

LIBERTARIAN CONSTRAINTS

The moral side constraints upon what we may do, I claim, reflect the fact of our separate existences. They reflect the fact that no moral balancing act can take place among us; there is no moral outweighing of one of our lives by others so as to lead to a greater overall *social* good. There is no justified sacrifice of some of us for others. This root idea, namely, that there are different individuals with separate lives and so no one may be sacrificed for others, underlies the existence of moral side constraints, but it also, I believe, leads to a libertarian side constraint that prohibits aggression against another. . . .

II

DISTRIBUTIVE JUSTICE

The minimal state is the most extensive state that can be justified. Any state more extensive violates people's rights. Yet many persons have put forth reasons purporting to justify a more extensive state. It is impossible within the compass of this book to examine all the reasons that have been put forth. Therefore, I shall focus upon those generally acknowledged to be most weighty and influential, to see precisely wherein they fail. Here we consider the claim that a more extensive state is justified, because necessary (or the best instrument) to achieve distributive justice; then we shall take up diverse other claims.

The term 'distributive justice' is not a neutral one. Hearing the term 'distribution', most people presume that some thing or mechanism uses some principle or criterion to give out a supply of things. Into this process of distributing shares some error may have crept. So it is an open question, at least, whether *re*distribution should take place; whether we should do again what has already been done once, though poorly. However, we are not in the position of children who have been given portions of pie by someone who now makes last minute adjustments to rectify careless cutting. There is no *central* distribution, no person or group entitled to control all the resources, jointly deciding how they are to be doled out. What each person gets, he gets from others who give to him in exchange for something, or as a gift. In a free society, diverse persons control different resources, and new holdings arise out of the voluntary exchanges and actions of persons. There is no more a distributing or distribution of shares than there is a distributing of mates in a society in which persons choose whom they shall marry. The total result is the product of many individual decisions which the different individuals involved are entitled to make. Some uses of the term 'distribution', it is true, do not imply a previous distributing appropriately judged by some criterion (for example, 'probability distribution'); nevertheless, despite the title of this chapter, it would be best to use a terminology that clearly is neutral. We shall speak of people's holdings; a principle of justice in holdings describes (part of) what justice tells us (requires) about holdings. I shall state first what I take to be the correct view about justice in holdings, and then turn to the discussion of alternate views.[8]

THE ENTITLEMENT THEORY

The subject of justice in holdings consists of three major topics. The first is the *original acquisition of holdings*, the appropriation of unheld things. This includes the issues of how unheld things may come to be held, the process, or processes, by which unheld things may come to be held, the things that may come to be held by these processes, the extent of what comes to be held by a particular process, and so on. We shall refer to the complicated truth about this topic, which we shall not formulate here, as the principle of justice in acquisition. The second topic concerns the *transfer of holdings* from one person to another. By what processes may a person transfer holdings to another? How may a person acquire a holding from another who holds it? Under this topic come general descriptions of voluntary exchange, and gift and (on the other hand) fraud, as well as reference to particular conventional details fixed upon in a given society. The complicated truth about this subject (with placeholders for conventional details) we shall call the principle of justice in transfer. (And we shall suppose it also includes principles governing how a person may divest himself of a holding, passing it into an unheld state.)

If the world were wholly just, the following inductive definition would exhaustively cover the subject of justice in holdings.

(1) A person who acquires a holding in accordance with the principle of justice in acquisition is entitled to that holding.

(2) A person who acquires a holding in accordance with the principle of justice in transfer, from someone else entitled to the holding, is entitled to the holding.

(3) No one is entitled to a holding except by (repeated) applications of 1 and 2.

The complete principle of distributive justice would say simply that a distribution is just if everyone is entitled to the holdings they possess under the distribution.

A distribution is just if it arises from another just distribution by legitimate means. The legitimate means of moving from one distribution to another are specified by the principle of justice in transfer. The legitimate first 'moves' are specified by the principle of justice in acquisition.[9] Whatever arises from a just situation by just steps is itself just. The means of change specified by the principle of justice in transfer preserve justice. As correct rules of inference are truth-preserving, and any conclusion deduced via repeated application of such rules from only true premises is itself true, so the means of transition from one situation to another specified by the principle of justice in transfer are justice-preserving, and any situation actually arising from repeated transitions in accordance with the principle from a just situation is itself just. The parallel between justice-preserving transformations and truth-preserving transformations illuminates where it fails as well as where it holds. That a conclusion could have been deduced by truth-preserving means from premises that are true suffices to show its truth. That from a just situation a situation *could* have arisen via justice-preserving means does *not* suffice to show its justice. The fact that a thief's victims voluntarily *could* have presented him with gifts does not entitle the thief to his ill-gotten gains. Justice in holdings is historical; it depends upon what actually has happened. We shall return to this point later.

Not all actual situations are generated in accordance with the two principles of justice in holdings: the principle of justice in acquisition and the principle of justice in transfer. Some people steal from others, or defraud them, or enslave them, seizing their product and preventing them from living as they choose, or forcibly exclude others from competing in exchanges. None of these are permissible modes of transition from one situation to another. And some persons acquire holdings by means not sanctioned by the principle of justice in acquisition. The existence of past injustice (previous violations of the first two principles of justice in holdings) raises the third major topic under justice in holdings: the rectification of injustice in holdings. If past injustice has shaped present holdings in various ways, some identifiable and some not, what now, if anything, ought to be done to rectify these injustices? What obligations do the performers of injustice have towards those whose position is worse than it would have been had the injustice not been done? Or, than it would have been had compensation been paid promptly? How, if at all, do things change if the beneficiaries and those made worse off are not the direct parties in the act of injustice, but, for example, their descendants? Is an injustice done to someone whose holding was itself based upon an unrectified injustice? How far back must one go in wiping clean the historical slate of injustices? What may victims of injustice permissibly do in order to rectify the injustices being done to them, including the many injustices done by persons acting through their government? I do not know of a thorough or theoretically sophisticated treatment of such issues.[10] Idealizing greatly, let us suppose theoretical investigation will produce a principle of rectification. This principle uses historical information about previous situations and injustices done in them (as defined by the first two principles of justice and rights against interference), and information about the actual course of events that flowed from these injustices, until the present, and it yields a description (or descriptions) of holdings in the society. The principle of rectification presumably will make use of its best estimate of subjunctive information about what would have occurred (or a probability distribution over what might have occurred, using the expected value) if the injustice had not taken place. If the actual description of holdings turns out not to be one of the descriptions yielded by the principle, then one of the descriptions yielded must be realized.[11]

The general outlines of the theory of justice in holdings are that the holdings of a person are just if he is entitled to them by the principles of justice in acquisition and transfer, or by the principle of rectification of injustice (as specified by the first two principles). If each person's holdings are just, then the total set (distribution) of holdings is just. To turn these general outlines into a specific theory we would have to specify the details of each of the three principles of justice in holdings: the principle of acquisition of holdings, the principle of transfer of holdings, and the principle of rectification of violations of the first two principles. I shall not attempt that task here.

HISTORICAL PRINCIPLES
AND END-RESULT PRINCIPLES

The general outlines of the entitlement theory illuminate the nature and defects of other conceptions of distributive justice. The entitlement theory of justice in distribution is *historical*; whether a distribution is just depends upon how it came about. In contrast, *current time-slice principles* of justice hold that the justice of a distribution is determined by how things are distributed (who has what) as judged by some *structural* principle(s) of just distribution. A utilitarian who judges between any two distributions by seeing which has the greater sum of utility and, if the sums tie, applies some fixed equality criterion to choose the more equal distribution, would hold a current time-slice principle of justice. As would someone who had a fixed schedule of trade-offs between the sum of happiness and equality. According to a current time-slice principle, all that needs to be looked at, in judging the justice of a distribution, is who ends up with what; in comparing any two distributions one need look only at the matrix presenting the distributions. No further information need be fed into a principle of justice. It is a consequence of such principles of justice that any two structurally identical distributions are equally just. (Two distributions are structurally identical if they present the same profile, but perhaps have different persons occupying the particular slots. My having ten and your having five, and my having five and your having ten are structurally identical distributions.) Welfare economics is the theory of current time-slice principles of justice. The subject is conceived as operating on matrices representing only current information about distribution. This, as well as some of the usual conditions (for example, the choice of distribution is invariant under relabelling of columns), guarantees that welfare economics will be a current time-slice theory, with all of its inadequacies.

Most persons do not accept current time-slice principles as constituting the whole story about distributive shares. They think it relevant in assessing the justice of a situation to consider not only the distribution it embodies, but also how that distribution came about. If some persons are in prison for murder or war crimes, we do not say that to assess the justice of the distribution in the society we must look only at what this person has, and that person has, and that person has . . . at the current time. We think it relevant to ask whether someone did something so that he *deserved* to be punished, deserved to have a lower share. Most will agree to the relevance of further information with regard to punishments and penalties. Consider also desired things. One traditional socialist view is that workers are entitled to the product and full fruits of their labour; they have earned it; a distribution is unjust if it does not give the workers what they are entitled to. Such entitlements are based upon some past history. No socialist holding this view would find it comforting to be told that because the actual distribution A happens to coincide structurally with the one he desires D, A therefore is no less just than D; it differs only in that the 'parasitic' owners of capital receive under A what the workers are entitled to under D, and the workers receive under A what the owners are entitled to under D, namely very little. This socialist rightly, in my view, holds on to the notions of earning, producing, entitlement, desert, and so forth, and he rejects current time-slice principles that look only to the structure of the resulting set of holdings. (The set of holdings resulting from what? Isn't it implausible that how holdings are produced and come to exist has no effect at all on who should hold what?) His mistake lies in his view of what entitlements arise out of what sorts of productive processes.

We construe the position we discuss too narrowly by speaking of *current* time-slice principles. Nothing is changed if structural principles operate upon a time sequence of current time-slice profiles and, for example, give someone more now to counterbalance the less he has had earlier. A utilitarian or an egalitarian or any mixture of the two over time will inherit the difficulties of his more myopic comrades. He is not helped by the fact that *some* of the information others consider relevant in assessing a distribution is reflected, unrecoverably, in past matrices. Henceforth, we shall refer to such unhistorical principles of distributive justice, including the current time-slice principles, as *end-result principles* or *end-state principles*.

In contrast to end-result principles of justice, *historical principles* of justice hold that past circumstances or actions of people can create differential entitlements or differential deserts to things. An injustice can be worked by moving from one distribution to another structurally identical one, for the second, in profile the same, may violate people's entitlements or deserts; it may not fit the actual history.

PATTERNING

The entitlement principles of justice in holdings that we have sketched are historical principles of justice. To better understand their precise character, we shall distinguish them from another subclass of the historical principles. Consider, as an example, the principle of distribution according to moral merit. This principle requires that total distributive shares vary directly with moral merit; no person should have a greater share than anyone whose moral merit is greater. (If moral merit could be not merely ordered but measured on an interval or ratio scale, stronger principles could be formulated.) Or consider the principle that results by substituting 'usefulness to society' for 'moral merit' in the previous principle. Or instead of 'distribute according to moral merit', or 'distribute according to usefulness to society', we might consider 'distribute according to the weighted sum of moral merit, usefulness to society, and need', with the weights of the different dimensions equal. Let us call a principle of distribution *patterned* if it specifies that a distribution is to vary along with some natural dimension, weighted sum of natural dimensions, or lexicographic ordering of natural dimensions. And let us say a distribution is patterned if it accords with some patterned principle. (I speak of natural dimensions, admittedly without a general criterion for them, because for any set of holdings some artificial dimensions can be gimmicked up to vary along with the distribution of the set.) The principle of distribution in accordance with moral merit is a patterned historical principle, which specifies a patterned distribution. 'Distribute according to IQ' is a patterned principle that looks to information not contained in distributional matrices. It is not historical, however, in that it does not look to any past actions creating differential entitlements to evaluate a distribution; it requires only distributional matrices whose columns are labeled by IQ scores. The distribution in a society, however, may be composed of such simple patterned distributions, without itself being simply patterned. Different sectors may operate different patterns, or some combination of patterns may operate in different proportions across a society. A distribution composed in this manner, from a small number of patterned distributions, we also shall term 'patterned'. And we extend the use of 'pattern' to include the overall designs put forth by combinations of end-state principles.

Almost every suggested principle of distributive justice is patterned: to each according to his moral merit, or needs, or marginal product, or how hard he tries, or the weighted sum of the foregoing, and so on. The principle of entitlement we have sketched is *not* patterned.[12] There is no one natural dimension or weighted sum or combination of a small number of natural dimensions that yields the distributions generated in accordance with the principle of entitlement. The set of holdings that results when some persons receive their marginal products, others win at gambling, others receive a share of their mate's income, others receive gifts from foundations, others receive interest on loans, others receive gifts from admirers, others receive returns on investment, others make for themselves much of what they have, others find things, and so on, will not be patterned. Heavy strands of patterns will run through it; significant portions of the variance in holdings will be accounted for by pattern-variables. If most people most of the time choose to transfer some of their entitlements to others only in exchange for something from them, then a large part of what many people hold will vary with what they held that others wanted. More details are provided by the theory of marginal productivity. But gifts to relatives, charitable donations, bequests to children, and the like, are not best conceived, in the first instance, in this manner. Ignoring the strands of pattern, let us suppose for the moment that a distribution actually arrived at by the operation of the principle of entitlement is random with respect to any pattern. Though the resulting set of holdings will be unpatterned, it will not be incomprehensible, for it can be seen as arising from the operation of a small number of principles. These principles specify how an initial distribution may arise (the principle of acquisition of holdings) and how distributions may be transformed into others (the principle of transfer of holdings). The process whereby the set of holdings is generated will be intelligible, though the set of holdings itself that results from this process will be unpatterned.

The writings of F. A. Hayek focus less than is usually done upon what patterning distributive justice requires. Hayek argues that we cannot know enough about each person's situation to distribute to each according to his moral merit (but would justice demand we do so if we did have this knowledge?); and he goes on to say, 'our objection is against all attempts to impress upon society a deliberately chosen pattern of distribution, whether it be an order of equality or of inequality.'[13] However, Hayek concludes that in a free society there will be distribution in accordance with value rather than moral merit; that is, in accordance with the perceived value of a person's actions and services to others. Despite his rejection of a patterned conception of distributive justice, Hayek himself suggests a pattern he thinks justifiable: distribution in accordance with the perceived benefits given to others, leaving room for the complaint that a free society does not realize exactly this pattern. Stating this pattern strand of a free capitalist society more precisely, we get 'To each according to how much he benefits others who have the resources for benefiting those who benefit them.' This will seem arbitrary unless some acceptable initial set of holdings is specified, or unless it is held that the operation of the system over time washes out any significant effects from the initial set of holdings. As an example of the latter, if almost anyone would have bought a car from Henry Ford, the supposition that it was an arbitrary matter who held the money (and so bought) would not place Henry Ford's earnings under a cloud. In any event, *his* coming to hold it is not arbitrary. Distribution according to benefits to others *is* a major patterned strand in a free capitalist society, as Hayek correctly points out, but it is only a strand and does not constitute the whole pattern of a system of entitlements (namely, inheritance, gifts for arbitrary reasons, charity, and so on) or a standard that one should insist a society fit. Will people tolerate for long a system yielding distributions that they believe are unpatterned?[14] No doubt people will not long accept a distribution they believe is *unjust*. People want their society to be and to look just. But must the look of justice reside in a resulting pattern rather than in the underlying generating principles? We are in no position to conclude that the inhabitants of a society embodying an entitlement conception of justice in holdings will find it unacceptable. Still, it must be granted that were people's reasons for transferring some of their holdings to others always irrational or arbitrary, we would find this disturbing. (Suppose people always determined what holdings they would transfer, and to whom, by using a random device.) We feel more comfortable upholding the justice of an entitlement system if most of the transfers under it are done for reasons. This does not mean necessarily that all deserve what holdings they receive. It means only that there is a purpose or point to someone's transferring a holding to one person rather than to another; that usually we can see what the transferrer thinks he's gaining, what cause he thinks he's serving, what goals he thinks he's helping to achieve, and so forth. Since in a capitalist society people often transfer holdings to others in accordance with how much they perceive these others benefiting them, the fabric constituted by the individual transactions and transfers is largely reasonable and intelligible.[15] (Gifts to loved ones, bequests to children, charity to the needy also are non-arbitrary components of the fabric.) In stressing the large strand of distribution in accordance with benefit to others, Hayek shows the point of many transfers, and so shows that the system of transfer of entitlements is not just spinning its gears aimlessly. The system of entitlements is defensible when constituted by the individual aims of individual transactions. No overarching aim is needed, no distributional pattern is required.

To think that the task of a theory of distributive justice is to fill in the blank in 'to each according to his ———' is to be predisposed to search for a pattern; and the separate treatment of 'from each according to his ———' treats production and distribution as two separate and independent issues. On an entitlement view these are *not* two separate questions. Whoever makes something, having bought or contracted for all other held resources used in the process (transferring some of his holdings for these co-operating factors), is entitled to it. The situation is *not* one of something's getting made, and there being an open question of who is to get it. Things come into the world already attached to people having entitlements over them. From the point of view of the historical entitlement conception of justice in holdings, those who start afresh to complete 'to each according to his ——' treat objects as if they appeared from nowhere, out of nothing. A complete theory of justice might cover this limit case as well; perhaps here is a use for the usual conceptions of distributive justice.[16]

So entrenched are maxims of the usual form that perhaps we should present the entitlement conception as a competitor. Ignoring acquisition and rectification, we might say:

> From each according to what he chooses to do, to each according to what he makes for himself (perhaps with the contracted aid of others) and what others choose to do for him and choose to give him of what they've been given previously (under this maxim) and haven't yet expended or transferred.

This, the discerning reader will have noticed, has its defects as a slogan. So as a summary and great simplification (and not as a maxim with any independent meaning) we have:

> *From each as they choose, to each as they are chosen.*

HOW LIBERTY UPSETS PATTERNS

It is not clear how those holding alternative conceptions of distributive justice can reject the entitlement conception of justice in holdings. For suppose a distribution favoured by one of these non-entitlement conceptions is realized. Let us suppose it is your favourite one and let us call this distribution D1; perhaps everyone has an equal share, perhaps shares vary in accordance with some dimension you treasure. Now suppose that Wilt Chamberlain is greatly in demand by basketball teams, being a great gate attraction. (Also suppose contracts run only for a year, with players being free agents.) He signs the following sort of contract with a team: In each home game, twenty-five cents from the price of each ticket of admission goes to him. (We ignore the question of whether he is 'gouging' the owners, letting them look out for themselves.) The season starts, and people cheerfully attend his team's games; they buy their tickets, each time dropping a separate twenty-five cents of their admission price into a special box with Chamberlain's name on it. They are excited about seeing him play; it is worth the total admission price to them. Let us suppose that in one season one million persons attend his home games, and Wilt Chamberlain winds up with $250,000, a much larger sum than the average income and larger even than anyone else has. Is he entitled to this income? Is this new distribution D2, unjust? If so, why? There is *no* question about whether each of the people was entitled to the control over the resources they held in D1; because that was the distribution (your favourite) that (for the purposes of argument) we assumed was acceptable. Each of these persons *chose* to give twenty-five cents of their money to Chamberlain. They could have spent it on going to the movies, or on candy bars, or on copies of *Dissent* magazine, or of *Monthly Review*. But they all, at least one million of them, converged on giving it to Wilt Chamberlain in exchange for watching him play basketball. If D1 was a just distribution, and people voluntarily moved from it to D2, transferring parts of their shares they were given under D1 (what was it for if not to do something with?), isn't D2 also just? If the people were entitled to dispose of the resources to which they were entitled (under D1), didn't this include their being entitled to give it to, or exchange it with, Wilt Chamberlain? Can anyone else complain on grounds of justice? Each other person already has legitimate share under D1. Under D1, there is nothing that anyone has that anyone else has a claim of justice against. After someone transfers something to Wilt Chamberlain, third parties *still* have their legitimate shares; *their* shares are not changed. By what process could such a transfer among two persons give rise to a legitimate claim of distributive justice of what was transferred, by a third party who had no claim of justice on any holding of the others *before* the transfer?[17] To cut off objections irrelevant here, we might imagine the exchanges occurring in a socialist society, after hours. After playing whatever basketball he does in his daily work, or doing whatever other daily work he does, Wilt Chamberlain decides to put in *overtime* to earn additional money. (First his work quota is set; he works time over that.) Or imagine it is a skilled juggler people like to see, who puts on shows after hours.

Why might someone work overtime in a society in which it is assumed their needs are satisfied? Perhaps because they care about things other than needs. I like to write in books that I read, and to have easy access to books for browsing at odd hours. It would be very pleasant and convenient to have the resources of Widener Library in my back yard. No society, I assume, will provide such resources close to each person who would like them as part of his regular allotment (under D1). Thus, persons either must do without some extra things that they want, or be allowed to do something extra to get some of these things. On what basis could the inequalities that would eventuate be forbidden? Notice also that small factories would spring up in a socialist society, unless forbidden. I melt down some of my personal possessions (under D1) and build a machine out of the material. I offer you, and others, a philosophy lecture once a week in exchange for your cranking the handle on my machine, whose products I exchange for yet other things, and so on. (The raw materials used by the machine are given to me by others who possess them under D1, in exchange for hearing lectures.) Each person might participate to gain things over and above their allotment under D1. Some persons even might want to leave their job in socialist industry and work full time in this private sector. I shall say something more about these issues elsewhere. Here I wish merely to note how private property even in means of production would occur in a socialist society that did not forbid people to use as they wished some of the resources they are given under the socialist distribution D1.[18] The socialist society would have to forbid capitalist acts between consenting adults.

The general point illustrated by the Wilt Chamberlain example and the example of the entrepreneur in a socialist society is that no end-state principle or distributional patterned principle of justice can be continuously realized without continuous interference with people's lives. Any favoured pattern would be transformed into one unfavoured by the principle, by people choosing to act in various ways; for example, by people exchanging goods and services with other people, or giving things to other people, things the transferrers are entitled to under the favoured distributional pattern. To maintain a pattern one must either continually interfere to stop people from transferring resources as they wish to, or continually (or periodically) interfere to take from some persons resources that others for some reason chose to transfer to them. (But if some time limit is to be set on how long people may keep resources others voluntarily transfer to them, why let them keep these resources for *any* period of time? Why not have immediate confiscation?) It might be objected that all persons voluntarily will choose to refrain from actions which would upset the pattern. This presupposes unrealistically (1) that all will most want to maintain the pattern (are those who don't, to be 're-educated' or forced to undergo 'self-criticism'?), (2) that each can gather enough information about his own actions and the ongoing activities of others to discover which of his actions will upset the pattern, and (3) that diverse and far-flung persons can co-ordinate their actions to dovetail into the pattern. Compare the manner in which the market is neutral among persons' desires, as it reflects and transmits widely scattered information via prices, and co-ordinates persons' activities.

It puts things perhaps a bit too strongly to say that every patterned (or end-state) principle is liable to be thwarted by the voluntary actions of the individual parties transferring some of their shares they receive under the principle. For perhaps some *very* weak patterns are not so thwarted.[19] Any distributional pattern with any egalitarian component is overturnable by the voluntary actions of individual persons over time; as is every patterned condition with sufficient content so as actually to have been proposed as presenting the central core of distributive justice. Still, given the possibility that some weak conditions or patterns may not be unstable in this way, it would be better to formulate an explicit description of the kind of interesting and contentful patterns under discussion, and to prove a theorem about their instability. Since the weaker the patterning, the more likely it is that the entitlement system itself satisfies it, a plausible conjecture is that any patterning either is unstable or is satisfied by the entitlement system.

NOTES

[1] Here and in the next section I draw upon and amplify my discussion of these issues in footnote 4 of 'On the Randian Argument', *The Personalist*, Spring, 1971.

[2] Milton Friedman, *Capitalism and Freedom* (Chicago: University of Chicago Press, 1962), ch. 6. Friedman's school vouchers, of course, allow a choice about who is to supply the product, and so differ from the protection vouchers imagined here.

[3] For a clear statement that this view is mistaken, see John Rawls, *A Theory of Justice* (Cambridge, Mass.: Harvard University Press, 1971), pp. 30, 565–6.

[4] Unfortunately, too few models of the structure of moral views have been specified heretofore, though there are surely other interesting structures. Hence an argument for a side-constraint structure that consists largely in arguing against an end-state maximization structure is inconclusive, for these alternatives are not exhaustive. An array of structures must be precisely formulated and investigated; perhaps some novel structure then will seem most appropriate.

   The issue of whether a side-constraint view can be put in the form of the goal-without-side-constraint view is a tricky one. One might think, for example, that each person could distinguish in his goal between *his* violating rights and someone else's doing it. Give the former infinite (negative) weight in his goal, and no amount of stopping others from violating rights can outweigh his violating someone's rights. In addition to a component of a goal receiving infinite weight, indexical expressions also appear, for example, '*my* doing something'. A careful statement delimiting 'constraint views' would exclude these gimmicky ways of transforming side constraints into the form of an end-state view as sufficient to constitute a view as end state. Mathematical methods of transforming a constrained minimization problem into a sequence of unconstrained minimizations of an auxiliary function are presented in Anthony Fiacco and Garth McCormick, *Nonlinear Programming: Sequential Unconstrained Minimization Techniques* (New York: Wiley, 1968). The book is interesting both for its methods and for their limitations in illuminating our area of concern; note the way in which the penalty functions include the constraints, the variation in weights of penalty functions (sec. 7.1), and so on.

The question of whether these side constraints are absolute, or whether they may be violated in order to avoid catastrophic moral horror, and if the latter, what the resulting structure might look like, is one I hope largely to avoid.

5 Which does which? Often a useful question to ask, as in the following:
'What is the difference between a Zen master and an analytic philosopher?'
'One talks riddles and the other riddles talks.'

6 *Groundwork of the Metaphysic of Morals.* Translated by H. J. Paton, *The Moral Law* (London: Hutchinson, 1956), p. 96.

7 See John Rawls, *A Theory of Justice*, sects 5, 6, 30.

8 The reader who has looked ahead and seen that the second part of this chapter discusses Rawls' theory mistakenly may think that every remark or argument in the first part against alternative theories of justice is meant to apply to, or anticipate, a criticism of Rawls' theory. This is not so; there are other theories also worth criticizing.

9 Applications of the principle of justice in acquisition may also occur as part of the move from one distribution to another. You may find an unheld thing now and appropriate it. Acquisitions also are to be understood as included when, to simplify, I speak only of transitions by transfers.

10 See, however, the useful book by Boris Bittker, *The Case for Black Reparations* (New York: Random House, 1973).

11 If the principle of rectification of violations of the first two principles yields more than one description of holdings, then some choice must be made as to which of these is to be realized. Perhaps the sort of considerations about distributive justice and equality that I argue against play a legitimate role in *this* subsidiary choice. Similarly, there may be room for such considerations in deciding which otherwise arbitrary features a statute will embody, when such features are unavoidable because other considerations do not specify a precise line; yet a line must be drawn.

12 One might try to squeeze a patterned conception of distributive justice

into the framework of the entitlement conception, by formulating a gimmicky obligatory 'principle of transfer' that would lead to the pattern. For example, the principle that if one has more than the mean income one must transfer everything one holds above the mean to persons below the mean so as to bring them up to (but not over) the mean. We can formulate a criterion for a 'principle of transfer' to rule out such obligatory transfers, or we can say that no correct principle of transfer, no principle of transfer in a free society will be like this. The former is probably the better course, though the latter also is true.

Alternatively, one might think to make the entitlement conception instantiate a pattern, by using matrix entries that express the relative strength of a person's entitlements as measured by some real-valued function. But even if the limitation to natural dimensions failed to exclude this function, the resulting edifice would *not* capture our system of entitlements to *particular* things.

[13] F. A. Hayek, *The Constitution of Liberty* (Chicago: University of Chicago Press, 1960), p. 87.

[14] This question does not imply that they will tolerate any and every patterned distribution. In discussing Hayek's views, Irving Kristol has recently speculated that people will not long tolerate a system that yields distributions patterned in accordance with value rather than merit. (' "When Virtue Loses All Her Loveliness" – Some Reflections on Capitalism and "The Free Society" ' *The Public Interest*, Fall, 1970, pp. 3–15.) Kristol, following some remarks of Hayek's, equates the merit system with justice. Since some case can be made for the external standard of distribution in accordance with benefit to others, we ask about a weaker (and therefore more plausible) hypothesis.

[15] We certainly benefit because great economic incentives operate to get others to spend much time and energy to figure out how to serve us by providing things we will want to pay for. It is not mere paradox mongering to wonder whether capitalism should be criticized for most rewarding and hence encouraging, not individualists like Thoreau who go about their own lives, but people who are occupied with serving others and winning them as customers. But to defend capitalism one need not think businessmen are the finest human types. (I do not mean to join here the general maligning of businessmen, either.) Those who think the finest should acquire the most can try to convince their fellows to transfer resources in accordance with *that* principle.

[16] Varying situations continuously from that limit situation to our own would force us to make explicit the underlying rationale of entitlements and to consider whether entitlement considerations lexicographically precede the considerations of the usual theories of distributive justice, so that the *slightest* strand of entitlement outweighs the considerations of the usual theories of distributive justice.

[17] Might not a transfer have instrumental effects on a third party, changing his feasible options? (But what if the two parties to the transfer independently had used their holdings in this fashion?) I discuss

this question below, but note here that this question concedes the point for distributions of ultimate intrinsic non-instrumental goods (pure utility experiences, so to speak) that are transferable. It also might be objected that the transfer might make a third party more envious because it worsens his position relative to someone else. I find it incomprehensible how this can be thought to involve a claim of justice.

Here and elsewhere in this chapter, a theory which incorporates elements of pure procedural justice might find what I say acceptable, *if* kept in its proper place; that is, if background institutions exist to ensure the satisfaction of certain conditions on distributive shares. But if these institutions are not themselves the sum or invisible-hand result of people's voluntary (non-aggressive) actions, the constraints they impose require justification. At no point does *our* argument assume any background institutions more extensive than those of the minimal night-watchman state, a state limited to protecting persons against murder, assault, theft, fraud, and so forth.

18 See the selection from John Henry MacKay's novel, *The Anarchists*, reprinted in Leonard Krimmerman and Lewis Perry, eds, *Patterns of Anarchy* (New York: Doubleday Anchor Books, 1966), in which an individualist anarchist presses upon a communist anarchist the following question: 'Would you, in the system of society which you call "free Communism" prevent individuals from exchanging their labour among themselves by means of their own medium of exchange? And further: Would you prevent them from occupying land for the purpose of personal use?' The novel continues: '[the] question was not to be escaped. If he answered "Yes!" he admitted that society had the right of control over the individual and threw overboard the autonomy of the individual which he had always zealously defended; if on the other hand, he answered "No!" he admitted the right of private property which he had just denied so emphatically. . . . Then he answered "In Anarchy any number of men must have the right of forming a voluntary association, and so realizing their ideas in practice. Nor can I understand how any one could justly be driven from the land and house which he uses and occupies . . . every serious man must declare himself: for Socialism, and thereby for force and against liberty or for Anarchism, and thereby for liberty and against force."' In contrast, we find Noam Chomsky writing, 'Any consistent anarchist must oppose private ownership of the means of production', 'the consistent anarchist then . . . will be a socialist . . . of a particular sort.' Introduction to Daniel Guerin, *Anarchism: From Theory to Practice* (New York: Monthly Review Press, 1970), pp. xiii, xv.

19 Is the patterned principle stable that requires merely that a distribution be Pareto-optimal? One person might give another a gift or bequest that the second could exchange with a third to their mutual benefit. Before the second makes this exchange, there is not Pareto-optimality. Is a stable pattern presented by a principle choosing that among the Pareto-optimal positions that satisfies some further condition C? It may seem

that there cannot be a counter-example, for won't any voluntary exchange made away from a situation show that the first situation wasn't Pareto-optimal? (Ignore the implausibility of this last claim for the case of bequests.) But principles are to be satisfied over time, during which new possibilities arise. A distribution that at one time satisfies the criterion of Pareto-optimality might not do so when some new possibilities arise (Wilt Chamberlain grows up and starts playing basketball); and though people's activities will tend to move then to a new Pareto-optimal position, *this* new one need not satisfy the contentful condition C. Continual interference will be needed to ensure the continual satisfaction of C. (The theoretical possibility of a pattern's being maintained by some invisible-hand process that brings it back to an equilibrium that fits the pattern when deviations occur should be investigated.)

PART II

6

Alasdair MacIntyre: The Virtues, the Unity of a Human Life and the Concept of a Tradition*

Any contemporary attempt to envisage each human life as a whole, as a unity, whose character provides the virtues with an adequate *telos* encounters two different kinds of obstacle, one social and one philosophical. The social obstacles derive from the way in which modernity partitions each human life into a variety of segments, each with its own norms and modes of behaviour. So work is divided from leisure, private life from public, the corporate from the personal. So both childhood and old áge have been wrenched away from the rest of human life and made over into distinct realms. And all these separations have been achieved so that it is the distinctiveness of each and not the unity of the life of the individual who passes through those parts in terms of which we are taught to think and to feel.

The philosophical obstacles derive from two distinct tendencies, one chiefly, though not only, domesticated in analytical philosophy and one at home in both sociological theory and in existentialism. The former is the tendency to think atomistically about human action and to analyse complex actions and transactions in terms of simple components. Hence the recurrence in more than one context of the notion of 'a basic action'. That particular actions derive their character as parts of larger wholes is a point of view alien to our dominant ways of thinking and yet one which it is necessary at least to consider if we are to begin to understand how a life may be more than a sequence of individual actions and episodes.

Equally the unity of a human life becomes invisible to us when a sharp separation is made either between the individual and the roles

*Alasdair MacIntyre, *After Virtue*. University of Notre Dame Press, Notre Dame, Indiana 46556. Copyright, 1981.

that he or she plays – a separation characteristic not only of Sartre's existentialism, but also of the sociological theory of Ralf Dahrendorf – or between the different role- and quasi-role-enactments of an individual life so that life comes to appear as nothing but a series of unconnected episodes – a liquidation of the self characteristic, as I noticed earlier, of Goffman's sociological theory. I already also suggested that both the Sartrian and the Goffmanesque conceptions of selfhood are highly characteristic of the modes of thought and practice of modernity. It is perhaps therefore unsurprising to realize that the self as thus conceived cannot be envisaged as a bearer of the Aristotelian virtues.

For a self separated from its roles in the Sartrian mode loses that arena of social relationships in which the Aristotelian virtues function if they function at all. The patterns of a virtuous life would fall under those condemnations of conventionality which Sartre put into a mouth of Antoine Roquentin in *La Nausée* and which he uttered in his own person in *L'Etre et le néant*. Indeed the self's refusal of the inauthenticity of conventionalized social relationships becomes what integrity is diminished into in Sartre's account.

At the same time the liquidation of the self into a set of demarcated areas of role-playing allows no scope for the exercise of dispositions which could genuinely be accounted virtues in any sense remotely Aristotelian. For a virtue is not a disposition that makes for success only in some one particular type of situation. What are spoken of as the virtues of a good committee man or of a good administrator or of a gambler or a pool hustler are professional skills professionally deployed in those situations where they can be effective, not virtues. Someone who genuinely possesses a virtue can be expected to manifest it in very different types of situation, many of them situations where the practice of a virtue cannot be expected to be effective in the way that we expect a professional skill to be. Hector exhibited one and the same courage in his parting from Andromache and on the battlefield with Achilles; Eleanor Marx exhibited one and the same compassion in her relationship with her father, in her work with trade unionists and in her entanglement with Aveling. And the unity of a virtue in someone's life is intelligible only as a characteristic of a unitary life, a life that can be conceived and evaluated as a whole. Hence just as in the discussion of the changes in and fragmentation of morality which accompanied the rise of modernity in the earlier parts of this book, each stage in the emergence of the characteristically modern views of the moral judgement was accompanied by a corresponding stage in the emergence of the characteristically modern conceptions of selfhood; so now, in defining the particular pre-modern concept of the virtues with which I have been preoccupied, it has become necessary to say something of the concomitant concept of selfhood, a concept of a self whose unity resides in the unity of a narrative which links birth to life to death as narrative beginning to middle to end.

Such a conception of the self is perhaps less unfamiliar than it may appear at first sight. Just because it has played a key part in the cultures which are historically the predecessors of our own, it would not be surprising if it turned out to be still an unacknowledged presence in many of our ways of thinking and acting. Hence it is not inappropriate to begin by scrutinizing some of our most taken-for-granted, but clearly correct conceptual insights about human actions and selfhood in order to show how natural it is to think of the self in a narrative mode.

It is a conceptual commonplace, both for philosophers and for ordinary agents, that one and the same segment of human behaviour may be correctly characterized in a number of different ways. To the question 'What is he doing?' the answers may with equal truth and appropriateness be 'Digging', 'Gardening', 'Taking exercise', 'Preparing for winter' or 'Pleasing his wife'. Some of these answers will characterize the agent's intentions, others unintended consequences of his actions, and of these unintended consequences some may be such that the agent is aware of them and others not. What is important to notice immediately is that any answer to the questions of how we are to understand or to explain a given segment of behaviour will presuppose some prior answer to the question of how these different correct answers to the question 'What is he doing?' are related to each other. For if someone's primary intention is to put the garden in order before the winter and it is only incidentally the case that in so doing he is taking exercise and pleasing his wife, we have one type of behaviour to be explained; but if the agent's primary intention is to please his wife by taking exercise, we have quite another type of behaviour to be explained and we will have to look in a different direction for understanding and explanation.

In the first place the episode has been situated in an annual cycle of domestic activity, and the behaviour embodies an intention which presupposes a particular type of household-cum-garden setting with the peculiar narrative history of that setting in which this segment of behaviour now becomes an episode. In the second instance the episode has been situated in the narrative history of a marriage, a very different, even if related, social setting. We cannot, that is to say, characterize behaviour independently of intentions, and we cannot characterize intentions independently of the settings which make those intentions intelligible both to agents themselves and to others.

I use the word 'setting' here as a relatively inclusive term. A social setting may be an institution, it may be what I have called a practice, or it may be a milieu of some other human kind. But it is central to the notion of a setting as I am going to understand it that a setting has a history, a history within which the histories of individual agents not only are, but have to be, situated, just because without the setting and its changes through time the history of the individual agent and his changes through time will be unintelligible. Of course one and the same piece of behaviour may belong to more than one setting. There are at least two different ways in which this may be so.

In my earlier example the agent's activity may be part of the history both of the cycle of household activity and of his marriage, two histories which have happened to intersect. The household may have its own history stretching back through hundreds of years, as do the histories of some European farms, where the farm has had a life of its own, even though different families have in different periods inhabited it; and the marriage will certainly have its own history, a history which itself presupposes that a particular point has been reached in the history of the institution of marriage. If we are to relate some particular segment of behaviour in any precise way to an agent's intentions and thus to the settings which that agent inhabits, we shall have to understand in a precise way how the variety of correct characterizations of the agent's behaviour relate to each other first by identifying which characteristics refer us to an intention and which do not and then by classifying further the items in both categories.

Where intentions are concerned, we need to know which intention or intentions were primary, that is to say, of which it is the case that, had the agent intended otherwise, he would not have performed that action. Thus if we know that a man is gardening with the self-avowed purposes of healthful exercise and of pleasing his wife, we do not yet know how to understand what he is doing until we know the answer to such questions as whether he would continue gardening if he continued to believe that gardening was healthful exercise, but discovered that his gardening no longer pleased his wife, *and* whether he would continue gardening, if he ceased to believe that gardening was healthful exercise, but continued to believe that it pleased his wife, *and* whether he would continue gardening if he changed his beliefs on both points. That is to say, we need to know both what certain of his beliefs are and which of them are causally effective; and, that is to say, we need to know whether certain contrary-to-fact hypothetical statements are true or false. And until we know this, we shall not know how to characterize correctly what the agent is doing.

Consider another equally trivial example of a set of compatibly correct answers to the question 'What is he doing?' 'Writing a sentence'; 'Finishing his book'; 'Contributing to the debate on the theory of action'; 'Trying to get tenure'. Here the intentions can be ordered in terms of the stretch of time to which reference is made. Each of the shorter-term intentions is, and can only be made, intelligible by reference to some longer-term intentions; and the characterization of the behaviour in terms of the longer-term intentions can only be correct if some of the characterizations in terms of shorter-term intentions are also correct. Hence the behaviour is only characterized adequately when we know what the longer and longest-term intentions invoked are and how the shorter-term intentions are related to the longer. Once again we are involved in writing a narrative history.

Intentions thus need to be ordered both causally and temporally and both orderings will make references to settings, references already made obliquely by such elementary terms as 'gardening', 'wife', 'book' and 'tenure'. Moreover the correct identification of the agent's beliefs will be an essential constituent of this task; failure at this point would mean failure in the whole enterprise. (The conclusion may seem obvious; but it already entails one important consequence. There is no such thing as 'behaviour', to be identified prior to and independently of intentions, beliefs and settings. Hence the project of a science of behaviour takes on a mysterious and somewhat outré character. It is not that such a science is impossible; but there is nothing for it to be but a science of uninterpreted physical movement such as B. E. Skinner aspires to. It is no part of my task here to examine Skinner's problems; but it is worth noticing that it is not at all clear what a scientific experiment could be, if one were a Skinnerian; since the conception of an experiment is certainly one of intention- and belief-informed behaviour. And what would be utterly doomed to failure would be the project of a science of, say, *political* behaviour, detached from a study of intentions, beliefs and settings. It is perhaps worth noting that when the expression 'the behavioural sciences' was given its first influential use in a Ford Foundation Report of 1953, the term 'behaviour' was defined so as to include what were called 'such subjective behaviour as attitudes, beliefs, expectations, motivations and aspirations' as well as 'overt acts'. But what the Report's wording seems to imply is that it is cataloguing two distinct sets of items, available for independent study. If the argument so far is correct, then there is only one set of items.)

Consider what the argument so far implies about the inter-relationships of the intentional, the social and the historical. We identify a particular action only by invoking two kinds of context, implicitly if not explicitly. We place the agent's intentions, I have suggested, in causal and temporal order with reference to their role in his or her history; and we also place them with reference to their role in the history of the setting or settings to which they belong. In doing this, in determining what causal efficacy the agent's inten-tions had in one or more directions, and how his short-term intentions succeeded or failed to be constitutive of long-term intentions, we ourselves write a further part of these histories. Narrative history of a certain kind turns out to be the basic and essential genre for the characterization of human actions.

It is important to be clear how different the standpoint pre-supposed by the argument so far is from that of those analytical philosophers who have constructed accounts of human actions which make central the notion of 'a' human action. A course of human events is then seen as a complex sequence of individual actions, and a natural question is: How do we individuate human actions? Now there are contexts in which such notions are at home. In the recipes of a cookery book for instance actions are individu-ated in just the way that some analytical philosophers have supposed to be possible of all actions. 'Take six eggs. Then break then into a bowl. Add flour, salt, sugar, etc.' But the point about such sequences is that each element in them is intelligible as an action only as a-possible-element-in-a-sequence. Moreover even such a sequence requires a context to be intelligible. If in the middle of my lecture on Kant's ethics I suddenly broke six eggs into a bowl and added flour and sugar, proceeding all the while with my Kantian exegesis, I have *not*, simply in virtue of the fact that I was following a sequence prescribed by Fanny Farmer, performed an intelligible action.

To this it might be related that I certainly performed an action or a set of actions, if not an intelligible action. But to this I want to reply that the concept of an intelligible action is a more funda-mental concept than that of an action as such. Unintelligible actions are failed candidates for the status of intelligible action; and to lump unintelligible actions and intelligible actions together in a single class of actions and then to characterize action in terms of what items of both sets have in common is to make the mistake of ignoring this. It is also to neglect the central importance of the concept of intelligibility.

The importance of the concept of intelligibility is closely related to the fact that the most basic distinction of all embedded in our discourse and our practice in this area is that between human beings and other beings. Human beings can be held to account for that of which they are the authors; other beings cannot. To identify an occurrence as an action is in the paradigmatic instances to identify it under a type of description which enables us to see that occurrence as flowing intelligibly from a human agent's intentions, motives, passions and purposes. It is therefore to understand an action as something for which someone is accountable, about which it is always appropriate to ask the agent for an intelligible account. When an occurrence is apparently the intended action of a human agent, but nonetheless we cannot so identify it, we are both intellectually and practically baffled. We do not know how to respond; we do not know how to explain; we do not even know how to characterize minimally as an intelligible action; our distinction between the humanly accountable and the merely natural seems to have broken down. And this kind of bafflement does indeed occur in a number of different kinds of situation; when we enter alien cultures or even alien social structures within our own culture, in our encounters with certain types of neurotic or psychotic patient (it is indeed the unintelligibility of such patient's actions that leads to their being treated as patients; actions unintelligible to the agent as well as to everyone else are understood – rightly – as a kind of suffering), but also in everyday situations. Consider an example.

I am standing waiting for a bus and the young man standing next to me suddenly says: 'The name of the common wild duck is *Histrionicus histrionicus histrionicus.*' There is no problem as to the meaning of the sentence he uttered: the problem is, how to answer the question, what was he doing in uttering it? Suppose he just uttered such sentences at random intervals; this would be one possible form of madness. We would render his act of utterance intelligible if one of the following turned out to be true. He has mistaken me for someone who yesterday had approached him in the library and asked: 'Do you by any chance know the Latin name of the common wild duck?' Or he has just come from a session with his psychotherapist who has urged him to break down his shyness by talking to strangers. 'But what shall I say?' 'Oh, anything at all.'

Or he is a Soviet spy waiting at a prearranged rendezvous and uttering the ill-chosen code sentence which will identify him to his contact. In each case the act of utterance becomes intelligible by finding its place in a narrative.

To this it may be replied that the supplying of a narrative is not necessary to make such an act intelligible. All that is required is that we can identify the relevant type of speech-act (e.g. 'He was answering a question') or some purpose served by his utterance (e.g. 'He was trying to attract your attention'). But speech-acts and purposes too can be intelligible or unintelligible. Suppose that the man at the bus stop explains his act of utterance by saying 'I was answering a question.' I reply: 'But I never asked you any question to which that could have been the answer.' He says, 'Oh, I know *that*.' Once again his action becomes unintelligible. And a parallel example could easily be constructed to show that the mere fact that an action serves some purpose of a recognized type is not sufficient to render an action intelligible. Both purposes and speech-acts require contexts.

The most familiar type of context in and by reference to which speech-acts and purposes are rendered intelligible is the conversation. Conversation is so all-pervasive a feature of the human world that it tends to escape philosophical attention. Yet remove conversation from human life and what would be left? Consider then what is involved in following a conversation and finding it intelligible or unintelligible. (To find a conversation intelligible is not the same as to understand it; for a conversation which I overhear may be intelligible, but I may fail to understand it.) If I listen to a conversation between two other people my ability to grasp the thread of the conversation will involve an ability to bring it under some one out of a set of descriptions in which the degree and kind of coherence in the conversation is brought out: 'a drunken, rambling quarrel', 'a serious intellectual disagreement', 'a tragic misunderstanding of each other', 'a comic, even farcical misconstrual of each other's motives', 'a penetrating interchange of views', 'a struggle to dominate each other', 'a trivial exchange of gossip'.

The use of words such as 'tragic', 'comic', and 'farcical' is not marginal to such evaluations. We allocate conversations to genres, just as we do literary narratives. Indeed a conversation is a dramatic work, even if a very short one, in which the participants are not only the actors, but also the joint authors, working out in agreement or disagreement the mode of their production. For it is not just that conversations belong to genres in just the way that plays and novels do; but they have beginnings, middles and endings just as do literary works. They embody reversals and recognitions; they move towards and away from climaxes. There may within a longer conversation be digressions and subplots, indeed digressions within digressions and subplots within subplots.

But if this is true of conversations, it is true also *mutatis mutandis* of battles, chess games, courtships, philosophy seminars, families at the dinner table, businessmen negotiating contracts – that is, of human transactions in general. For conversation, understood widely enough, is the form of human transactions in general. Conversational behaviour is not a special sort or aspect of human behaviour, even though the forms of language-using and of human life are such that the deeds of others speak for them as much as do their words. For that is possible only because they are the deeds of those who have words.

I am presenting both conservations in particular then and human actions in general as enacted narratives. Narrative is not the work of poets, dramatists and novelists reflecting upon events which had no narrative order before one was imposed by the singer or the writer; narrative form is neither disguise nor decoration. Barbara Hardy has written that 'we dream in narrative, day-dream in narrative, remember, anticipate, hope, despair, believe, doubt, plan, revise, criticise, construct, gossip, learn, hate and love by narrative' in arguing the same point (Hardy, 1968, p. 5).

At the beginning of this chapter I argued that in successfully identifying and understanding what someone else is doing we always move towards placing a particular episode in the context of a set of narrative histories, histories both of the individuals concerned and of the settings in which they act and suffer. It is now becoming clear that we render the actions of others intelligible in this way because action itself has a basically historical character. It is because we all live out narratives in our lives and because we understand our own lives in terms of the narratives that we live out that the form of narrative is appropriate for understanding the actions of others. Stories are lived before they are told – except in the case of fiction.

This has of course been denied in recent debates. Louis O. Mink, quarrelling with Barbara Hardy's view, has asserted: 'Stories are not lived but told. Life has no beginnings, middles, or ends; there are meetings, but the start of an affair belongs to the story we tell ourselves later, and there are partings, but final partings only in the story. There are hopes, plans, battles and ideas, but only in retrospective stories are hopes unfulfilled, plans miscarried, battles decisive, and ideas seminal. Only in the story is it America which Columbus discovers and only in the story is the kingdom lost for want of a nail' (Mink, 1970, pp. 557–8).

What are we to say to this? Certainly we must agree that it is only retrospectively that hopes can be characterized as unfulfilled or battles as decisive and so on. But we so characterize them in life as much as in art. And to someone who says that in life there are no endings, or that final partings take place only in stories, one is tempted to reply, 'But have you never heard of death?' Homer did not have to tell the tale of Hector before Andromache could lament unfulfilled hope and final parting. There are countless Hectors and countless Andromaches whose lives embodied the form of their Homeric namesakes, but who never came to the attention of any poet. What is true is that in taking an event as a beginning or an ending we bestow a significance upon it which may be debatable. Did the Roman republic end with the death of Julius Caesar, or at Philippi, or with the founding of the principate? The answer is surely that, like Charles II, it was a long time a-dying; but this answer implies the reality of its ending as much as do any of the former. There is a crucial sense in which the principate of Augustus, or the taking of the oath in the tennis court, or the decision to construct an atomic bomb at Los Alamos constitute beginnings; the peace of 404 B.C., the abolition of the Scottish Parliament and the battle of Waterloo equally constitute endings; while there are many events which are both endings and beginnings.

As with beginnings, middles and endings, so also with genres and with the phenomenon of embedding. Consider the question of to what genre the life of Thomas Becket belongs, a question which has to be asked and answered before we can decide how it is to be written. (On Mink's paradoxical view this question could not be asked until *after* the life had been written.) In some of the medieval versions, Thomas's career is presented in terms of the canons of medieval hagiography. In the Icelandic *Thomas Saga* he is presented as a saga hero. In Dom David Knowles's modern biography the story is a tragedy, the tragic relationship of Thomas and Henry II, each of whom satisfies Aristotle's demand that the hero be a great man with a fatal flaw. Now it clearly makes sense to ask who is right, if anyone: the monk William of Canterbury, the author of the saga, or the Cambridge Regius Professor Emeritus? The answer appears to be clearly the last. The true genre of the life is neither hagiography nor saga, but tragedy. So of such modern narrative subjects as the life of Trotsky or that of Lenin, of the history of the Soviet Communist Party or the American presidency, we may also ask: To what genre does their history belong? And this is the same question as: What type of account of their history will be both true and intelligible?

Or consider again how one narrative may be embedded in another. In both plays and novels there are well-known examples: the play within the play in *Hamlet*, Wandering Willie's Tale in *Redgauntlet*, Aeneas' narrative to Dido in book 2 of the *Aeneid*, and so on. But there are equally well-known examples in real life. Consider again the way in which the career of Becket as archbishop and chancellor is embedded within the reign of Henry II, or the way in which the tragic life of Mary Stuart is embedded in that of Elizabeth I, or the history of the Confederacy within the history of the United States. Someone may discover (or not discover) that he or she is a character in a number of narratives at the same time, some of them embedded in others. Or again, what seemed to be an intelligible narrative in which one was playing a part may be transformed wholly or partly into a story of unintelligible episodes. This last is what happened to Kafka's character K. in both *The Trial* and *The Castle*. (It is no accident that Kafka could not end his novels, for the notion of an ending like that of a beginning has its sense only in terms of intelligible narrative.)

I spoke earlier of the agent as not only an actor, but an author. Now I must emphasize that what the agent is able to do and say intelligibly as an actor is deeply affected by the fact that we are never more (and sometimes less) than the co-authors of our own narratives. Only in fantasy do we live what story we please. In life, as both Aristotle and Engels noted, we are always under certain constraints. We enter upon a stage which we did not design and we find ourselves part of an action that was not of our making. Each of us being a main character in his own drama plays subordinate parts in the dramas of others, and each drama constrains the others. In my drama, perhaps, I am Hamlet or Iago or at least the swineherd who may yet become a prince, but to you I am only A Gentleman or at best Second Murderer, while you are my Polonius or my Gravedigger, but your own hero. Each of our dramas exerts constraints on each other's, making the whole different from the parts, but still dramatic.

It is considerations as complex as these which are involved in making the notion of intelligibility the conceptual connecting link between the notion of action and that of narrative. Once we have understood its importance the claim that the concept of an action is secondary to that of an intelligible action will perhaps appear less bizarre and so too will the claim that the notion of 'an' action, while of the highest practical importance, is always a potentially misleading abstraction. An action is a moment in a possible or actual history or in a number of such histories. The notion of a history is as fundamental a notion as the notion of an action. Each requires the other. But I cannot say this without noticing that it is precisely this that Sartre denies – as indeed his whole theory of the self, which captures so well the spirit of modernity, requires that he should. In *La Nausée*, Sartre makes Antoine Roquentin argue not just what Mink argues, that narrative is very different from life, but that to present human life in the form of a narrative is always to falsify it. There are not and there cannot be any true stories. Human life is composed of discrete actions which lead nowhere, which have no order; the story-teller imposes on human events retrospectively an order which they did not have while they were lived. Clearly if Sartre/Roquentin is right – I speak of Sartre/Roquentin to distinguish him from such other well-known characters as Sartre/Heidegger and Sartre/Marx – my central contention must be mistaken. There is nonetheless an important point of agreement between my thesis and that of Sartre/Roquentin. We agree in identifying the intelligibility of an action with its place in a narrative sequence. Only Sartre/Roquentin takes it that human actions are as such unintelligible occurrences: it is to a realization of the metaphysical implications of this that Roquentin is brought in the course of the novel and the practical effect upon him is to bring to an end his own project of writing an historical biography. This project no longer makes sense. Either he will write what is true or he will write an intelligible history, but the one possibility excludes the other. Is Sartre/Roquentin right?

We can discover what is wrong with Sartre's thesis in either of two ways. One is to ask: what would human actions deprived of any falsifying narrative order be like? Sartre himself never answers this question; it is striking that in order to show that there are no true narratives, he himself writes a narrative albeit a fictional one. But the only picture that I find myself able to form of human nature *an-sich*, prior to the alleged misinterpretation by narrative is the kind of dislocated sequence which Dr Johnson offers us in his notes of his travels in France: 'There we waited on the ladies – Morville's. – Spain. Country towns all beggars. At Dijon he could not find the way to Orleans. – Cross roads of France very bad. – Five soldiers. – Women. – Soldiers escaped. – The Colonel would not lose five men for the sake of one woman. – The magistrate cannot seize a soldier but by the Colonel's permission, etc., etc.' (quoted in Hobsbaum, 1973, p. 32). What this suggests is what I take to be true, namely that the characterization of actions allegedly prior to any narrative form being imposed upon them will always turn out to be the presentation of what are plainly the disjointed parts of some possible narrative. We can also approach the question in another way. What I have called a history is an enacted dramatic narrative in which the characters are also the authors. The characters of course never start literally *ab initio*; they plunge *in medias res*, the beginnings of their story already made for them by what and who has gone before. But when Julian Grenfell or Edward Thomas went off to France in the 1914–18 war they no less enacted a narrative than did Menelaus or Odysseus when *they* went off. The difference between imaginary characters and real ones is not in the narrative form of what they do; it is in the degree of their authorship of that form and of their own deeds. Of course just as they do not begin where they please, they cannot go on exactly as they please either; each character is constrained by the actions of others and by the social settings presupposed in his and their actions, a point forcibly made by Marx in the classical, if not entirely satisfactory account of human life as enacted dramatic narrative, *The Eighteenth Brumaire of Louis Bonaparte*.

I call Marx's account less than satisfactory partly because he wishes to present the narrative of human social life in a way that will be compatible with a view of that life as law-governed and predictable in a particular way. But it is crucial that at any given point in an enacted dramatic narrative we do not know what will happen next. The kind of unpredictability for which I argued [in chapter 8, *After Virtue*] is required by the narrative structure of human life, and the empirical generalizations and explorations which social scientists discover provide a kind of understanding of human life which is perfectly compatible with that structure.

This unpredictability coexists with a second crucial characteristic of all lived narratives, a certain teleological character. We live out our lives, both individually and in our relationships with each other, in the light of certain conceptions of a possible shared future, a future in which certain possibilities beckon us forward and others repel us, some seem already foreclosed and others perhaps inevitable. There is no present which is not informed by some image of some future and an image of the future which always presents itself in the form of a *telos* – or of a variety of ends or goals – towards which we are either moving or failing to move in the present. Unpredictability and teleology therefore coexist as part of our lives; like characters in a fictional narrative we do not know what will happen next, but none the less our lives have a certain form which projects itself towards our future. Thus the narratives which we live out have both an unpredictable and a partially teleological character. If the narrative of our individual and social lives is to continue intelligibly – and either type of narrative may lapse into unintelligibility – it is always both the case that there are constraints on how the story can continue *and* that within those constraints there are indefinitely many ways that it can continue.

A central thesis then begins to emerge: man is in his actions and practice, as well as in his fictions, essentially a story-telling animal. He is not essentially, but becomes through his history, a teller of stories that aspire to truth. But the key question for men is not about their own authorship; I can only answer the question 'What am I to do?' if I can answer the prior question 'Of what story or stories do I find myself a part?' We enter human society, that is, with one or more imputed characters – roles into which we have been drafted – and we have to learn what they are in order to be able to understand how others respond to us and how our responses to them are apt to be construed. It is through hearing stories about wicked stepmothers, lost children, good but misguided kings, wolves that suckle twin boys, youngest sons who receive no inheritance but must make their own way in the world and eldest sons who waste their inheritance on riotous living and go into exile to live with the swine, that children learn or mislearn both what a child and what a parent is, what the cast of characters may be in the drama into which they have been born and what the ways of the world are. Deprive children of stories and you leave them unscripted, anxious stutterers in their actions as in their words. Hence there is no way to give us an understanding of any society, including our own, except through the stock of stories which constitute its initial dramatic resources. Mythology, in its original sense, is at the heart of things. Vico was right and so was Joyce. And so too of course is that moral tradition from heroic society to its medieval heirs according to which the telling of stories has a key part in educating us into the virtues.

I suggested earlier that 'an' action is always an episode in a possible history: I would now like to make a related suggestion about another concept, that of personal identity. Derek Parfit and others have recently drawn our attention to the contrast between the criteria of strict identity, which is an all-or-nothing matter (*either* the Tichborne claimant *is* the last Tichborne heir; *either* all the properties of the last heir belong to the claimant *or* the claimant is not the heir – Leibniz's Law applies) and the psychological continuities of personality which are a matter of more or less. (Am I the same man as fifty I was at forty in respect of memory, intellectual powers, critical responses? More or less.) But what is crucial to human beings as characters in enacted narratives is that, possessing only the resources of psychological continuity, we have to be able to respond to the imputation of strict identity. I am forever whatever I have been at any time for others – and I may at any time be called upon to answer for it – no matter how changed I may be now. There is no way of *founding* my identity – or lack of it – on the psychological continuity or discontinuity of the self. The self inhabits a character whose unity is given as the unity of a character. Once again there is a crucial disagreement with empiricist or analytical philosophers on the one hand and with existentialists on the other.

Empiricists, such as Locke or Hume, tried to give an account of personal identity solely in terms of psychological states or events. Analytical philosophers, in so many ways their heirs as well as their critics, have wrestled with the connection between those states and events and strict identity understood in terms of Leibniz's Law. Both have failed to see that a background has been omitted, the lack of which makes the problems insoluble. That background is provided by the concept of a story and of that kind of unity of character which a story requires. Just as a history is not a sequence of actions, but the concept of an action is that of a moment in an actual or possible history abstracted for some purpose from that history, so the characters in a history are not a collection of persons, but the concept of a person is that of a character abstracted from a history.

What the narrative concept of selfhood requires is thus twofold. On the one hand, I am what I may justifiably be taken by others to be in the course of living out a story that runs from my birth to my death; I am the *subject* of a history that is my own and no one else's, that has its own peculiar meaning. When someone complains – as do some of those who attempt or commit suicide – that his or her life is meaningless, he or she is often and perhaps characteristically complaining that the narrative of their life has become unintelligible to them, that it lacks any point, any movement towards a climax or a *telos*. Hence the point of doing any one thing rather than another at crucial junctures in their lives seems to such a person to have been lost.

To be the subject of a narrative that runs from one's birth to one's death is, I remarked earlier, to be accountable for the actions and experiences which compose a narratable life. It is, that is, to be open to being asked to give a certain kind of account of what one did or what happened to one or what one witnessed at any earlier point in one's life the time at which the question is posed. Of course someone may have forgotten or suffered brain damage or simply not attended sufficiently at the relevant times to be able to give the relevant account. But to say of someone under some one description ('The prisoner of the Château d'If') that he is the same person as someone characterized quite differently ('The Count of Monte Cristo') is precisely to say that it makes sense to ask him to give an intelligible narrative account enabling us to understand how he could at different times and different places be one and the same person and yet be so differently characterized. Thus personal identity is just that identity presupposed by the unity of the character which the unity of a narrative requires. Without such unity there would not be subjects of whom stories could be told.

The other aspect of narrative selfhood is correlative: I am not only accountable, I am one who can always ask others for an account, who can put others to the question. I am part of their story, as they are part of mine. The narrative of any one life is part of an interlocking set of narratives. Moreover this asking for and giving of accounts itself plays an important part in constituting narratives. Asking you what you did and why, saying what I did and why, pondering the differences between your account of what I did and my account of what I did, and vice versa, these are essential constituents of all but the very simplest and barest of narratives. Thus without the accountability of the self those trains of events that constitute all but the simplest and barest of narratives could not occur; and without that same accountability narratives would lack that continuity required to make both them and the actions that constitute them intelligible.

It is important to notice that I am not arguing that the concepts of narrative or of intelligibility or of accountability are *more* fundamental than that of personal identity. The concepts of narrative, intelligibility and accountability presuppose the applicability of the concept of personal identity, just as it presupposes their applicability and just as indeed each of these three presupposes the applicability of the two others. The relationship is one of mutual presupposition. It does follow of course that all attempts to elucidate the notion of personal identity independently of and in isolation from the notions of narrative, intelligibility and accountability are bound to fail. As all such attempts have.

It is now possible to return to the question from which this enquiry into the nature of human action and identity started: In what does the unity of an individual life consist? The answer is that its unity is the unity of a narrative embodied in a single life. To ask 'What is the good for me?' is to ask how best I might live out that unity and bring it to completion. To ask 'What is the good for man?' is to ask what all answers to the former question must have in common. But now it is important to emphasize that it is the systematic asking of these two questions and the attempt to answer them in deed as well as in word which provide the moral life with its unity. The unity of a human life is the unity of a narrative quest. Quests sometimes fail, are frustrated, abandoned or dissipated into distractions; and human lives may in all these ways also fail. But the only criteria for success or failure in a human life as a whole are the criteria of success or failure in a narrated or to-be-narrated quest. A quest for what?

Two key features of the medieval conception of a quest need to be recalled. The first is that without some at least partly determinate conception of the final *telos* there could not be any beginning to a quest. Some conception of the good for man is required. Whence is such a conception to be drawn? Precisely from those questions which led us to attempt to transcend that limited conception of the virtues which is available in and through practices. It is in looking for a conception of *the* good which will enable us to order other goods, for a conception of *the* good which will enable us to extend our understanding of the purpose and content of the virtues, for a conception of *the* good which will enable us to understand the place of integrity and constancy in life, that we initially define the kind of life which is a quest for the good. But secondly it is clear the medieval conception of a quest is not at all that of a search for something already adequately characterized, as miners search for gold or geologists for oil. It is in the course of the quest and only through encountering and coping with the various particular harms, dangers, temptations and distractions which provide any quest with its episodes and incidents that the goal of the quest is finally to be understood. A quest is always an education both as to the character of that which is sought and in self-knowledge.

The virtues therefore are to be understood as those dispositions which will not only sustain practices and enable us to achieve the goods internal to practices, but which will also sustain us in the relevant kind of quest for the good, by enabling us to overcome the harms, dangers, temptations and distractions which we encounter, and which will furnish us with increasing self-knowledge and increasing knowledge of the good. The catalogue of the virtues will therefore include the virtues required to sustain the kind of households and the kind of political communities in which men and women can seek for the good together and the virtues necessary for philosophical enquiry about the character of the good. We have then arrived at a provisional conclusion about the good life for man: the good life for man is the life spent in seeking for the good life for man, and the virtues necessary for the seeking are those which will enable us to understand what more and what else the good life for man is. We have also completed the second stage in our account of the virtues, by situating them in relation to the good life for man and not only in relation to practices. But our enquiry requires a third stage.

For I am never able to seek for the good or exercise the virtues only *qua* individual. This is partly because what it is to live the good life concretely varies from circumstance to circumstances even when it is one and the same conception of the good life and one and the same set of virtues which are being embodied in a human life. What the good life is for a fifth-century Athenian general will not be the same as what it was for a medieval nun or a seventeenth-century farmer. But it is not just that different individuals live in different social circumstances; it is also that we all approach our own circumstances as bearers of a particular social identity. I am someone's son or daughter, someone else's cousin or uncle; I am a citizen of this or that city, a member of this or that guild or profession; I belong to this clan, that tribe, this nation. Hence what is good for me has to be the good for one who inhabits these roles. As such, I inherit from the past of my family, my city, my tribe, my nation, a variety of debts, inheritances, rightful expectations and obligations. These constitute the given of my life, my moral starting point. This is in part what gives my life its own moral particularity.

This thought is likely to appear alien and even surprising from the standpoint of modern individualism. From the standpoint of individualism I am what I myself choose to be. I can always, if I wish to, put in question what are taken to be the merely contingent social features of my existence. I may biologically be my father's son; but I cannot be held responsible for what he did unless I choose implicitly or explicitly to assume such responsibility. I may legally be a citizen of a certain country; but I cannot be held responsible for what my country does or has done unless I choose implicitly or explicitly to assume such responsibility. Such individualism is expressed by those modern Americans who deny any responsibility for the effects of slavery upon black Americans, saying 'I never owned any slaves'. It is more subtly the standpoint of those other modern Americans who accept a nicely calculated responsibility for such effects measured precisely by the benefits they themselves as individuals have indirectly received from slavery. In both cases 'being an American' is not in itself taken to be part of the moral identity of the individual. And of course there is nothing peculiar to modern Americans in this attitude: the Englishman who says, *'I* never did any wrong to Ireland; why bring up that old history as though it had something to do with *me?'* or the young German who believes that being born after 1945 means that what Nazis did to Jews has no moral relevance to his relationship to his Jewish contemporaries, exhibit the same attitude, that according to which the self is detachable from its social and historical roles and statuses. And the self so detached is of course a self very much at home in either Sartre's or Goffman's perspective, a self that can have no history. The contrast with the narrative view of the self is clear. For the story of my life is always embedded in the story of those communities from which I derive my identity. I am born with a past; and to try to cut myself off from that past, in the individualist mode, is to deform my present relationships. The possession of an historical identity and the possession of a social identity coincide. Notice that rebellion against my identity is always one possible mode of expressing it.

Notice also that the fact that the self has to find its moral identity in and through its membership in communities such as those of the family, the neighbourhood, the city and the tribe does not entail that the self has to accept the moral *limitations* of the particularity of those forms of community. Without those moral particularities to begin from there would never be anywhere to begin; but it is in moving forward from such particularity that the search for the good, for the universal, consists. Yet particularity can never be simply left behind or obliterated. The notion of escaping from it into a realm of entirely universal maxims which belong to man as such, whether in its eighteenth-century Kantian form or in the presentation of some modern analytical moral philosophies, is an illusion and an illusion with painful consequences. When men and women identify what are in fact their partial and particular causes too easily and too completely with the cause of some universal principle, they usually behave worse than they would otherwise do.

What I am, therefore, is in key part what I inherit, a specific past that is present to some degree in my present. I find myself part of a history and that is generally to say, whether I like it or not, whether I recognize it or not, one of the bearers of a tradition. It was important when I characterized the concept of a practice to notice that practices always have histories and that at any given moment what a practice is depends on a mode of understanding it which has been transmitted often through many generations. And thus, insofar as the virtues sustain the relationships required for practices, they have to sustain relationships to the past – and to the future – as well as in the present. But the traditions through which particular practices are transmitted and reshaped never exist in isolation for larger social traditions. What constitutes such traditions?

We are apt to be misled here by the ideological uses to which the concept of a tradition has been put by conservative political theorists. Characteristically such theorists have followed Burke in contrasting tradition with reason and the stability of tradition with conflict. Both contrasts obfuscate. For all reasoning takes place within the context of some traditional mode of thought, transcending through criticism and invention the limitations of what had hitherto been reasoned in that tradition; this is as true of modern physics as of medieval logic. Moreover when a tradition is in good order it is always partially constituted by an argument about the goods the pursuit of which gives to that tradition its particular point and purpose.

So when an institution – a university, say, or a farm, or a hospital – is the bearer of a tradition of practice or practices, its common life will be partly, but in a centrally important way, constituted by a continuous argument as to what a university is and ought to be or what good farming is or what good medicine is. Traditions, when vital, embody continuities of conflict. Indeed when a tradition becomes Burkean, it is always dying or dead.

The individualism of modernity could of course find no use for the notion of tradition within its own conceptual scheme except as an adversary notion; it therefore all too willingly abandoned it to the Burkeans, who, faithful to Burke's own allegiance, tried to combine adherence in politics to a conception of tradition which would vindicate the oligarchical revolution of property of 1688 and adherence in economics to the doctrine and institutions of the free market. The theoretical incoherence of this mismatch did not deprive it of ideological usefulness. But the outcome has been that modern conservatives are for the most part engaged in conserving only older rather than later versions of liberal individualism. Their own core doctrine is as liberal and as individualist as that of self-avowed liberals.

A living tradition then is an historically extended, socially embodied argument, and an argument precisely in part about the goods which constitute that tradition. Within a tradition the pursuit of goods extends through generations, sometimes through many generations. Hence the individual's search for his or her good is generally and characteristically conducted within a context defined by those traditions of which the individual's life is a part, and this is true both of those goods which are internal to practices and of the goods of a single life. Once again the narrative phenomenon of embedding is crucial: the history of a practice in our time is generally and characteristically embedded in and made intelligible in terms of the larger and longer history of the tradition through which the practice in its present form was conveyed to us; the history of each of our own lives is generally and characteristically embedded in and made intelligible in terms of the larger and longer histories of a number of traditions. I have to say 'generally and characteristically' rather than 'always', for traditions decay, disintegrate and disappear. What then sustains and strengthens traditions? What weakens and destroys them?

The answer in key part is: the exercise or the lack of exercise of the relevant virtues. The virtues find their point and purpose not only in sustaining those relationships necessary if the variety of goods internal to practices are to be achieved and not only in sustaining the form of an individual life in which that individual may seek out his or her good as the good of his or her whole life, but also in sustaining those traditions which provide both practices and individual lives with their necessary historical context. Lack of justice, lack of truthfulness, lack of courage, lack of the relevant intellectual virtues – these corrupt traditions, just as they do those institutions and practices which derive their life from the traditions of which they are the contemporary embodiments. To recognize this is of course also to recognize the existence of an additional virtue, one whose importance is perhaps most obvious when it is least present, the virtue of having an adequate sense of the traditions to which one belongs or which confront one. This virtue is not to be confused with any form of conservative antiquarianism; I am not praising those who choose the conventional conservative role of *laudator temporis acti*. It is rather the case that an adequate sense of tradition manifests itself in a grasp of those future possibilities which the past has made available to the present. Living traditions, just because they continue a not-yet-completed narrative, confront a future whose determinate and determinable character, so far as it possesses any, derives from the past.

In practical reasoning the possession of this virtue is not manifested so much in the knowledge of a set of generalizations or maxims which may provide our practical inferences with major premises; its presence or absence rather appears on the kind of capacity for judgement which the agent possesses in knowing how to select among the relevant stack of maxims and how to apply them in particular situations. Cardinal Pole possessed it, Mary Tudor did not; Montrose possessed it, Charles I did not. What Cardinal Pole and the Marquis of Montrose possessed were in fact those virtues which enable their possessors to pursue both their own good and the good of the tradition of which they are the bearers even in situations defined by the necessity of tragic, dilemmatic choice.

It has often been suggested – by J. L. Austin, for example – that *either* we can admit the existence of rival and contingently incompatible goods which make incompatible claims to our practical allegiance *or* we can believe in some determinate conception of *the* good life for man, but that these are mutually exclusive alternatives. No one can consistently hold both these views. What this contention is blind to is that there may be better or worse ways for individuals to live through the tragic confrontation of good with good. And that to know what the good life for man is may require knowing what are the better and what are the worse ways of living in and through such situations. Nothing *a priori* rules out this possibility; and this suggests that within a view such as Austin's there is concealed an unacknowledged empirical premise about the character of tragic situations.

One way in which the choice between rival goods in a tragic situation differs from the modern choice between incommensurable moral premises is that *both* of the alternative courses of action which confront the individual have to be recognized as leading to some authentic and substantial good. By choosing one I do nothing to diminish or derogate from the claims upon me of the other; and therefore, whatever I do, I shall have left undone what I ought to have done. The tragic protagonist, unlike the moral agent as depicted by Sartre or Hare, is not choosing between allegiance to one moral principle rather than another, nor is he or she deciding upon some principle of priority between moral principles. Hence the 'ought' involved has a different meaning and force from that of the 'ought' in moral principles understood in a modern way. For the tragic protagonist cannot do everything that he or she ought to do. This 'ought', unlike Kant's, does not imply 'can'. Moreover any attempt to map the logic of such 'ought' assertions on to some modal calculus so as to produce a version of deontic logic has to fail. (See, from a very different point of view, Bas C. Van Fraasen, 1973.)

Yet it is clear that the moral task of the tragic protagonist may be performed better or worse, independently of the choice between alternatives that he or she makes – *ex hypothesi* he or she has no *right* choice to make. The tragic protagonist may behave heroically or unheroically, generously or ungenerously, gracefully or gracelessly, prudently or imprudently. To perform his or her task better rather than worse will be to do both what is better for him or her *qua* individual or *qua* parent or child or *qua* citizen or member of a profession, or perhaps *qua* some or all of these. The existence of tragic dilemmas casts no doubt upon and provides no counterexamples to the thesis that assertions of the form 'To do this in this way would be better for X and/or for his or her family, city or profession' are susceptible of objective truth and falsity, any more than the existence of alternative and contingently incompatible forms of medical treatment casts doubt on the thesis that assertions of the form 'To undergo this medical treatment in this way would be better for X and/or his or her family' are susceptible of objective truth and falsity. (See, from a different point of view, the illuminating discussion in Samuel Guttenplan, 1979–80, pp. 61–80.)

The presupposition of this objectivity is of course that we can understand the notion of 'good for X' and cognate notions in terms of some conception of the unity of X's life. What is better or worse for X depends upon the character of that intelligible narrative which provides X's life with its unity. Unsurprisingly it is the lack of any such unifying conception of a human life which underlies modern denials of the factual character of moral judgements and more especially of those judgements which ascribe virtues or vices to individuals.

I argued earlier that every moral philosophy has some particular sociology as its counterpart. What I have tried to spell out here is the kind of understanding of social life which the tradition of the virtues requires, a kind of understanding very different from those dominant in the culture of bureaucratic individualism. Within that culture conceptions of the virtues become marginal and the tradition of the virtues remains central only in the lives of social groups whose existence is on the margins of the central culture. Within the central culture of liberal or bureaucratic individualism new conceptions of the virtues emerge and the concept of a virtue is itself transformed.

BIBLIOGRAPHY

Samuel Guttenplan, 'Moral Realism and Moral Dilemmas', *Proceedings of the Aristotelian Society*, 1979–80: pp. 61–80.
Barbara Hardy, 'Towards a Poetics of Fiction: An Approach Through Narrative', *Novel*, 2, 1968: pp. 5–14.
Philip Hobsbaum, *A Reader's Guide to Charles Dickens*, 1973.
Louis O. Mink, 'History and Fiction as Modes of Comprehension', *New Literary History*, 1, 1970: pp. 541–58.
John Rawls, *A Theory of Justice*, 1971.
Bas C. Van Frassen, 'Values and the Heart's Command', *Journal of Philosophy*, 70, 1973: pp. 5–19.

7

Peter Berger: On the Obsolescence of the Concept of Honour*

Honour occupies about the same place in contemporary usage as chastity. An individual asserting it hardly invites admiration, and one who claims to have lost it is an object of amusement rather than sympathy. Both concepts have an unambiguously outdated status in the *Weltanschauung* of modernity. Especially intellectuals, by definition in the vanguard of modernity, are about as likely to admit to honour as to be found out as chaste. At best, honour and chastity are seen as ideological leftovers in the consciousness of obsolete classes, such as military officers or ethnic grandmothers.

The obsolescence of the concept of honour is revealed very sharply in the inability of most contemporaries to understand insult, which in essence is an assault on honour. In this, at least in America, there is a close parallel between modern consciousness and modern law. Motives of honour have no standing in American law and legal codes that still admit them, as in some countries of Southern Europe, are perceived as archaic. In modern consciousness, as in American law (shaped more than any other by that prime force of modernization which is capitalism), insult in itself is not actionable, is not recognized as a real injury. The insulted party must be able to prove material damage. There are cases, indeed, where psychic harm may be the basis for a legal claim, but that too is a far cry from a notion of offence against honour. The *Weltanschauung* of everyday life closely conforms in this to the legal definitions of reality. If an individual is insulted and, as a result, is harmed in his career or his capacity to earn an income, he may not only have recourse to the courts but may count on the sympathy of his friends. His friends, and in some cases the courts,

* The complete text of the above article has been previously printed in *European Journal of Sociology*, xi (1970), pp. 339–47. Reprinted with permission.

will come to his support if, say, the insult so unsettles him that he loses his self-esteem or has a nervous breakdown. If, however, neither kind of injury pertains, he will almost certainly be advised by lawyers and friends alike to just forget the whole thing. In other words, the *reality* of the offence will be denied. If the individual persists in maintaining it, he will be negatively categorized, most probably in psychiatric terms (as 'neurotic', 'overly sensitive', or the like), or if applicable in terms that refer to cultural lag (as 'hopelessly European', perhaps, or as the victim of a 'provincial mentality').

The contemporary denial of the reality of honour and of offences against honour is so much part of a taken-for-granted world that a deliberate effort is required to even see it as a problem. The effort is worthwhile, for it can result in some, perhaps unexpected, new insights into the structure of modern consciousness.

The problem of the obsolescence of the concept of honour can be brought into better focus by comparing it with a most timely concept – that of dignity. Taken by itself, the demise of honour might be interpreted as part of a process of moral coarsening, of a lessening of respect for persons, even of dehumanization. Indeed, this is exactly how it looked to a conservative mind at the beginning of the modern era – for example, to the fifteenth-century French poet Eustache Deschamps: 'Age of decline nigh to the end, / Time of horror which does all things falsely, / Lying age, full of pride and of envy, / *Time without honour and without true judgement.*'[1] Yet it seems quite clear in retrospect that this pessimistic estimate was, to say the least, very one-sided. The age that saw the decline of honour also saw the rise of new moralities and of a new humanism, and most specifically of a historically unprecedented concern for the dignity and the rights of the individual. The same modern men who fail to understand an issue of honour are immediately disposed to concede the demands for dignity and for equal rights by almost every new group that makes them – racial or religious minorities, exploited classes, the poor, the deviant, and so on. Nor would it be just to question the genuineness of this disposition. A little thought, then, should make clear that the problem is not clarified by ethical pessimism. It is necessary to ask more fundamentally: What is honour? What is dignity? What can be learned about modern consciousness by the obsolescence of the one and the unique sway of the other?

Honour is commonly understood as an aristocratic concept, or at least associated with a hierarchical order of society. It is certainly true that Western notions of honour have been strongly influenced by the medieval codes of chivalry and that these were rooted in the social structures of feudalism. It is also true that concepts of honour have survived into the modern era best in groups retaining a hierarchical view of society, such as the nobility, the military, and traditional professions like law and medicine. In such groups honour is a direct expression of status, a source of solidarity among social equals and a demarcation line against social inferiors. Honour, indeed, also dictates certain standards of behaviour in dealing with inferiors, but the full code of honour only applies among those who share the same status in the hierarchy. In a hierarchically ordered society the etiquette of everyday life consists of ongoing transactions of honour, and different groups relate differently to this process according to the principle of 'To each his due'. It would be a mistake, however, to understand honour *only* in terms of hierarchy and its delineations. To take the most obvious example, the honour of women in many traditional societies, while usually differentiated along class lines, may pertain in principle to women of *all* classes.

J. K. Campbell, in his study of contemporary rural culture in Greece,[2] makes this very clear. While the obligations of honour (*timi*) differ as between different categories of individuals, notably between men and women, everyone within the community exists within the same all-embracing system of honour. Those who have high status in the community have particular obligations of honour, but even the lowly are differentiated in terms of honour and dishonour. Men should exhibit manliness and women shame, but the failure of either implies dishonour for the individual, the family and, in some cases, the entire community. For all, the qualities enjoined by honour provide the link, not only between self and community, but between self and the idealized norms of the community: 'Honour considered as the possession by men and women of these qualities is the attempt to relate existence to certain archetypal patterns of behaviour.'[3] Conversely, dishonour is a fall from grace in the most comprehensive sense – loss of face in the community, but also loss of self and separation from the basic norms that govern human life.

It is valid to view such a culture as essentially pre-modern, just as it is plausible to predict its disintegration under the impact of modernization. Historically, there are several stages in the latter process. The decline of medieval codes of honour did not lead directly to the contemporary situation in which honour is an all but meaningless concept. There took place first the *embourgeoisement* of honour, which has been defined by Norbert Elias as the process of 'civilization', both a broadening and a mellowing process.[4] The contents had changed, but there was still a conception of honour in the age of the triumphant bourgeoisie. Yet it was with the rise of the bourgeoisie, particularly in the consciousness of its critical intellectuals, that not only the honour of the *ancien régime* and its hierarchical prototypes was debunked, but that an understanding of man and society emerged that would eventually liquidate *any* conception of honour.

Thus Cervantes' *Quixote* is the tragi-comedy of a particular obsolescence, that of the knight-errant in an age in which chivalry has become an empty rhetoric. The greatness of the *Quixote*, however, transcends this particular time-bound debunking job. It unmasks not only the 'madness' of chivalry but, by extension, the folly of *any* identification of self with 'archetypal patterns of behaviour'. Put differently, Don Quixote's 'enchanters' (whose task, paradoxically, is precisely what Max Weber had in mind as '*dis*enchantment') cannot be stopped so easily once they have started their terrible task. As Don Quixote tells Sancho in one of his innumerable homilies:

> Is it possible that in the time you have been with me you have not yet found out that all the adventures of a knight-errant appear to be illusion, follies, and dreams, and turn out to be the reverse? Not because things are really so, but because in our midst there is a host of enchanters, forever changing, disguising and transforming our affairs as they please, according to whether they wish to favor or destroy us. So, what you call a barber's basin is to me Mambrino's helmet, and to another person it will appear to be something else.[5]

These 'enchanters', alas, have not stopped with chivalry. Every human adventure, in which the self and its actions have been identified and endowed with the honour of collective prototypes has, finally, been debunked as 'illusion, follies, and dreams'. Modern man is Don Quixote on his deathbed, denuded of the multicoloured banners that previously enveloped the self and revealed to be *nothing but a man*: 'I was mad, but I am now in my senses; I was once Don Quixote of La Mancha, but I am now, as I said before, Alonso Quixano the Good.'[6] The same self, deprived or, if one prefers, freed from the mystifications of honour is hailed in Falstaff's 'catechism': 'Honour is a mere scutcheon.'[7] It is modern consciousness that unmasks it as such, that, 'enchants' or 'disenchants' it (depending on one's point of view) until it is shown as nothing but a painted artifact. Behind the 'mere scutcheon' is the face of modern man – man bereft of the consolation of prototypes, *man alone.*

It is important to understand that it is precisely this solitary self that modern consciousness has perceived as the bearer of human dignity and of inalienable human rights. The modern discovery of dignity took place precisely amid the wreckage of debunked conceptions of honour. Now, it would be a mistake to ascribe to modern consciousness alone the discovery of a fundamental dignity underlying all possible social disguises. The same discovery can be found in the Hebrew Bible, as in the confrontation between Nathan and David ('Thou art the man'); in Sophocles, in the confrontation between Antigone and Creon; and, in a different form, in Mencius' parable of a criminal stopping a child from falling into a well. The understanding that there is a humanity behind or beneath the roles and the norms imposed by society, and that this humanity has profound dignity, is not a modern prerogative. What is peculiarly modern is the manner in which the reality of this intrinsic humanity is related to the realities of society.

Dignity, as against honour, always relates to the intrinsic humanity divested of all socially imposed roles or norms. It pertains to the self as such, to the individual regardless of his position in society. This becomes very clear in the classic formulations of human rights, from the Preamble to the Declaration of Independence to the Universal Declaration of Human Rights of the United Nations. These rights always pertain to the individual 'irrespective of race, colour or creed' – or, indeed, of sex, age, physical condition or any conceivable social status. There is an implicit sociology and an implicit anthropology here. The implicit sociology views all biological and historical differentiations among men as either downright unreal or essentially irrelevant. The implicit anthropology locates the real self over and beyond all these differentiations.

It should now be possible to see these two concepts somewhat more clearly. Both honour and dignity are concepts that bridge self and society. While either pertains to the individual in a very intimate way, it is in relations with others that both honour and dignity are attained, exchanged, preserved or threatened. Both require a deliberate effort of the will for their maintenance – one must *strive* for them, often against the malevolent opposition of others – thus honour and dignity become goals of moral enterprise. Their loss, always a possibility, has far-reaching consequences for the self. Finally, both honour and dignity have an infectious quality that

extends beyond the moral person of the individual possessing them.
The infection involves his body ('a dignified gait'), his material
ambience (from clothing to the furnishings of his house) and other
individuals closely associated with him ('He brought honour on his
whole family'). What, then, is the difference between these two
concepts of the social self? Or, substituting a more current term to
avoid the metaphysical associations of 'self', how do these two
conceptions of identity differ?

*The concept of honour implies that identity is essentially, or at
least importantly, linked to institutional roles. The modern concept
of dignity, by contrast, implies that identity is essentially independent of institutional roles.* To return to Falstaff's image, in a world
of honour the individual *is* the social symbols emblazoned on his
escutcheon. The true self of the knight is revealed as he rides out to
do battle in the full regalia of his role; by comparison, the naked
man in bed with a woman represents a lesser reality of the self. In
a world of dignity, in the modern sense, the social symbolism
governing the interaction of men is a disguise. The escutcheons *hide*
the true self. It is precisely the naked man, and even more
specifically the naked man expressing his sexuality, who represents
himself more truthfully. Consequently, the understanding of self-
discovery and self-mystification is reversed as between these two
worlds. In a world of honour, the individual discovers his true
identity in his roles, and to turn away from the roles is to turn away
from himself – in 'false consciousness', one is tempted to add. In a
world of dignity, the individual can only discover his true identity
by emancipating himself from his socially imposed roles – the latter
are only masks, entangling him in illusion, 'alienation' and 'bad
faith'. It follows that the two worlds have a different relation to
history. It is through the performance of institutional roles that
the individual participates in history, not only the history of a
particular institution but that of his society as a whole. It is
precisely for this reason that modern consciousness, in its conception of the self, tends towards a curious ahistoricity. In a world of
honour, identity is firmly linked to the past through the reiterated
performance of prototypical acts. In a world of dignity, history is
the succession of mystifications from which the individual must free
himself to attain 'authenticity'.

It is important not to lose sight here of continuities in the
constitution of man – of 'anthropological constants', if one prefers.
Modern man is not a total innovation or a mutation of the species.
Thus he shares with any version of archaic man known to us both
his intrinsic sociality and the reciprocal process with society

through which his various identities are formed, maintained and changed. All the same, within the parameters set by his fundamental constitution, man has considerable leeway in constructing, dismantling and reassembling the worlds in which he lives. Inasmuch as identity is always part of a comprehensive world, and a humanly *constructed* world at that, there are far-reaching differences in the ways in which identity is conceived and, consequently, experienced. Definitions of identity vary with overall definitions of reality. Each such definition, however, has reality-generating power: Men not only define themselves, but they actualize these definitions in real experience – *they live them*.

No monocausal theory is likely to do justice to the transformation that has taken place. Very probably most of the factors commonly cited have in fact played a part in the process – technology and industrialization, bureaucracy, urbanization and population growth, the vast increase in communication between every conceivable human group, social mobility, the pluralization of social worlds and the profound metamorphosis in the social contexts in which children are reared. Be this as it may, the resultant situation has been aptly characterized by Arnold Gehlen with the terms 'deinstitutionalization' and 'subjectivization'. The former term refers to a global weakening in the holding power of institutions over the individual. The institutional fabric, whose basic function has always been to provide meaning and stability for the individual, has become incohesive, fragmented and thus progressively deprived of plausibility. The institutions then confront the individual as fluid and unreliable, in the extreme case as unreal. Inevitably, the individual is thrown back upon himself, on his own subjectivity, from which he must dredge up the meaning and the stability that he requires to exist. Precisely because of man's intrinsic sociality, this is a very unsatisfactory condition. Stable identities (and this also means identities that will be subjectively plausible) can only emerge in reciprocity with stable social contexts (and this means contexts that are structured by stable institutions). Therefore, there is a deep uncertainty about contemporary identity. Put differently, there is a built-in identity crisis in the contemporary situation.

It is in this connection that one begins to understand the implicit sociology and the implicit anthropology mentioned above. Both are rooted in actual experience of the modern world. The literary, philosophical and even social-scientific formulations are *ex post facto* attempts to come to terms with this experience. Gehlen has shown this convincingly for the rise of the modern novel as the literary form most fully reflecting the new subjectivism. But the conceptualizations of man and society of, for instance, Marxism and existentialism are equally rooted in this experience. So is the perspective of modern social science, especially of sociology. Marx's 'alienation' and 'false consciousness', Heidegger's 'authenticity' and Sartre's 'bad faith', and such current sociological notions as David Reisman's 'other-direction' or Erving Goffman's 'impression management' could only arise and claim credibility in a situation in which the identity-defining power of institutions has been greatly weakened.

The obsolescence of the concept of honour may now be seen in a much more comprehensive perspective. The social location of honour lies in a world of relatively intact, stable institutions, a world in which individuals can with subjective certainty attach their identities to the institutional roles that society assigns to them. The disintegration of this world as a result of the forces of modernity has not only made honour an increasingly meaningless notion, but has served as the occasion for a redefinition of identity and its intrinsic dignity apart from and often *against* the institutional roles through which the individual expresses himself in society. The reciprocity between individual and society, between subjective identity and objective identification through roles, now comes to be experienced as a sort of struggle. Institutions cease to be the 'home' of the self; instead they become oppressive realities that distort and estrange the self. Roles no longer actualize the self, but serve as a 'veil of *maya*' hiding the self not only from others but from the individual's own consciousness. Only in the interstitial areas left vacant, as it were, by the institutions (such as the so-called private sphere of social life) can the individual hope to discover or define himself. Identity ceases to be an objectively and subjectively given fact, and instead becomes the goal of an often devious and difficult quest. Modern man, almost inevitably it seems, is ever in search of himself. If this is understood, it will also be clear why both the sense of 'alienation' and the concomitant identity crisis are most vehement among the young today. Indeed, 'youth' itself, which is a matter of social definition rather than biological fact, will be seen as an interstitial area vacated or 'left over' by the large institutional structures of modern society. For this reason it is, simultaneously, the locale of the most acute experiences of self-estrangement and of the most intensive quest for reliable identities.

A lot will depend, naturally, on one's basic assumptions about man whether one will bemoan or welcome these transformations. What to one will appear as a profound loss will be seen by another as the prelude to liberation. Among intellectuals today, of course, it is the latter viewpoint that prevails and that forms the implicit anthropological foundation for the generally 'left' mood of the time. The threat of chaos, both social and psychic, whichever lurks behind the disintegration of institutions, will then be seen as a necessary stage that must precede the great 'leap into freedom' that is to come. It is also possible, in a conservative perspective, to view the same process as precisely the root pathology of the modern era, as a disastrous loss of the very structures that enable men to be free and to be themselves. Such pessimism is expressed forcefully, if somewhat petulantly, in Gehlen's latest book, a conservative manifesto in which modernity appears as an all-engulfing pestilence.[8]

We would contend here that both perspectives – the liberation myth of the 'left' and the nostalgia of the 'right' for an intact world – fail to do justice to the anthropological and indeed the ethical dimensions of the problem. It seems clear to us that the unrestrained enthusiasm for total liberation of the self from the 'repression' of institutions fails to take account of certain fundamental requirements of man, notably those of *order* – that institutional order of society without which both collectivities and individuals must descend into dehumanizing chaos. In other words, the demise of honour has been a very costly price to pay for whatever liberations modern man may have achieved. On the other hand, the unqualified denunciation of the contemporary constellation of institutions and identities fails to perceive the vast moral achievements made possible by just this constellation – the discovery of the autonomous individual, with a dignity deriving from his very being, over and above all and any social identifications. Anyone denouncing the modern world *tout court* should pause and question whether he wishes to include in that denunciation the specifically modern discoveries of human dignity and human rights. The conviction that even the weakest members of society have an inherent right to protection and dignity; the proscription of slavery in all its forms, of racial and ethnic oppression; the staggering discovery of the dignity and rights of the child; the new sensitivity to cruelty, from the abhorrence of torture to the codification of the crime of genocide – a sensitivity that has become politically significant in the outrage against the cruelties of the war in Vietnam; the new recognition of individual responsibility for all actions, even those assigned to the individual with specific institutional roles, a recognition that attained the force of law at Nuremberg – all these, and others, are moral achievements that would be unthinkable without the peculiar constellations of the modern world. To reject them is unthinkable ethically. By the same token, it is not possible to simply trace them to a false anthropology. The task before us, rather, is to understand the empirical processes that have made modern man lose sight of honour at the expense of dignity – and then to think through both the anthropological and the ethical implications of this. Obviously these remarks can do no more than point up some dimensions of the problem. It may be allowed, though, to speculate that a rediscovery of honour in the future development of modern society is both empirically plausible and morally desirable. Needless to say, this will hardly take the form of a regressive restoration of traditional codes. But the contemporary mood of anti-institutionalism is unlikely to last, as Anton Zijderveld implies.[9] Man's fundamental constitution is such that, just about inevitably, he will once more construct institutions to provide an ordered reality for himself. A return to institutions will *ipso facto* be a return to honour. It will then be possible again for individuals to identify themselves with the escutcheons of their institutional roles, experienced now not as self-estranging tyrannies but as freely chosen vehicles of self-realization. The ethical question, of course, is what these institutions will be like. Specifically, the ethical test of any future institutions, and of the codes of honour they will entail, will be whether they succeed in embodying and in stabilizing the discoveries of human dignity that are the principle achievements of modern man.

NOTES

[1] Cited in J. Huizinga, *The Waning of the Middle Ages* (New York: Doubleday-Anchor, 1954), p. 33 (my italics).
[2] J. K. Campbell, *Honour, Family and Patronage* (Oxford, 1964).
[3] Ibid., pp. 271.
[4] Norbert Elias, *Der Prozess der Zivilisation* (Bern: Francke, 1969).
[5] Cervantes, *Don Quixote*, trans. Walter Starkie (New York: New American Library, 1964), i:25, p. 243.
[6] Ibid., ii:74.
[7] W. Shakespeare, *Henry IV*, Part I, v:i.
[8] Arnold Gehlen, *Moral and Hypermoral* (Frankfurt: Athenäum, 1969).
[9] Anton Zijderveld, *Abstract Society* (New York: Doubleday, 1970).

8

Michael J. Sandel: Justice and the Good*

I

THE STATUS OF THE GOOD

The difficulty with Rawls' theory of the good is epistemological as well as moral, and in this it recalls a problem that arose in connection with the concept of right – that of distinguishing a standard of assessment from the thing being assessed. If my fundamental values and final ends are to enable me, as surely they must, to evaluate and regulate my immediate wants and desires, these values and ends must have a sanction independent of the mere fact that I happen to hold them with a certain intensity. But if my conception of the good is simply the product of my immediate wants and desires, there is no reason to suppose that the critical standpoint it provides is any more worthy or valid than the desires it seeks to assess; as the product of those desires, it would be governed by the same contingencies.

Rawls responds to this difficulty in the case of the right by seeking in justice as fairness an Archimedean point that 'is not at the mercy, so to speak, of existing wants and interests' (1971, p. 261). But as we have seen, Rawls' concept of right does not extend to private morality, nor does any other instrument of detachment save the good from thoroughgoing implication in the agent's existing wants and desires. 'Purely preferential choice' is thoroughly heteronomous choice, and no person's values or conception of the good can possibly reach beyond it. As Rawls strikingly concedes, 'That we have one conception of the good rather than another is not relevant from a moral standpoint. In

* © 1982 Cambridge University Press. Reprinted from *Liberalism and the Limits of Justice* by Michael Sandel, by permission of the publishers.

acquiring it we are influenced by the same sort of contingencies that lead us to rule out a knowledge of our sex and class' (1975, p. 537).

The limited scope for reflection on Rawls' account, and the problematic, even impoverished theory of the good that results reveal the extent to which deontological liberalism accepts an essentially utilitarian account of the good, however its theory of right may differ. This utilitarian background first appeared in our discussion of Dworkin's defence of affirmative action; once no individual rights were seen to be at stake, utilitarian considerations automatically prevailed. Although Dworkin defends what he calls an 'anti-utilitarian concept of right', the scope of this right is strictly (if elusively) circumscribed, such that 'the vast bulk of the laws that diminish my liberty are justified on utilitarian grounds as being in the general interest or for the general welfare' (1977, p. 269).[1]

The utilitarian background to Rawls' conception most clearly appears in his references to individual moral life. Where justice as fairness rejects utilitarianism as the basis of social, or public morality, it has no apparent argument with utilitarianism as the basis of individual, or private morality, the Kantian notion of 'duty to oneself' to the contrary. Rawls describes the utilitarian account of private morality, without discernible objection, as follows:

> A person quite properly acts, at least when others are not affected, to achieve his own greatest good, to advance his rational ends as far as possible. . . . [T]he principle for an individual is to advance as far as possible his own welfare, his own system of desires' (1971, p. 23).

> To be sure there is one formal principle that seems to provide a general answer [to an individual's choice of life plan]. This is the principle to adopt that plan which maximizes the expected net balance of satisfaction (1971, p. 416).

For Rawls, utilitarianism goes wrong not in conceiving the good as the satisfaction of arbitrarily-given desires undifferentiated as to worth — for justice as fairness shares in this — but only in being indifferent to the way these consummations are spread across individuals. Its mistake as he sees it is to adopt 'for society as a whole the principle of rational choice for one man', to combine 'the desires of all persons into one coherent system of desire', and to seek its overall satisfaction (1971, pp. 26–7). In so doing, it 'fuses' or 'conflates' all persons into one, it reduces social choice to 'essentially a question of efficient administration' (as, presumably, individual choice can properly be reduced), and so fails to take seriously the distinction between persons (1971, pp. 27, 33).

Justice as fairness seeks to remedy these shortcomings by emphasizing the distinction between persons and by insisting on the separateness of those diverse 'systems of desires' that utilitarianism conflates. But the grounds for Rawls' departure from utilitarianism in this respect are not immediately apparent. Although he seems firm in his view that to each individual human being there corresponds exactly one 'system of desires', he never says why this must be so, or what exactly a 'system of desires' consists in, or why it is wrong to conflate them. Is a 'system of desires' a set of desires *ordered* in a certain way, arranged in a hierarchy of relative worth or essential connection with the identity of the agent, or is it simply a concatenation of desires arbitrarily arrayed, distinguishable only by their relative intensity and accidental location? If it is the second, if a *system* of desires means nothing more than an arbitrary collection of desires accidentally embodied in some particular human being, then it is unclear why the integrity of such a 'system' should be taken so morally and metaphysically seriously. If desires can properly be conflated within persons, why not between persons as well?

If, on the other hand, what makes a *system* of desires is a hierarchical ordering of qualitatively distinguishable desires, then it would be no more justifiable to 'conflate' desires within a person than between persons, and what is wrong with utilitarianism would also be wrong, in this respect at least, with justice as fairness. The tendency to conflate desires, whether within persons or between them, would reflect the failure to *order* them, or to acknowledge the qualitative distinctions between them. But this failure cuts across the distinction between individual and social choice, for there is no reason to suppose that a 'system of desires' in *this* sense corresponds in all cases to the empirically-individuated person. Communities of various sorts could count as distinct 'systems of desires' in this sense, so long as they were identifiable in part by an order or structure of shared values partly constitutive of a common identity or form of life. From this point of view, the utilitarian failure to take seriously the distinction between persons would appear a mere symptom of its larger failure to take seriously the qualitative distinctions of worth between different orders of desires, a failure rooted in an impoverished account of the good which justice as fairness has been seen to share.

For a deontological doctrine such as Rawls' it might be thought that viewing the good as wholly mired in contingency, despite its implausibility generally, would have at least the redeeming advantage of making the primacy of right all the more compelling. If the good is nothing more than the indiscriminate satisfaction of arbitrarily-given preferences, regardless of worth, it is not difficult to imagine that the right (and for that matter a good many other sorts of claims) must outweigh it. But in fact the morally diminished status of the good must inevitably call into question the status of justice as well. For once it is conceded that our conceptions of the good are morally arbitrary, it becomes difficult to see why the highest of all (social) virtues should be the one that enables us to pursue these arbitrary conceptions 'as fully as circumstances permit'.

THE MORAL EPISTEMOLOGY OF JUSTICE

Our discussion of the good thus brings us back to the question of justice and the claim for its priority, and with this we return to the circumstances of justice in the original position. Here, the distinctness or separateness of persons on which Rawls insists as a corrective to utilitarianism is installed as the key assumption of mutual disinterest, the notion that individuals take no interest in one another's interests (1971, p. 218). When first we surveyed the conditions in the original position, this assumption in particular and the empiricist rendering of the circumstances of justice in general seemed to undermine the primacy of justice in various ways. Where justice depended for its virtue on the existence of certain empirical pre-conditions, the virtue of justice was no longer absolute, as truth to theories, but only conditional, as physical courage to a war zone; it presupposed a rival virtue or set of virtues of at least correlative status; it assumed in certain circumstances a remedial dimension; ˙ finally, where inappropriately displayed, justice appeared as a vice rather than a virtue. In sum, a Humean account of the circumstances of justice – such as Rawls explicitly adopts – seemed incompatible with the privileged status of justice required by Rawls and defended by Kant only by recourse to a moral metaphysic Rawls found unacceptable.

Hume's own view of justice confirms its partiality, at least in so far as it is derived from premises which Hume and Rawls seem to share. For Hume, the circumstances of justice describe certain unfortunate if unavoidable material and motivational conditions of actual human societies, most notably moderate scarcity and 'limited generosity'. Together, these circumstances demonstrate the sense in which the arrival of justice signifies the absence of certain nobler but rarer virtues.

'If every man had a tender regard for another, or if nature supplied abundantly all our wants and desires . . . the jealousy of interest, which justice supposes, could no longer have place'; nor, says Hume, would there be any occasion for distinctions of property and possession. 'Encrease to a sufficient degree the benevolence of men, or the bounty of nature, and you render justice useless, by supplying its place with much nobler virtues, and more valuable blessings.' If material scarcity were replaced with abundance, 'or if everyone had the same affection and tender regard for everyone as for himself; justice and injustice would be equally unknown among mankind.' And so, Hume concludes, ''tis only from the scanty provision nature has made for his wants, that justice derives its origin' (1739, pp. 494–5).

For Hume, justice cannot be the first virtue of social institutions (at least not in any categorical sense), and in some cases is doubtfully a virtue at all. In the institution of the family, for example, affections may be enlarged to such an extent that justice is scarcely engaged, much less as 'the first virtue'. And even in the wider society, where generosity is more limited and justice more extensively engaged, its virtue can only be accounted for against a background of higher or nobler virtues whose absence calls justice into being. In so far as mutual benevolence and enlarged affections could be cultivated more widely, the need for 'the cautious, jealous virtue of justice' would diminish in proportion, and mankind would be the better for it. Were scarcity or selfishness overcome altogether, then 'justice, being totally useless . . . could never possibly have place in the catalogue of virtue' (1777, p. 16), much less the first place to which Rawls would assign it.

But despite the parallel Rawls himself invites between Hume's account and his own, the assumption of mutual disinterest has a different meaning for Rawls. It does not imply that human beings are typically governed by 'selfishness and confined generosity'; indeed it is not meant as a claim about human motivations at all. It is rather a claim about the subject of motivations. It assumes interests *of* a self, not necessarily *in* a self, a subject of possession individuated in advance and given prior to its ends.

From this there follow important consequences for the status of justice. No longer is benevolence prior to justice and in some cases able to supplant it. Since for Rawls, the virtue of justice does not presuppose egoistic motivations to begin with, it need not await the fading of benevolence to find its occasion, and even the full flowering of 'enlarged affections' cannot displace it. Justice ceases to be merely remedial with respect to the 'nobler virtues', for its virtue no longer depends on their absence. To the contrary, where persons are individuated in Rawls' sense, justice not only wins its independence from prevailing sentiments and motivations, but comes to stand above them as primary. For given the nature of the subject as Rawls conceives it, justice is not merely a sentiment or a feeling like other, lesser virtues, but above all a framework that constrains these virtues and is 'regulative' with respect to them.

> Therefore in order to realize our nature we have no alterna-
> tive but to plan to preserve our sense of justice as governing
> our other aims. This sentiment cannot be fulfilled if it is
> compromised and balanced against other ends as but one
> desire among the rest. . . . To the contrary, how far we
> succeed in expressing our nature depends on how consistently
> we act from our sense of justice as finally regulative. What we
> cannot do is express our nature by following a plan that views
> the sense of justice as but one desire to be weighed against
> others. For this sentiment reveals what the person is, and to
> compromise it is not to achieve for the self free reign but to
> give way to the contingencies and accidents of the world
> (1971, pp. 574–5).

We have seen how the priority of justice, like the priority of the self, derives in large part from its freedom from the contingencies and accidents of the world. This much emerged in our discussion of right and the bounds of the self. In the light of our discussion of the good we can now also see why on Rawls' theory of the subject, such virtues as benevolence and even love are not self-sufficient moral ideals but must await justice for their completion.

Given the limited role for reflection on Rawls' account, the virtues of benevolence and love, as features of the good, are forms of sentiment rather than insight, ways of feeling rather than knowing. Unlike personal or first-order sentiments and feelings, whose objects are given more or less directly to my awareness, benevolence and love are desires whose object is the good of another. But given the separateness of persons and the intractability of the bounds between them, the content of *this* good (that is, the good I wish another) must be largely opaque to me. On Rawls' view, love is blind, not for its intensity but rather for the opacity of the good that is the object of its concern. 'The reason why the situation remains obscure is that love and benevolence are second-order notions: they seek to further the good of beloved individuals that is already given' (1971, p. 191).

If arriving at one's own good is primarily a matter of surveying existing preferences and assessing their relative intensities, it is not the sort of enquiry in which another, even an intimate other, can readily participate. Only the person himself can 'know' what he really wants or 'decide' what he most prefers. 'Even when we take up another's point of view and attempt to estimate what would be to his advantage, we do so as an adviser, so to speak' (1971, p. 448), and given the limited cognitive access Rawls' conception allows, a rather unprivileged adviser at that.

Although we may at times overcome the difficulty of knowing the good of a beloved individual whose interests we would advance, the problem becomes hopelessly compounded when we would extend our love or benevolence to a plurality of persons whose interests may conflict. For we could not hope to know their respective goods well enough to sort them out and assess their relative claims. Even if benevolence could be as widely cultivated as Hume in his hypothetical vision suggests, its virtue would still not be self-sufficient, for it would remain unclear, without more, what the love of mankind would enjoin. 'It is quite pointless to say that one is to judge the situation as benevolence dictates. This assumes that we are wrongly swayed by self-concern. Our problem lies elsewhere. Benevolence is at sea as long as its many loves are in opposition in the persons of its many objects' (1971, p. 190). Not surprisingly, the anchor this benevolence requires is supplied by the virtue of justice; benevolence, even at its most expansive, depends on justice for its completion. 'A love of mankind that wishes to preserve the distinction of persons, to recognize the separateness of life and experience, will use the two principles of justice to determine its aims when the many goods it cherishes are in opposition' (1971, p. 191). Even in the face of so noble a virtue as the love of mankind, the primacy of justice prevails, although the love that remains is of an oddly judicial spirit.

> This love is guided by what individuals themselves would consent to in a fair initial situation which gives them equal representation as moral persons (1971, p. 191).

Thus we see that the assumption of the mutual disinterestedness of the parties does not prevent a reasonable interpretation of benevolence and of the love of mankind *within the framework of justice as fairness* [emphasis added] (1971, p. 192).

For Rawls, the consequences of taking seriously the distinction between persons are not directly moral but more decisively epistemological. What the bounds between persons confine is less the reach of our sentiments – this they do not prejudge – than the reach of our understanding, of our cognitive access to others. And it is this *epistemic* deficit (which derives from the nature of the subject) more than any shortage of benevolence (which is in any case variable and contingent) that requires justice for its remedy and so accounts for its pre-eminence. Where for Hume, we need justice because we do not *love* each other well enough, for Rawls we need justice because we cannot *know* each other well enough for even love to serve alone.

But as our discussion of agency and reflection suggests, we are neither as transparent to ourselves nor as opaque to others as Rawls' moral epistemology requires. If our agency is to consist in something more than the exercise in 'efficient administration' which Rawls' account implies, we must be capable of a deeper introspection than a 'direct self-knowledge' of our immediate wants and desires allows. But to be capable of a more thoroughgoing reflection, we cannot be wholly unencumbered subjects of possession, individuated in advance and given prior to our ends, but must be subjects constituted in part by our central aspirations and attachments, always open, indeed vulnerable, to growth and transformation in the light of revised self-understandings. And in so far as our constitutive self-understandings comprehend a wider subject than the individual alone, whether a family or tribe or city or class or nation or people, to this extent they define a community in the constitutive sense. And what marks such a community is not merely a spirit of benevolence, or the prevalence of communitarian values, or even certain 'shared final ends' alone, but a common vocabulary of discourse and a background of implicit practices and understandings within which the opacity of the participants is reduced if never finally dissolved. In so far as justice depends for its pre-eminence on the separateness or boundedness of persons in the cognitive sense, its priority would diminish as that opacity faded and this community deepened.

JUSTICE AND COMMUNITY

Of any society it can always be asked to what extent it is just, or 'well-ordered' in Rawls' sense, and to what extent it is a community, and the answer can in neither case fully be given by reference to the sentiments and desires of the participants alone. As Rawls observes, to ask whether a particular society is just is not simply to ask whether a large number of its members happen to have among their various desires the desire to act justly – although this may be one feature of a just society – but whether the society is itself a society of a certain kind, ordered in a certain way, such that justice describes its 'basic structure' and not merely the dispositions of persons within the structure. Thus Rawls writes that although we call the attitudes and dispositions of persons just and unjust, for justice as fairness the 'primary subject of justice is the basic structure of society' (1971, p. 7). For a society to be just in this strong sense, justice must be constitutive of its framework and not simply an attribute of certain of the participants' plans of life.

Similarly, to ask whether a particular society is a community is not simply to ask whether a large number of its members happen to have among their various desires the desire to associate with others or to promote communitarian aims – although this may be one feature of a community – but whether the society is itself a society of a certain kind, ordered in a certain way, such that community describes its basic structure and not merely the dispositions of persons within the structure. For a society to be a community in this strong sense, community must be constitutive of the shared self-understandings of the participants and embodied in their institutional arrangements, not simply an attribute of certain of the participants' plans of life.

Rawls might object that a constitutive conception of community such as this should be rejected 'for reasons of clarity among others', or on the grounds that it supposes society to be 'an organic whole with a life of its own distinct from and superior to that of all its members in their relations with one another' (1971, p. 264). But a constitutive conception of community is no more metaphysically problematic than a constitutive conception of justice such as Rawls defends. For if this notion of community describes a framework of self-understandings that is distinguishable from and in some sense prior to the sentiments and dispositions of individuals within the framework, it is only in the same sense that justice as fairness describes a 'basic structure' or framework that is likewise distinguishable from and prior to the sentiments and dispositions of individuals within it.

If utilitarianism fails to take seriously our distinctness, justice as fairness fails to take seriously our commonality. In regarding the bounds of the self as prior, fixed once and for all, it relegates our commonality to an aspect of the good, and relegates the good to a mere contingency, a product of indiscriminate wants and desires 'not relevant from a moral standpoint'. Given a conception of the good that is diminished in this way, the priority of right would seem an unexceptionable claim indeed. But utilitarianism gave the good a bad name, and in adopting it uncritically, justice as fairness wins for deontology a false victory.

II

For justice to be the first virtue, certain things must be true of us. We must be creatures of a certain kind, related to human circumstance in a certain way. We must stand at a certain distance from our circumstance, whether as transcendental subject in the case of Kant, or as essentially unencumbered subject of possession in the case of Rawls. Either way, we must regard ourselves as independent: independent from the interests and attachments we may have at any moment, never identified by our aims but always capable of standing back to survey and asssess and possibly to revise them (Rawls, 1979, p. 7; 1980, pp. 544–5).

DEONTOLOGY'S LIBERATING PROJECT

Bound up with the notion of an independent self is a vision of the moral universe this self must inhabit. Unlike classical Greek and medieval Christian conceptions, the universe of the deontological ethic is a place devoid of inherent meaning, a world 'disenchanted' in Max Weber's phrase, a world without an objective moral order. Only in a universe empty of *telos*, such as seventeenth-century science and philosophy affirmed,[2] is it possible to conceive a subject apart from and prior to its purposes and ends. Only a world ungoverned by a purposive order leaves principles of justice open to human construction and conceptions of the good to individual choice. In this the depth of opposition between deontological liberalism and teleological world views most fully appears.

Where neither nature nor cosmos supplies a meaningful order to be grasped or apprehended, it falls to human subjects to constitute meaning on their own. This would explain the prominence of contract theory from Hobbes onward, and the corresponding emphasis on voluntarist as against cognitive ethics culminating in Kant. What can no longer be found remains somehow to be created.[3] Rawls describes his own view in this connection as a version of Kantian 'constructivism'.

The parties to the original position do not agree on what the moral facts are, as if there were already such facts. It is not that, being situated impartially, they have a clear and undistorted view of a prior and independent moral order. Rather (for constructivism), *there is no such order*, and therefore no such facts apart from the procedure as a whole [emphasis added] (1980, p. 568).

Similarly for Kant, the moral law is not a discovery of theoretical reason but a deliverance of practical reason, the product of pure will. 'The elementary practical concepts have as their foundation the form of a pure will given in reason', and what makes this will authoritative is that it legislates in a world where meaning has yet to arrive. Practical reason finds its advantage over theoretical reason precisely in this voluntarist faculty, in its capacity to generate practical precepts directly, without recourse to cognition. 'Since in all precepts of the pure will it is only a question of the determination of will', there is no need for these precepts 'to wait upon intuitions in order to acquire a meaning. This occurs for the noteworthy reason that *they themselves produce the reality of that to which they refer*' [emphasis added] (1788, pp. 67–8).

It is important to recall that, on the deontological view, the notion of a self barren of essential aims and attachments does not imply that we are beings wholly without purpose or incapable of moral ties, but rather that the values and relations we have are the products of choice, the possessions of a self given prior to its ends. It is similar with deontology's universe. Though it rejects the possibility of an objective moral order, this liberalism does not hold that just anything goes. It affirms justice, not nihilism. The notion of a universe empty of intrinsic meaning does not, on the deontological view, imply a world wholly ungoverned by regulative principles, but rather a moral universe inhabited by subjects capable of constituting meaning on their own – as agents of *construction* in case of the right, as agents of *choice* in the case of the good. *Qua* noumenal selves, or parties to the original position, we arrive at principles of justice; *qua* actual, individual selves, we arrive at conceptions of the good. And the principles we construct as noumenal selves constrain (but do not determine) the purposes we choose as individual selves. This reflects the priority of the right over the good.

The deontological universe and the independent self that moves within it, taken together, hold out a liberating vision. Freed from the dictates of nature and the sanction of social roles, the deontological subject is installed as sovereign, cast as the author of the only moral meanings there are. As inhabitants of a world without *telos*, we are free to construct principles of justice unconstrained by an order of value antecedently given. Although the principles of justice are not strictly speaking a matter of choice, the society they define 'comes as close as a society can to being a voluntary scheme' (1976, p. 13), for they arise from a pure will or act of construction not answerable to a prior moral order. And as independent selves, we are free to choose our purposes and ends unconstrained by such an order, or by custom or tradition or inherited status. So long as they are not unjust, our conceptions of the good carry weight, whatever they are, simply in virtue of our having chosen them. We are 'self-originating sources of valid claims' (Rawls, 1980, p. 543).

Now justice is the virtue that embodies deontology's liberating vision and allows it to unfold. It embodies this vision by describing those principles the sovereign subject is said to construct while situated prior to the constitution of all value. It allows the vision to unfold in that, equipped with these principles, the just society regulates each person's choice of ends in a way compatible with a similar liberty for all. Citizens governed by justice are thus enabled to realize deontology's liberating project – to exercise their capacity as 'self-originating sources of valid claims' – as fully as circumstances permit. So the primacy of justice at once expresses and advances the liberating aspirations of the deontological world view and conception of the self.

But the deontological vision is flawed, both within its own terms and more generally as an account of our moral experience. Within its own terms, the deontological self, stripped of all possible constitutive attachments, is less liberated than disempowered. As we have seen, neither the right nor the good admits of the voluntarist derivation deontology requires. As agents of construction we do not really construct (Sandel, 1982, chapter 3) and as agents of choice we do not really choose (Sandel, 1982, chapter 4). What goes on behind the veil of ignorance is not a contract or an agreement but if anything a kind of discovery; and what goes on in 'purely preferential choice' is less a choosing of ends than a matching of pre-existing desires, undifferentiated as to worth, with the best available means of satisfying them. For the parties to the original position, as for the parties to ordinary deliberative rationality, the liberating moment fades before it arrives; the sovereign subject is left at sea in the circumstances it was thought to command. The moral frailty of the deontological self also appears at the level of first-order principles. Here we found that the independent self, being essentially dispossessed, was too thin to be capable of desert in the ordinary sense (Sandel, 1982, chapter 2). For claims of desert presuppose thickly-constituted selves, beings capable of possession in the constitutive sense, but the deontological self is wholly without possessions of this kind. Acknowledging this lack, Rawls would found entitlements on legitimate expectations instead. If we are incapable of desert, at least we are entitled that institutions honour the expectations to which they give rise.

But the difference principle requires more. It begins with the thought, congenial to the deontological view, that the assets I have are only accidentally mine. But it ends by assuming that these assets are therefore common assets and that society has a prior claim on the fruits of their exercise. This either disempowers the deontological self or denies its independence. Either my prospects are left at the mercy of institutions established for 'prior and independent social ends' (*Liberalism and the Limits of Justice, p. 313*), ends which may or may not coincide with my own, or I must count myself a member of a community defined in part by those ends, in which case I cease to be unencumbered by constitutive attachments. Either way, the difference principle contradicts the liberating aspiration of the deontological project. We cannot be persons for whom justice is primary and also be persons for whom the difference principle is a principle of justice.

CHARACTER, SELF-KNOWLEDGE, AND FRIENDSHIP

If the deontological ethic fails to redeem its own liberating promise, it also fails plausibly to account for certain indispensable aspects of our moral experience. For deontology insists that we view ourselves as independent selves, independent in the sense that our identity is never tied to our aims and attachments. Given our 'moral power to form, to revise, and rationally to pursue a conception of the good'

(Rawls, 1980, p. 544), the continuity of our identity is unproblematically assured. No transformation of my aims and attachments could call into question the person I am, for no such allegiances, however deeply held, could possibly engage my identity to begin with.

But we cannot regard ourselves as independent in this way without great cost to those loyalties and convictions whose moral force consists partly in the fact that living by them is inseparable from understanding ourselves as the particular persons we are – as members of this family or community or nation or people, as bearers of this history, as sons and daughters of that revolution, as citizens of this republic. Allegiances such as these are more than values I happen to have or aims I 'espouse at any given time'. They go beyond the obligations I voluntarily incur and the 'natural duties' I owe to human beings as such. They allow that to some I owe more than justice requires or even permits, not by reason of agreements I have made but instead in virtue of those more or less enduring attachments and commitments which taken together partly define the person I am.

To imagine a person incapable of constitutive attachments such as these is not to conceive an ideally free and rational agent, but to imagine a person wholly without character, without moral depth. For to have character is to know that I move in a history I neither summon nor command, which carries consequences none the less for my choices and conduct. It draws me closer to some and more distant from others; it makes some aims more appropriate, others less so. As a self-interpreting being, I am able to reflect on my history and in this sense to distance myself from it, but the distance is always precarious and provisional, the point of reflection never finally secured outside the history itself. A person with character thus knows that he is implicated in various ways even as he reflects, and feels the moral weight of what he knows.

This makes a difference for agency and self-knowledge. For, as we have seen, the deontological self, being wholly without character, is incapable of self-knowledge in any morally serious sense. Where the self is unencumbered and essentially dispossessed, no person is left for *self*-reflection to reflect upon. This is why, on the deontological view, deliberation about ends can only be an exercise in arbitrariness. In the absence of constitutive attachments, deliberation issues in 'purely preferential choice', which means the ends we seek, being mired in contingency, 'are not relevant from a moral standpoint' (Rawls, 1975, p. 537).

When I act out of more or less enduring qualities of character, by contrast, my choice of ends is not arbitrary in the same way. In consulting my preferences, I have not only to weigh their intensity but also to assess their suitability to the person I (already) am. I ask, as I deliberate, not only what I really want but who I really am, and this last question takes me beyond an attention to my desires alone to reflect on my identity itself. While the contours of my identity will in some ways be open and subject to revision, they are not wholly without shape. And the fact that they are not enables me to discriminate among my more immediate wants and desires; some now appear essential, others merely incidental to my defining projects and commitments. Although there may be a certain ultimate contingency in my having wound up the person I am – only theology can say for sure – it makes a moral difference none the less that, being the person I am, I affirm these ends rather than those, turn this way rather than that. While the notion of constitutive attachments may at first seem an obstacle to agency – the self, now encumbered, is no longer strictly prior – some relative fixity of character appears essential to prevent the lapse into arbitrariness which the deontological self is unable to avoid.

The possibility of character in the constitutive sense is also indispensable to a certain kind of friendship, a friendship marked by mutual insight as well as sentiment. By any account, friendship is bound up with certain feelings. We like our friends; we have affection for them, and wish them well. We hope that their desires find satisfaction, that their plans meet with success, and we commit ourselves in various ways to advancing their ends.

But for persons presumed incapable of constitutive attachments, acts of friendship such as these face a powerful constraint. However much I might hope for the good of a friend and stand ready to advance it, only the friend himself can know what that good is. This restricted access to the good of others follows from the limited scope for self-reflection, which betrays in turn the thinness of the deontological self to begin with. Where deliberating about my good means no more than attending to wants and desires given directly to my awareness, I must do it on my own; it neither requires nor admits the participation of others. Every act of friendship thus becomes parasitic on a good identifiable in advance. 'Benevolence and love are second-order notions: they seek to further the good of beloved individuals that is already given' (Rawls, 1971, p. 191). Even the friendliest sentiments must await a moment of introspection itself inaccessible to friendship. To expect more of any friend, or to offer more, can only be a presumption against the ultimate privacy of self-knowledge.

For persons encumbered in part by a history they share with others, by contrast, knowing oneself is a more complicated thing. It is also a less strictly private thing. Where seeking my good is bound up with exploring my identity and interpreting my life history, the knowledge I seek is less transparent to me and less opaque to others. Friendship becomes a way of knowing as well as liking. Uncertain which path to take, I consult a friend who knows me well, and together we deliberate, offering and assessing by turns competing descriptions of the person I am, and of the alternatives I face as they bear on my identity. To take seriously such deliberation is to allow that my friend may grasp something I have missed, may offer a more adequate account of the way my identity is engaged in the alternatives before me. To adopt this new description is to see myself in a new way; my old self-image now seems partial or occluded, and I may say in retrospect that my friend knew me better than I knew myself. To deliberate with friends is to admit this possibility, which presupposes in turn a more richly-constituted self than deontology allows. While there will of course remain times when friendship requires deference to the self-image of a friend, however flawed, this too requires insight; here the need to defer implies the ability to know.

So to see ourselves as deontology would see us is to deprive us of those qualities of character, reflectiveness, and friendship that depend on the possibility of constitutive projects and attachments. And to see ourselves as given to commitments such as these is to admit a deeper commonality than benevolence describes, a commonality of shared self-understanding as well as 'enlarged affections'. As the independent self finds its limits in those aims and attachments from which it cannot stand apart, so justice finds its limits in those forms of community that engage the identity as well as the interests of the participants.

To all of this, deontology might finally reply with a concession and a distinction: it is one thing to allow that 'citizens in their personal affairs . . . have attachments and loves that they believe they would not, or could not, stand apart from', that they 'regard it as unthinkable . . . to view themselves without certain religious and philosophical convictions and commitments' (Rawls, 1980, p. 545). But with public life it is different. There, no loyalty or allegiance could be similarly essential to our sense of who we are. Unlike our ties to family and friends, no devotion to city or nation, to party or cause, could possibly run deep enough to be defining. By contrast with our private identity, our 'public identity' as moral persons 'is not affected by changes over time' in our conceptions of the good (Rawls, 1980, pp. 544–5). While we may be thickly-constituted selves in private, we must be wholly unencumbered selves in public, and it is there that the primacy of justice prevails. But once we recall the special status of the deontological claim, it is unclear what the grounds for this distinction could be. It might seem at first glance a psychological distinction; detachment comes more easily in public life, where the ties we have are typically less compelling; I can more easily step back from, say, my partisan allegiances than certain personal loyalties and affections. But as we have seen from the start, deontology's claim for the independence of the self must be more than a claim of psychology or sociology. Otherwise, the primacy of justice would hang on the degree of benevolence and fellow-feeling any particular society managed to inspire. The independence of the self does not mean that I can, as a psychological matter, summon in this or that circumstance the detachment required to stand outside my values and ends, rather that I must regard myself as the bearer of a self distinct from my values and ends, whatever they may be. It is above all an epistemological claim, and has little to do with the relative intensity of feeling associated with public or private relations.

Understood as an epistemological claim, however, the deonto-logical conception of the self cannot admit the distinction required. Allowing constitutive possibilities where 'private' ends are at stake would seem unavoidably to allow at least the possibility that 'public' ends could be constitutive as well. Once the bounds of the self are no longer fixed, individuated in advance and given prior to experience, there is no saying in principle what sorts of experiences could shape or reshape them, no guarantee that only 'private' and never 'public' events could conceivably be decisive.

Not egoists but strangers, sometimes benevolent, make for citizens of the deontological republic; justice finds its occasion because we cannot know each other, or our ends, well enough to govern by the common good alone. This condition is not likely to fade altogether, and so long as it does not, justice will be necessary. But neither is it guaranteed always to predominate, and in so far as it does not, community will be possible, and an unsettling presence for justice.

Liberalism teaches respect for the distance of self and ends, and when this distance is lost, we are submerged in a circumstance that ceases to be ours. But by seeking to secure this distance too completely, liberalism undermines its own insight. By putting the self beyond the reach of politics, it makes human agency an article of faith rather than an object of continuing attention and concern, a premise of politics rather than its precarious achievement. This misses the pathos of politics and also its most inspiring possibilities. It overlooks the danger that when politics goes badly, not only disappointments but also dislocations are likely to result. And it forgets the possibility that when politics goes well, we can know a good in common that we cannot know alone.

NOTES

[1] For a compelling critique of Dworkin's view in this respect, see H. L. A. Hart (1979, pp. 86–9).

[2] For discussion of the moral, political, and epistemological consequences of the seventeenth-century scientific revolution and world-view, see Strauss, 1953; Arendt, 1958, pp. 248–325; Wolin, 1960, pp. 239–85; and Taylor, 1975, pp. 3–50.

[3] As one liberal writer boldly asserts, 'The hard truth is this: There is no moral meaning hidden in the bowels of the universe. . . . Yet there is no need to be overwhelmed by the void. We may create our own meanings, you and I' (Ackerman, 1980, p. 368). Oddly enough, he insists none the less that liberalism is committed to no particular metaphysic or epistemology, nor any 'Big Questions of a highly controversial character' (pp. 356–7, 361).

BIBLIOGRAPHY

Ackerman, B.A. 1980. *Social Justice in the Liberal State*, New Haven.
Arendt, H. 1958. *The Human Condition*, Chicago.
Dworkin, R. 1977. *Taking Rights Seriously*, London.
Hart, H.L.A. 1979. Between utility and rights. In *The Idea of Freedom*, ed. A. Ryan, pp.77–98. Oxford.
Hume, D. 1739. *A Treatise of Human Nature*, 2nd edn, ed. L. A. Selby-Bigge, 1978. Oxford.
Hume, D. 1777. *An Enquiry Concerning the Principles of Morals*, 1966 edn, La Salle, Illinois.
Kant, I. 1788. *Critique of Practical Reason*, translated by L. W. Beck, 1956. Indianapolis.
Rawls, J. 1971. *A Theory of Justice*, Oxford.
Rawls, J. 1975. Fairness to goodness, *Philosophical Review*, 84, pp.536–54.
Rawls, J. 1979. A well-ordered society. In *Philosophy, Politics, and Society*, 5th series, eds P. Laslett and J. Fishkin, pp.6–20. Oxford.
Rawls, J. 1980. Kantian constructivism in moral theory, *Journal of Philosophy*, 77, pp.515–72.
Sandel, M. 1982. *Liberalism and the Limits of Justice*, Cambridge.
Strauss, L. 1953. *Natural Right and History*, Chicago.
Taylor, C. 1975. *Hegel*, Cambridge.
Wolin, S. 1960. *Politics and Vision*, Boston.

9

Charles Taylor: Hegel: History and Politics*

I

. . . Kant's moral theory remained at the edges of politics, as it were, setting limits beyond which states or individuals should not tread. For Hegel, in contrast, morality can only receive a concrete content in politics, in the design of the society we have to further and sustain.

This set of obligations which we have to further and sustain a society founded on the Idea is what Hegel calls '*Sittlichkeit*'. This has been variously translated in English, as 'ethical life', 'objective ethics', 'concrete ethics', but no translation can capture the sense of this term of art, and I propose to use the original here. '*Sittlichkeit*' is the usual German term for 'ethics', with the same kind of etymological origin, in the term '*Sitten*' which we might translate 'customs'. But Hegel gives it a special sense, in contrast to '*Moralität*' (which of course has a parallel etymological origin in 'mores', although being Latin it would not be so evident to German readers).

'*Sittlichkeit*' refers to the moral obligations I have to an ongoing community of which I am part. These obligations are based on established norms and uses, and that is why the etymological root in '*Sitten*' is important for Hegel's use.[1] The crucial characteristic of *Sittlichkeit* is that it enjoins us to bring about what already is. This is a paradoxical way of putting it, but in fact the common life which is the basis of my *sittlich* obligation is already there in existence. It is in virtue of its being an ongoing affair that I have these obligations; and my fulfilment of these obligations is what sustains

*© 1975 Cambridge University Press. Reprinted from *Hegel* by Charles Taylor © 1975, by permission of the publisher.

it and keeps it in being. Hence in *Sittlichkeit*, there is no gap between what ought to be and what is, between *Sollen* and *Sein*. With *Moralität*, the opposite holds. Here we have an obligation to realize something which does not exist. What ought to be contrasts with what is. And connected with this, the obligation holds of me not in virtue of being part of a larger community life, but as an individual rational will.

Hegel's critique of Kant can then be put in this way: Kant identifies ethical obligation with *Moralität*,[2] and cannot get beyond this. For he presents an abstract, formal notion of moral obligation, which holds of man as an individual, and which being defined in contrast to nature is in endless opposition to what is.

We can see how all of Hegel's reproaches against Kant's moral philosophy are systematically connected. Because it remained with a purely formal notion of reason, it could not provide a content to moral obligation. Because it would not accept the only valid content, which comes from an ongoing society to which we belong, it remained an ethic of the individual. Because it shied away from that larger life of which we are a part, it saw the right as forever opposed to the real; morality and nature are always at loggerheads.

The doctrine of *Sittlichkeit* is that morality reaches its completion in a community. This both give obligation its definitive content, as well as realizing it, so that the gap between *Sollen* and *Sein* is made up. Hegel started off as we saw, following Kant in distinguishing will and freedom from nature. But the fulfilment of freedom is when nature (here society, which started in a raw, primitive form) is made over to the demands of reason.

Because the realization of the Idea requires that man be part of a larger life in a society, moral life reaches its highest realization in *Sittlichkeit*. This highest realization is an achievement, of course, it is not present throughout history, and there are even periods where public life has been so emptied of spirit, that *Moralität* expresses something higher. But the fulfilment of morality comes in a realized *Sittlichkeit*.

This is the point where Hegel runs counter to the moral instinct of liberalism then and now. Between obligations which are founded on our membership of some community and those which are not so contingent we tend to think of the latter as transcending the former, as the truly universal moral obligations. Hegel's reversal of the order and his exalted view of political society is what has inspired accusations of 'Prussianism', state-worship, even proto-Fascism. We can see already how wide of the mark these are. We tend to think of *Moralität* as more fundamental because we see the moral man as being ever in danger of being asked by his community to do the unconscionable. And particularly so in an age of nationalism. We are probably right in feeling this in our age, but it was not what Hegel foresaw. The community which is the locus of our fullest moral life is a state which comes close to a true embodiment of the Idea. Hegel thought that the states of his day were building towards that. He was wrong, and we shall discuss this more later on. But it is ludicrous to attribute a view like 'my government right or wrong' to Hegel, or to think that he would have approved the kind of blind following of orders of German soldiers and functionaries under the Third Reich, which was a time if ever there was one when *Moralität* had the higher claim.

We should not forget that two of Hegel's 'heroes', i.e. pivotal figures, in history are Socrates and Jesus, both of whom undermined or broke with the *Sittlichkeit* of their people, and struck off on their own. Hegel's point is, however, that man's (and *Geist's*) true realization cannot come like this. No matter what great spiritual truths a man discovered, they could not be made real, i.e. embodied, if he remains on his own. As an individual he depends on his society in a host of ways, and if it is unregenerate, then he cannot realize the good. If he does not want to compromise his truth and corrupt his message, then he must either withdraw, and/or offer a challenge to his society which will earn him the fate of Christ or Socrates.

Full realization of freedom requires a society for the Aristotelian reason that a society is the minimum self-sufficient human reality. In putting *Sittlichkeit* at the apex, Hegel is – consciously – following Aristotle. And in following Aristotle, the ancient Greek world. For the last time that the world saw an effortless and undivided *Sittlichkeit* was among the Greeks. Hegel's notion of *Sittlichkeit* is in part a rendering of that expressive unity which his whole generation saw in the Greek polis, where – it was believed – men had seen the collective life of their city as the essence and meaning of their own lives, had sought their glory in its public life, their rewards in power and reputation within it, and immortality in its memory. It was his expression for that *vertu* which Montesquieu had seen as the mainspring of republics. In common with his generation he recognized that this *Sittlichkeit* was lost forever in its original form, but along with many of his contemporaries he aspired to see it reborn in a new way.

The idea that our highest and most complete moral existence is one we can only attain to as members of a community obviously takes us beyond the contract theory of modern natural law, or the utilitarian conception of society as an instrument of the general happiness. For these societies are not the focus of independent obligations, let alone the highest claims which can be made on us. Their existence simply gives a particular shape to pre-existing moral obligations, e.g. the keeping of promises, or the furtherance of the greatest happiness of the greatest number. The doctrine which puts *Sittlichkeit* at the apex of moral life requires a notion of society as a larger community life, to recall the expression used above, in which man participates as a member.

Now this notion displaces the centre of gravity, as it were, from the individual on to the community, which is seen as the locus of a life or subjectivity, of which the individuals are phases. The community is an embodiment of *Geist*, and a fuller, more substantial embodiment than the individual. This idea of a subjective life beyond the individual has been the source of much resistance to Hegel's philosophy. For it has seemed to the common sense at least of the Anglo-Saxon world (nurtured by a certain philosophical tradition) as both wildly extravagant in a speculative sense, and morally very dangerous in its 'Prussian' or even 'Fascist' consequences, sacrificing the individual and his freedom on the altar of some 'higher' communal deity. Before going further, therefore, we should examine this notion of the society and the relation of individuals to it. We shall see, indeed, that Hegel's notion of objective *Geist* is not without difficulty; but the extravagance is not where the atomistic mentality of the empiricist world thought it was.

Hegel uses a number of terms to characterize this relation of man to the community.

One of the most common is 'substance'. The state, or the people is the 'substance' of individuals. This idea is clearly expressed in the *Encyclopaedia*.

> The substance which knows itself free, in which absolute *'Ought'* is equally well *being*, has reality as the spirit of a *people*. The abstract diremption of this spirit is the individuation into persons, of whose independent existence spirit is the inner power and necessity. But the person as thinking intelligence knows this substance as his own essence – in this conviction [Gesinnung] he ceases to be a mere accident of it – rather he looks on it at his absolute and final goal existing in reality, as something which is attained in the *here and now*,

while at the same time he *brings it about through his activity*, but as something which in fact simply is.   (*EG*, §514)[3]

We can notice here at the end a reference to that basic feature of *Sittlichkeit*, that it provides a goal which is at the same time already realized, which is brought about, and yet is. But what is worth noticing here is the set of related concepts which help to explain 'substance'. The community, says Hegel, is also 'essence', and also 'final goal' for the individuals.

The notion behind 'substance' and 'essence' is that the individuals only are what they are by their inherence in the community. This idea is put in a passage of *VG*. 'Everything that man is he owes to the state; only in it can he find his essence. All value that a man has, all spiritual reality, he has only through the state' (*VG*, 111). Or more directly 'the individual *is* an individual in this substance. . . . No individual can step beyond [it]; he can separate himself certainly from other particular individuals, but not from the *Volksgeist*' (*VG*, 59–60).

The notion behind 'final goal' [Endzweck] seems to be more sinister, for it seems to imply that individuals only exist to serve the state as some pitiless Moloch. This seems even more clearly to be the message of *PR*, §258, 'this substantial unity is an absolute unmoved end in itself, in which freedom comes into its supreme right. On the other hand this final end has supreme right against the individual, whose supreme duty is to be a member of the state.' But this reading is based on a serious misinterpretation. Hegel denies that the state exists for the individuals, in other words he rejects the Enlightenment utilitarian idea that the state has only an instrumental function, that the ends it must serve are those of individuals. But he cannot really accept the inverse proposition.

> The state is not there for the sake of the citizens; one could say, it is the goal and they are its instruments. But this relation of ends and means is quite inappropriate here. For the state is not something abstract, standing over against the citizens; but rather they are moments as in organic life, where no member is end and none means. . . . The essence of the state is ethical life [die sittliche Lebendigkeit] (*VG*, 112).

Rather we see here that the notion of ends and means gives way to the image of a living being. The state or the community has a higher life; its parts are related as the parts of an organism.[4] Thus the individual is not serving an end separate from him, rather he is serving a large goal which is the ground of his identity, for he only is the individual he is in this larger life. We have gone beyond the opposition self-goal/other-goal.

Hegel adds to this notion of the community as living that of the community as 'self-consciousness'. And it is this, together with the use of the words 'Geist', 'Volksgeist' which has given rise to the idea that the Hegelian state or community is a super-individual. But in the passage of VG where he introduces the terms 'self-consciousness', Hegel makes clear that he is not talking about it in connection with Volksgeistei in the sense that it applies to individuals. Rather it is a 'philosophical concept' (VG, 61). Like any Geist larger than the individual it only has existence through the vehicle of individual concrete subjects.[5] It is thus not a subject like them.

But why does Hegel want to speak of a spirit which is larger than the individual? What does it mean to say that the individual is part of, inheres in, a larger life; and that he is only what he is by doing so?

These ideas only appear mysterious because of the powerful hold on us of atomistic prejudices, which have been very important in modern political thought and culture. We can think that the individual is what he is in abstraction from his community only if we are thinking of him qua organism. But when we think of a human being, we do not simply mean a living organism, but a being who can think, feel, decide, be moved, respond, enter into relations with others; and all this implies a language, a related set of ways of experiencing the world, of interpreting his feelings, understanding his relation to others, to the past, the future, the absolute, and so on. It is the particular way he situates himself within this cultural world that we call his identity.

But now a language, and the related set of distinctions underlying our experience and interpretation, is something that can only grow in and be sustained by a community. In that sense, what we are as human beings, we are only in a cultural community. Perhaps, once we have fully grown up in a culture, we can leave it and still retain much of it. But this kind of case is exceptional, and in an important sense marginal. Emigrés cannot fully live their culture, and are always forced to take on something of the ways of the new society they have entered. The life of a language and culture is one whose locus is larger than that of the individual. It happens in the community. The individual possesses this culture, and hence his identity, by participating in this larger life.

When I say that a language and the related distinctions can only be sustained by a community, I am not thinking only of language as a medium of communication; so that our experience could be entirely private, and just need a public medium to be communicated from one to another. Rather the fact is that our experience is what it is, is shaped in part, by the way we interpret it; and this has a lot to do with the terms which are available to us in our culture. But there is more; many of our most important experiences would be impossible outside of society, for they relate to objects which are social. Such are, for instance, the experience of participating in a rite, or of taking part in the political life of our society, or of rejoicing at the victory of the home team, or of national mourning for a dead hero; and so on. All these experiences and emotions have objects which are essentially social, i.e. would not be outside of (this) society.

So the culture which lives in our society shapes our private experience and constitutes our public experience, which in turn interacts profoundly with the private. So that it is no extravagant proposition to say that we are what we are in virtue of participating in the larger life of our society – or at least, being immersed in it, if our relationship to it is unconscious and passive, as is often the case.

But of course Hegel is saying something more than this. For this inescapable relation to the culture of my society does not rule out the most extreme alienation. This comes about when the public experience of my society ceases to have any meaning for me.

Far from wishing to deny this possibility, Hegel was one of the first to develop a theory of alienation. The point is that the objects of public experience, rite, festival, election, etc., are not like facts of nature. For they are not entirely separable from the experience they give rise to. They are partly constituted by the ideas and interpretations which underlie them. A given social practice, like voting in the ecclesia, or in a modern election, is what it is because of a set of commonly understood ideas and meanings, by which the depositing of stones in an urn, or the marking of bits of paper, counts as the making of a social decision. These ideas about what is going on are essential to define the institution. They are essential if there is to be *voting* here, and not some quite other activity which could be carried on by putting stones in the urns.

Now these ideas are not universally acceptable or even understandable. They involve a certain view of man, society, and decision, for instance, which may seem evil or unintelligible to other societies. To take a social decision by voting implies that it is right, appropriate and intelligible to build the community decision out of a concatenation of individual decisions. In some societies, e.g. many traditional village societies throughout the world, social decisions can (could) only be taken by consensus. An atomistic decision procedure of this kind is tantamount to dissolving the social bond. Whatever else it is it could not be a *social* decision.

Thus a certain view of man and his relation to society is embedded in some of the practices and institutions of a society. So that we can think of these as expressing certain ideas. And indeed, they may be the only, or the most adequate expression of these ideas, if the society has not developed a relatively articulate and accurate theory about itself. The ideas which underlie a certain practice and make it what it is, e.g. those which make the marking of papers the taking of a social decision, may not be spelled out adequately in propositions about man, will, society, and so on. Indeed, an adequate theoretical language may be as yet undeveloped.

In this sense we can think of the institutions and practices of a society as a kind of language in which its fundamental ideas are expressed. But what is 'said' in this language is not ideas which could be in the minds of certain individuals only, they are rather common to a society, because embedded in its collective life, in practices and institutions which are of the society indivisibly. In these the spirit of the society is in a sense objectified. They are, to use Hegel's term, 'objective spirit'.

These institutions and practices make up the public life of a society. Certain norms are implicit in them, which they demand to be maintained and properly lived out. Because of what voting is as a concatenating procedure of social decision, certain norms about falsification, the autonomy of the individual decision, etc., flow inescapably from it. The norms of a society's public life are the content of *Sittlichkeit*.

We can now see better what Hegel means when he speaks of the norms or ends of society as sustained by our action, and yet as already there, so that the member of society 'brings them about through his activity, but as something which rather simply is' (*EG*, §514). For these practices and institutions are maintained only by ongoing human activity in conformity to them; and yet they are in a sense there already before this activity, and must be, for it is only the ongoing practice which defines what the norm is our future action must seek to sustain. This is especially the case if there is as yet no theoretical formulation of the norm, as there was not in Hegel's view in the Greek city-states at their apogee. The Athenian acted 'as it were, out of instinct' (*VG*, 115) his *Sittlichkeit* was a 'second nature'. But even if there is a theory, it cannot substitute for the practice as a criterion, for it is unlikely that any formulation can entirely render what is involved in a social practice of this kind. Societies refer to theoretical 'value' formulations as their norms rather than to practices, when they are trying to make themselves over to meet an unrealized standard; e.g. they are trying to 'build socialism', or become fully 'democratic'. But these goals are, of course, of the domain of *Moralität*. *Sittlichkeit* presupposes that the living practices are an adequate 'statement' of the basic norms, although in the limit case of the modern philosophy of the state, Hegel sees the theoretical formulation as catching up. Hence we see the importance of Hegel's insistence that the end sought by the highest ethics is already realized. It means that the highest norms are to be discovered in the real, that the real is rational, and that we are to turn away from chimaeric attempts to construct a new society from a blue-print. Hegel strongly opposes those who hold

> that a philosophy of state . . . [has] . . . the task of discovering and promulgating still another theory. . . . In examining this idea and the activity in conformity with it, we might suppose that no state or constitution has ever existed in the world at all, but that nowadays . . . we had to start all over again from the beginning, and that the ethical world had just been waiting for such present-day projects, proofs and investigations.
>
> (*PR*, preface, 4)

The happiest, unalienated life for man, which the Greeks enjoyed, is where the norms and ends expressed in the public life of a society are the most important ones by which its members define their identity as human beings. For then the institutional matrix in which they cannot help living is not felt to be foreign. Rather it is the essence, the 'substance' of the self. 'Thus in universal spirit each man has self-certainty, the certainty that he will find nothing other in existing reality than himself' (*PhG*, 258).

And because this substance is sustained by the activity of the citizens, they see it as their work. 'This substance is also the universal work [Werk], which creates itself through the action of each and all as their unity and equality, because it is Being-for-self [Fürsichsein], the self, the act of doing [das Tun]' (*PhG*, 314).

To live in a state of this kind is to be free. The opposition between social necessity and individual freedom disappears. 'The rational is necessary as what belongs to substance, and we are free in so far as we recognize it as law and follow it as the substance of our own essence; objective and subjective will are then reconciled and form one and the same untroubled whole' (*VG*, 115).

But alienation arises when the goals, norms or ends which define the common practices or institutions begin to seem irrelevant or even monstrous, or when the norms are redefined so that the practices appear a travesty of them. A number of public religious practices have suffered the first fate in history; they have 'gone dead' on subsequent generations, and may even be seen as irrational or blasphemous. To the extent that they remain part of the public ritual there is widespread alienation in society – we can think of contemporary societies like Spain, which remains officially Catholic while a good part of the population is rabidly anti-clerical; or communist societies, which have a public religion of atheism, even though many of their citizens believe in God.

But the democratic practices of Western society seem to be suffering something like the second fate in our time. Many people can no longer accept the legitimacy of voting and the surrounding institutions, elections, parliaments, etc., as vehicles of social decision. They have redrawn their conception of the relation of individual to society, so that the mediation and distance which any large-scale voting system produces between individual decision and social outcome seems unacceptable. Nothing can claim to be a real social decision which is not arrived at in a full and intense discussion in which all participants are fully conscious of what is at stake. Decisions made by elected representatives are branded as sham, as manipulation masquerading as consensus. With this redefinition of the norm of collective decision (that is, of a decision made *by* people, and not just for them), our present representative institutions begin to be portrayed as an imposture; and a substantial proportion of the population is alienated from them.

In either case, norms as expressed in public practices cease to hold our allegiance. They are either seen as irrelevant or are decried as usurpation. This is alienation. When this happens men have to turn elsewhere to define what is centrally important to them. Sometimes they turn to another society, for instance a smaller, more intense religious community. But another possibility, which had great historical importance in Hegel's eyes, is that they strike out on their own and define their identity as individuals. Individualism comes, as Hegel puts it in the *VG*, when men cease to identify with the community's life, when they 'reflect', that is, turn back on themselves, and see themselves most importantly as individuals with individual goals. This is the moment of dissolution of a *Volk* and its life.

What happens here is that the individual ceases to define his identity principally by the public experience of the society. On the contrary, the most meaningful experience, which seems to him most vital, to touch most the core of his being, is private. Public experience seems to him secondary, narrow, and parochial, merely touching a part of himself. Should that experience try to make good its claim to centrality as before, the individual enters into conflict with it and has to fight it.

This kind of shift has of course been instantiated many times in history, but the paradigm event of this kind for Hegel occurs with the break-up of the Greek city-state. Thus in the Greek polis, men identified themselves with its public life; its common experiences were for them the paradigm ones. Their most basic, unchallengeable values were those embodied in this public life, and hence their major duty and virtue was to continue and sustain this life. In other words, they lived fully by their *Sittlichkeit*. But the public life of each of these polis was narrow and parochial. It was not in conformity with universal reason. With Socrates arises the challenge of a man who cannot agree to base his life on the parochial, on the merely given, but requires a foundation in universal reason. Socrates himself expresses a deep contradiction since he accepts the idea of *Sittlichkeit*, of laws that one should hold allegiance to; he derives this from universal reason as well. And yet because of his allegiance to reason he cannot live with the actual law of Athens. Rather he undermines them, he corrupts the youth not to take them as final, but to question them. He has to be put to death, a death which he accepts because of his allegiance to the laws.

But now a new type of man arises who cannot identify with this public life. He begins to relate principally not to the public life but to his own grasp of universal reason. The norms that he now feels compelling are quite unsubstantiated in any reality; they are ideas that go beyond the real. The reflecting individual is in the domain of *Moralität*.

Of course, even the self-conscious individual related to some society. Men thought of themselves *qua* moral beings as belonging to some community, the city of men and Gods of the Stoics, the city of God of the Christian. But they saw this city as quite other than and beyond the earthly city. And the actual community of philosophers or believers in which they worked out and sustained the language by which they identified themselves was scattered and powerless. The common life on which their identity as rational or

God-fearing individuals was founded was or could be very attenu-
ated. So that what was most important in a man's life was that he
did or thought as an individual, not his participation in the public
life of a real historical community. (This was not really true of the
Christian church for which the Eucharist was of central importance, but certainly applies to the sage of the late ancient world.)

In any case, the community of the wise, as that of the saints, was
without external, self-subsistent existence in history. Rather, the
public realm was given over to private, unjustified power. This is
Hegel's usual description of the ancient period of universal empires
which succeeded the city-state, particularly the Roman empire. The
unity and fulfilment of *Sittlichkeit*, lost from this world, was
transposed out of it into an ethereal beyond.

What then is Hegel saying with his thesis of the primacy of
Sittlichkeit, and the related notion of the community as 'ethical
substance', a spiritual life in which man must take part? We can
express it in three propositions, put in ascending order of contesta-
bility. First, that what is most important for man can only be
attained in relation to the public life of a community, not in the
private self-definition of the alienated individual. Second, this
community must not be a merely partial one, e.g. a conventicle or
private association, whose life is conditioned, controlled and
limited by a larger society. It must be co-terminous with the
minimum self-sufficient human reality, the state. The public life
which expresses at least some of our important norms must be that
of a state.

Thirdly, the public life of the state has this crucial importance for
men because the norms and ideas it expresses are not just human
inventions. On the contrary, the state expresses the Idea, the
ontological structure of things. In the final analysis it is of vital
importance because it is one of the indispensable ways in which
man recovers his essential relation to this ontological structure, the
other being in the modes of consciousness which Hegel calls
'absolute spirit', and this real relation through the life of the
community is essential to the completion of the return to conscious
identity between man and the Absolute (which means also the
Absolute's self-identity).

Obviously these three propositions arc linked. The third gives the
underlying ground of the first and second. If man achieves his true
identity as a vehicle of cosmic spirit, and if one of the indispensable
media in which this identity is expressed is the public life of his
political society, then evidently, it is essential that he come to
identify himself in relation to this public life. He must transcend the

alienation of a private or sectarian identity, since these can never link him fully to the Absolute. This is the complex of ideas which lies behind the Hegelian use of terms like 'substance', 'essence', '*Endzweck*', '*Selbstzweck*' in speaking of the community. First of all that the set of practices and institutions which make up the public life of the community express the most important norms, most central to its members' identity, so that they are only sustained in their identity by their participation in these practices and institutions, which in their turn they perpetuate by this participation. Secondly, that the community concerned is the state, that is, a really self-sufficient community. And thirdly, that this community has this central role because it expresses the Idea, the formula of rational necessity underlying man and his world.

Thus what is strange and contestable in Hegel's theory of the state is not the idea of a larger life in which men are immersed, or the notion that the public life of a society expresses certain ideas, which are thus in a sense the ideas of the society as a whole and not just of the individuals, so that we can speak of a people as having a certain 'spirit'. For throughout most of human history men have lived most intensely in relation to the meanings expressed in the public life of their societies. Only an exaggerated atomism could make the condition of alienated men seem the inescapable human norm.

But where Hegel does make a substantial claim which is not easy to grant is in his basic ontological view, that man is the vehicle of cosmic spirit, and the corollary, that the state expresses the underlying formula of necessity by which this spirit posits the world.

In other words, the idea of a '*Volksgeist*', the spirit of a people, whose ideas are expressed in their common institutions, by which they define their identity, this is intelligible enough. And something like it is essential if we are to understand what has gone on in human history. What is harder to credit is the thesis that men – and hence in their own way these *Volksgeister* – are vehicles of a cosmic spirit which is returning to self-consciousness through man.

Thus there is no specially odd Hegelian doctrine of a super-individual subject of society, as is often believed. There is only a very difficult doctrine of a cosmic subject whose vehicle is man. This is woven into a theory of man in society which by itself is far from implausible or bizarre. Indeed, it is much superior to the atomistic conceptions of some of Hegel's liberal opponents.

But it is his ontological view which makes Hegel take a turn which goes against the mainstream of liberal thought. This latter tends to assume that individualism is the ultimate in human evolution. Even if civilized men are not alienated from the state, still their highest foci of identity are thought to be beyond it, in religion, or some personal moral ideal, or the human race as a whole. Thus the condition in which men identify themselves primarily in relation to the common life of their society must be a more primitive stage, and especially where this common life is thought to embody cosmic or religious significance. For this kind of society to *succeed* an age of individualism could only represent regression. And this is, of course, why Hegel has been harshly judged by those in this strand of liberalism (which does not exhaust what can justifiably be called liberal thought: Montesquieu, de Tocqueville, Herder, von Humboldt, and others have been concerned about the quality of public life, with which men must identify themselves).

But the attempt to understand Hegel within the terms of this liberal tradition has just led to distortion. A notorious example is Hegel's doctrine of the state. In the atomist liberal tradition, 'state' can only mean something like 'organs of government'. To talk of these as 'essence' or 'final goal' of the citizens can only mean subjection to irresponsible tyranny. But what Hegel means by 'state' is the politically organized community. His model is not the *Machstaat* of Frederick the Great, which he never admired,[6] but the Greek polis. Thus his ideal is not a condition in which individuals are means to an end, but rather a community in which like a living organism, the distinction between means and ends is overcome, everything is both means and end. In other words the state should be an application of the category of internal teleology (cf. quote from *VG*, 112, p. 388).

Thus the state which is fully rational will be one which expresses in its institutions and practices the most important ideas and norms which its citizens recognize, and by which they define their identity. And this will be the case because the state expresses the articulations of the Idea, which rational man comes to see as the formula of necessity underlying all things, which is destined to come to self-consciousness in man. So that the rational state will restore *Sittlichkeit*, the embodiment of the highest norms in an ongoing public life. It will recover what was lost with the Greeks, but on a higher level. For the fully developed state will incorporate the principle of the individual rational will judging by universal criteria, the very principle that undermined and eventually destroyed the Greek polis.

This integration of individuality and *Sittlichkeit* is a requirement we can deduce from the Idea. But this is also Hegel's way of formulating and answering the yearning of his age to unite somehow the radical moral autonomy of Kant and the expressive unity of the Greek polis. Hegel's answer to this conundrum was, as we saw, an extraordinary and original combination of the ultra-modern aspiration to autonomy, and a renewed vision of cosmic order as the foundation of society; a derivation, we might say, of cosmic order from the idea of radical autonomy itself, via a displacement of its centre of gravity from man to *Geist*. This synthesis he saw as the goal of history. . . .

II

We can see the aspiration to what Hegel calls 'absolute freedom', or universal and total participation, as the attempt to meet an endemic need of modern society. Traditional societies were founded on differentiation: royalty, aristocracy, common folk; priests and laymen; free and serf, and so on. This differentiation was justified as a reflection of a hierarchical order of things. After the revolution of modern, self-defining subjectivity, these conceptions of cosmic order came to be seen as fictions, and were denounced as fraudulent inventions of kings, priests, aristocrats, etc., to keep their subjects submissive. But however much they may have been used, con-sciously or not, as justifications of the status quo, these conceptions also were the ground of men's identification with the society in which they lived. Man could only be himself in relation to a cosmic order; the state claimed to body forth this order and hence to be one of men's principal channels of contact with it. Hence the power of organic and holistic metaphors: men saw themselves as parts of society in something like the way that a hand, for instance, is part of the body.

The revolution of modern subjectivity gave rise to another type of political theory. Society was justified not by what it was or expressed, but by what it achieved, the fulfilment of men's needs, desires and purposes. Society came to be seen as an instrument and its different modes and structures were to be studied scientifically for their effects on human happiness. Political theory would banish myth and fable. This reached clearest expression in utilitarianism.

But this modern theory has not provided a basis for men's identification with their society. In the intermittent crises of alienation which have followed the breakdown of traditional society, utilitarian theories have been powerless to fill the gap. So that modern societies have actually functioned with a large part of their traditional outlook intact, or only slowly receding, as in the case of Britain, for instance. Or when some radical break is sought, they have had recourse to more powerful stuff, some variant of the general will tradition (Jacobinism, Marxism, anarchism) as a revolutionary ideology. Or modern societies have had recourse either in revolutionary or 'normal' times to the powerful secular religion of nationalism. And even societies which seem to be founded on the utilitarian tradition, or an earlier, Lockeian variant, like the United States, in fact have recourse to 'myth', e.g. the myth of the frontier, of the perpetual new beginning, the future as boundlessly open to self-creation.

This last is the greatest irony of all, in that the utilitarian theory itself leaves no place for myth of this kind, that is, speculative interpretation of the ends of human life in their relation to society, nature and history, as part of the justifying beliefs of a mature society. These are thought to belong to earlier, less evolved ages. Mature men are attached to their society because of what it produces for them. As recently as a decade ago this perspective was widely believed in by the liberal intelligentsia of America and the Western world, who announced an imminent 'end of ideology'. But they turned out to be latter-day, inverted variants of Monsieur Jourdain, who were speaking not prose, but myth without knowing it. It is now clearer that the utilitarian perspective is no less an ideology than its major rivals, and no more plausible. Utilitarian man whose loyalty to his society would be contingent only on the satisfactions it secured for him is a species virtually without members. And the very notion of satisfaction is now not so firmly anchored, once we see that it is interwoven with 'expectations', and beliefs about what is appropriate and just. Some of the richest societies in our day are among the most teeming with dissatisfaction, for instance, the USA.

The aspiration to absolute freedom can be seen as an attempt to fill this lack in modern political theory, to find grounds for identification with one's society which are fully in the spirit of modern subjectivity. We have grounds for identifying ourselves with our society and giving our full allegiance to it when it is ours in the strong sense of being our creation, and moreover the creation of what is best in us and mostly truly ourselves: our moral will (Rousseau, Fichte), or our creative activity (Marx). From Rousseau through Marx and the anarchist thinkers to contemporary theories of participatory democracy, there have been recurrent demands to reconstruct society, so as to do away with heteronomy, or overcome alienation, or recover spontaneity. Only a society which was an emanation of free moral will could recover a claim on our allegiance comparable to that of traditional society. For once more society would reflect or embody something of absolute value. Only this would no longer be a cosmic order, but in keeping with the modern revolution, the absolute would be human freedom itself.

The aspiration to absolute freedom is therefore born of a deep dissatisfaction with the utilitarian model of society as an instrument for the furtherance/adjustment of interests. Societies built on this model are experienced as a spiritual desert, or as a machine. They express nothing spiritual, and their regulations and discipline are felt as an intolerable imposition by those who aspire to absolute freedom. It is therefore not surprising that the theorists of absolute freedom have often been close to the reactionary critics of liberal society, and have often themselves expressed admiration for earlier societies.

Hegel understood this aspiration. As we saw he made the demand for radical autonomy a central part of his theory. He had indeed, an important place in the line of development of this aspiration to absolute freedom as it develops from Rousseau through Marx and beyond. For he wove the demand for radical autonomy of Rousseau and Kant together with the expressivist theory which came from Herder, and this provided the indispensable background for Marx's thought. And yet he was a strong critic of radical freedom. This alone would make it worthwhile to examine his objections.

Disentangled from Hegel's particular theory of social differentiation, the basic point of this critique is this: absolute freedom requires homogeneity. It cannot brook differences which would prevent everyone participating totally in the decisions of the society. And what is even more, it requires some near unanimity of will to emerge from this deliberation, for otherwise the majority would just be imposing its will on the minority, and freedom would not be universal. But differentiation of some fairly essential kinds are ineradicable. (Let us leave aside for the moment the objection that Hegel did not identify the right ones.) And moreover, they are recognized in our post-Romantic climate as essential to human identity. Men cannot simply identify themselves as men, but they define themselves more immediately by their partial community, cultural, linguistic, confessional, etc. Modern democracy is therefore in a bind.

I think a dilemma of this kind can be seen in contemporary society. Modern societies have moved towards much greater homogeneity and greater interdependence, so that partial communities lose their autonomy and to some extent their identity. But great differences remain; only because of the ideology of homogeneity, these differential characteristics no longer have meaning and value for those who have them. Thus the rural population is taught by the mass media to see itself as just lacking in some of the advantages of a more advanced life style. The poor are seen as marginal to the society, for instance, in America, and in some ways have a worse lot than in more recognizedly class-divided societies.

Homogenization thus increases minority alienation and resentment. And the first response of liberal society is to try even more of the same: programmes to eliminate poverty, or assimilate Indians, move population out of declining regions, bring an urban way of life to the countryside, etc. But the radical response is to convert this sense of alienation into a demand for 'absolute freedom'. The idea is to overcome alienation by creating a society in which everyone, including the present 'out' groups, participate fully in the decisions.

But both these solutions would simply aggravate the problem, which is that homogenization has undermined the communities or characteristics by which people formerly identified themselves and put nothing in their place. What does step into the gap almost everywhere is ethnic or national identity. Nationalism has become the most powerful focus of identity in modern society. The demand for radical freedom can and frequently does join up with nationalism, and is given a definite impetus and direction from this.

But unless this happens, the aspiration to absolute freedom is unable to resolve the dilemma. It attempts to overcome the alienation of a mass society by mass participation. But the very size, complexity and inter-dependence of modern society makes this increasingly difficult on technical grounds alone. What is more serious, the increasing alienation in a society which has eroded its traditional foci of allegiance makes it harder and harder to achieve the basic consensus, to bring everyone to the 'general will', which is essential for radical democracy. As the traditional limits fade with the grounds for accepting them, society tends to fragment, partial groups become increasingly truculent in their demands, as they see less reason to compromise with the 'system'.

But the radical demand for participation can do nothing to stem this fragmentation. Participation of *all* in a decision is only possible if there is a ground of agreement, or of underlying common purpose. Radical participation cannot create this; it presupposes it.

This is the point which Hegel repeatedly makes. The demand for absolute freedom by itself is empty. Hegel stresses one line of possible consequences, that emptiness leads to pure destructiveness. But he also mentions another in his discussion in the *PhG*. For in fact some direction has to be given to society, and hence a group can take over and imprint its own purpose on society claiming to represent the general will. They thus 'solve' the problem of diversity by force. Contemporary communist societies provide examples of this. And whatever can be said for them they can certainly not be thought of as models of freedom. Moreover their solution to the emptiness of absolute freedom is in a sense only provisional. The problem of what social goals to choose or structures to adopt is solved by the exigencies of mobilization and combat towards the free society. Society can be set a definite task because it has to build the *preconditions* of communism, either in defeating class enemies or in constructing a modern economy. Such societies would be in disarray if ever the period of mobilization were to end (which is why it would end only over the dead bodies of the ruling party).

But an ideology of participation which does not want to take this totalitarian road of general mobilization cannot cope with the complexity and fragmentation of a large-scale contemporary society. Many of its protagonists see this, and return to the original Rousseauian idea of a highly decentralized federation of communities. But in the meantime the growth of a large homogeneous society has made this much less feasible. It is not just that with our massive concentrations of population and economic interdependence a lot of decisions have to be taken for the whole society, and decentralization gives us no way of coping with these. More serious is the fact that homogenization has undermined the partial communities which would naturally have been the basis of such a decentralized federation in the past. There is no advantage in an artificial carving up of society into manageable units. If in fact no one identifies strongly with these units, participation will be minimal, as we see in much of our urban politics today.

Thus Hegel's dilemma for modern democracy, put as its simplest, is this: The modern ideology of equality and of total participation leads to a homogenization of society. This shakes men loose from their traditional communities, but cannot replace them as a focus of identity. Or rather, it can only replace them as such a focus under the impetus of militant nationalism or some totalitarian ideology which would depreciate or even crush diversity and individuality. It would be a focus for some and would reduce the others to mute alienation. Hegel constantly stresses that the tight unity of the

Greek city-state cannot be recaptured in the modern world that has known the principle of individual freedom.

Thus the attempt to fill the gap by moving towards a society of universal and total participation, where it is not actually harmful in suppressing freedom, is vain. It can only aggravate the problem by intensifying homogenization, while offering no relief since absolute freedom by itself is empty and cannot offer a focus of identity. And besides, total participation is unrealizable in a large-scale society. In fact ideologies of absolute freedom only produce something in the hands of a minority with a powerful vision which it is willing to impose.

The only real cure for this malady, a recovery of meaningful differentiation, is closed for modern society precisely because of its commitment to ideologies which constantly press it towards greater homogeneity. Some of the differences which remain are depreciated, and are breeding grounds for alienation and resentment. Others in fact fill the gap and become foci of identity. These are principally ethnic or national differences. But they tend to be exclusive and divisive. They can only with difficulty form the basis of a differentiated society. On the contrary, multi-national states have great trouble surviving in the modern world. Nationalism tends to lead to single homogeneous states. Where nationalism is strong, it tends to provide the common focus of identity and to fend off fragmentation. But then it is in danger of suppressing dissent and diversity and falling over into a narrow and irrational chauvinism.

Hegel gave, as we shall see again below, little importance to nationalism. And this was the cause of his failure to foresee its pivotal role in the modern world. As an allegiance it was not rational enough, too close to pure sentiment, to have an important place in the foundations of the state. But it is also true that it cannot provide what modern society needs in his view. And this is a ground for differentiation, meaningful to the people concerned, but which at the same time does not set the partial communities against each other, but rather knits them together in a larger whole.

This in a single formula is what modern society would require to resolve its dilemma. It is something which traditional societies had. For the point about conceptions of cosmic order or organic analogies is that they gave a meaning to differences between social groups which also bound them into one. But how to recover this in modern society? Hegel's answer, as we saw it, is to give social and political differentiation a meaning by seeing them as expressive of cosmic order, but he conceives this order as the final and complete fulfilment of the moderrn aspiration to autonomy. It is an order founded on reason alone, and hence is the ultimate object of the free will.

We can see now more clearly how the two levels of Hegel's thought on the necessary differentiation of society meshed with each other. On one level, there is the set of considerations drawn from a comparison with the Greek polis: the size of the modern state, the great differences which a state must encompass once all the functions are to be performed by citizens, the modern notion of individuality. These will be generally accepted by everyone though their significance might be disputed. On the other level, there is the necessary articulation of the Idea which has to be reflected in society. In Hegel's mind these do not operate as quite separate orders of consideration, as I have set them out here. They are intricated in each other, so that Hegel sees the existing social differentiations of his time as reflecting the articulations of the Idea, or rather as preparing a perfectly adequate reflection as the Idea realizes itself in history. And that is of course why he did not see these differences as remnants of earlier history destined to wither away, as the radical thinkers of this time thought, but rather as approaching the lineaments of a state which would finally be 'adequate to the concept'.

We cannot accept Hegel's solution today. But the dilemma it was meant to solve remains. It was the dilemma which de Tocqueville tried to grapple with in different terms, when he saw the immense importance to a democratic polity of vigorous constituent communities in a decentralized structure of power, while at the same time the pull of equality tended to take modern society towards uniformity, and perhaps also submission under an omnipotent government. This convergence is perhaps not all that surprising in two thinkers who were both deeply influenced by Montesquieu, and both had a deep and sympathetic understanding of the past as well as of the wave of the future. But whether we take it in Hegel's reading or in de Tocqueville's, one of the great needs of the modern democratic polity is to recover a sense of significant differentiation, so that its partial communities, be they geographical, or cultural, or occupational, can become again important centres of concern and activity for their members in a way which connects them to the whole.

NOTES

1 Cf. *Schriften zur Politik und Rechtsphilosophie*, ed. G. Lasson (Leipzig, 1923), p. 388.

2 Once again, this is Hegel's term of art; Kant himself used the usual word '*Sittlichkeit*' in his works on ethics.

3 Cf. also *PR*, §§145, 156, 258.

4 In the language of the *Logic*, the category of External Teleology is inadequate here. The state can only be understood by Internal Teleology.

5 Thus in *PR*, §258, Hegel speaks of the state possessing 'the actuality of the substantial will . . . *in the particular self-consciousness* once that consciousness has been raised to consciousness of its universality' (my italics).

6 In a work of the early 1800s, which has been published since his death under the title, *The German Constitution*, Hegel expresses his opposition to the modern theory that a state should be a 'machine with a single spring which imparts movement to all the rest of the infinite wheelwork' (*Schriften zur Politik und Rechtsphilosophie*, ed. G. Lasson, Leipzig 1923, p. 28; *Hegel's Political Writings*, translated T. M. Knox, ed. Z. A. Pelczynski, Oxford, 1964, p. 161). Prussia, as well as revolutionary France, is cited as an example later in this passage. (*Schriften* p. 31, *Political Writings* pp. 163–4. Cf. discussion in Schlomo Avineri, *Hegel's Theory of the Modern State*, Cambridge, 1970, pp. 47–9).

REFERENCES GIVEN IN ABBREVIATED FORM

Abbreviation	Work	Comment
PhG	*Phänomenologie des Geistes*, G. Lasson edition, Hamburg, 1952	The *Phenomenology of Spirit* published by Hegel in 1807 at the end of his Jena period.
EG	*System der Philosophie*, dritter teil. Die Philosophie des Geistes, SW x.	References are to paragraph numbers (§ . . .). Hegel's paragraphs consisted of a principal statement, sometimes followed by an explanatory remark, sometimes in turn followed by an addition inserted by the later editors. Where useful I distinguish in my references between the principal statement

		and the remark, and where remark or addition are very long, I give the page reference in the SW edition.
PR	Grundlinien der Philosophie des Rechts, ed. J. Hoffmeister, Hamburg, 1955, or *Hegel's Philosophy of Right*, trans. T. M. Knox (Oxford, 1942).	References to this work, first published in 1821, are also to paragraph numbers (§ . . .). Here also the main text of a paragraph is sometimes followed by an explanatory remark (sometimes referred to with an 'E' after the paragraph number), and also sometimes by an addition inserted by later editors on the basis of lecture notes. I have usually quoted the text of Knox's edition, but the references to paragraph number makes it easy to find the texts in the German edition as well. Where remarks or additions are long, I have given page references to the Knox edition.
VG	*Die Vernunft in der Geschichte*, ed. J. Hoffmeister (Hamburg, 1955).	The introductory part of Hegel's lectures on the philosophy of history, put together from various cycles of lecture notes after his death.

10

Michael Walzer: Welfare, Membership and Need*

Membership is important because of what the members of a political community owe to one another and to no one else, or to no one else in the same degree. And the first thing they owe is the communal provision of security and welfare. This claim might be reversed: communal provision is important because it teaches us the value of membership. If we did not provide for one another, if we recognized no distinction between members and strangers, we would have no reason to form and maintain political communities. 'How shall men love their country', Rousseau asked, 'if it is nothing more for them than for strangers, and bestows on them only that which it can refuse to none?'[1] Rousseau believed that citizens ought to love their country and therefore that their country ought to give them particular reasons to do so. Membership (like kinship) is a special relation. It's not enough to say, as Edmund Burke did, that 'to make us love our country, our country ought to be lovely.'[2] The crucial thing is that it be lovely for us – though we always hope that it will be lovely for others (we also love its reflected loveliness).

Political community for the sake of provision, provision for the sake of community: the process works both ways, and that is perhaps its crucial feature. Philosophers and political theorists have been too quick to turn it into a simple calculation. Indeed, we are rationalists of everyday life; we come together, we sign the social contract or reiterate the signing of it, in order to provide for our needs. And we value the contract insofar as those needs are met. But one of our needs is community itself: culture, religion, and politics. It is only under the aegis of these three that all the other things we need become *socially recognized needs*, take on historical and determinate form. The social contract is an agreement to reach decisions together about what goods are necessary to our common life, and then to provide those goods for one another. The signers

* From *Spheres of Justice* by Michael Walzer. © 1983 by Basic Books, Inc., Publishers. Reprinted by permission of the publisher.

own one another more than mutual aid, for that they owe or can owe to anyone. They owe mutual provision of all those things for the sake of which they have separated themselves from mankind as a whole and joined forces in a particular community. *Amour social* is one of those things; but though it is a distributed good – often unevenly distributed – it arises only in the course of other distributions (and of the political choices that the other distributions require). Mutual provision breeds mutuality. So the common life is simultaneoulsy the prerequisite of provision and one of its products.

Men and women come together because they literally cannot live apart. But they can live together in many different ways. Their survival and then their well-being require a common effort: against the wrath of the gods, the hostility of other people, the indifference and malevolence of nature (famine, flood, fire, and disease), the brief transit of a human life. Not army camps alone, as David Hume wrote, but temples, storehouses, irrigation works, and burial grounds are the true mothers of cities.[3] As the list suggests, origins are not singular in character. Cities differ from one another, partly because of the natural environments in which they are built and the immediate dangers their builders encounter, partly because of the conceptions of social goods that the builders hold. They recognize but also create one another's needs and so give a particular shape to what I will call the 'sphere of security and welfare'. The sphere itself is as old as the oldest human community. Indeed, one might say that the original community is a sphere of security and welfare, a system of communal provision, distorted, no doubt, by gross inequalities of strength and cunning. But the system has, in any case, no natural form. Different experiences and different conceptions lead to different patterns of provision. Though there are some goods that are needed absolutely, there is no good such that once we see it, we know how it stands *vis-à-vis* all other goods and how much of it we owe to one another. The nature of a need is not self-evident.

Communal provision is both general and particular. It is general whenever public funds are spent so as to benefit all or most of the members without any distribution to individuals. It is particular whenever goods are actually handed over to all or any of the members.* Water, for example, is one of 'the bare requirements of

---

* I don't mean to reiterate here the technical distinction that economists make between public and private goods. General provision is always public, at least on the less stringent definitions of that term (which specify

civil life', and the building of reservoirs is a form of general provision.[4] But the delivery of water to one rather than to another neighbourhood (where, say, the wealthier citizens live) is particular. The securing of the food supply is general; the distribution of food to widows and orphans is particular. Public health is most often general, the care of the sick, most often particular. Sometimes the criteria for general and particular provision will differ radically. The building of temples and the organization of religious services is an example of general provision designed to meet the needs of the community as a whole, but communion with the gods may be allowed only to particularly meritorious members (or it may be sought privately in secret or in nonconformist sects). The system of justice is a general good, meeting common needs; but the actual distribution of rewards and punishments may serve the particular needs of a ruling class, or it may be organized, as we commonly think it should be, to give individuals what they individually deserve. Simone Weil has argued that, with regard to justice, need operates at both the general and the particular levels, since criminals need to be punished.[5] But that is an idiosyncratic use of the word *need*. More likely, the punishment of criminals is something only the rest of us need. But need does operate both generally and particularly for other goods: health care is an obvious example that I will later consider in some detail.

Despite the inherent forcefulness of the word, needs are elusive. People don't just have needs, they have ideas about their needs; they have priorities, they have degrees of need; and these priorities and degrees are related not only to their human nature but also to their history and culture. Since resources are always scarce, hard choices have to be made. I suspect that these can only be political choices. They are subject to a certain philosophical elucidation, but the idea of need and the commitment to communal provision do not by themselves yield any clear determination of priorities or degrees. Clearly we can't meet, and we don't have to meet, every need to the same degree or any need to

only that public goods are those that can't be provided to some and not to other members of the community). So are most forms of particular provision, for even goods delivered to individuals generate non-exclusive benefits for the community as a whole. Scholarships to orphans, for example, are private to the orphans, public to the community of citizens within which the orphans will one day work and vote. But public goods of this latter sort, which depend upon prior distributions to particular persons or groups, have been controversial in many societies; and I have designed my categories so as to enable me to examine them closely.

the ultimate degree. The ancient Athenians, for example, provided public baths and gymnasiums for the citizens but never provided anything remotely resembling unemployment insurance or social security. They made a choice about how to spend public funds, a choice shaped presumably by their understanding of what the common life required. It would be hard to argue that they made a mistake. I suppose there are notions of need that would yield such a conclusion, but these would not be notions acceptable to – they might not even be comprehensible to – the Athenians themselves.

The question of degree suggests even more clearly the importance of political choice and the irrelevance of any merely philosophical stipulation. Needs are not only elusive; they are also expansive. In the phrase of the contemporary philosopher Charles Fried, needs are voracious; they eat up resources.[6] But it would be wrong to suggest that therefore need cannot be a distributive principle. It is, rather, a principle subject to political limitation; and the limits (within limits) can be arbitrary, fixed by some temporary coalition of interests or majority of voters. Consider the case of physical security in a modern American city. We could provide absolute security, eliminate every source of violence except domestic violence, if we put a street light every ten yards and stationed a policeman every thirty yards throughout the city. But that would be very expensive, and so we settle for something less. How much less can only be decided politically.* One can imagine the sorts of things that would figure in the debates. Above all, I think, there would be a certain understanding – more or less widely shared, controversial only at the margins – of what constitutes 'enough' security or of what level of insecurity is simply intolerable. The decision would also be affected by other factors: alternative needs, the state of the economy, the agitation of the policemen's union, and so on. But whatever decision is ultimately reached, for whatever reasons, security is provided because the citizens need it. And because, at some level, they all need it, the criterion of need remains a critical standard (as we shall see) even though it cannot determine priority and degree. . . .

---

* And should be decided politically: that is what democratic political arrangements are for. Any philosophical effort to stipulate in detail the rights or the entitlements of individuals would radically constrain the scope of democratic decision making. I have argued this point elsewhere.[7]

THE EXTENT OF PROVISION

Distributive justice in the sphere of welfare and security has a twofold meaning: it refers, first to the recognition of need and, second, to the recognition of membership. Goods must be provided to needy members because of their neediness, but they must also be provided in such a way as to sustain their membership. It's not the case, however, that members have a claim on any specific set of goods. Welfare rights are fixed only when a community adopts some programme of mutual provision. There are strong arguments to be made that, under given historical conditions, such-and-such a programme should be adopted. But these are not arguments about individual rights; they are arguments about the character of a particular political community. No one's rights were violated because the Athenians did not allocate public funds for the education of children. Perhaps they believed, and perhaps they were right, that the public life of the city was education enough.

The right that members can legitimately claim is of a more general sort. It undoubtedly includes some version of the Hobbesian right to life, some claim on communal resources for bare subsistence. No community can allow its members to starve to death when there is food available to feed them; no government can stand passively by at such a time – not if it claims to be a government of or by or for the community. The indifference of Britain's rulers during the Irish potato famine in the 1840s is a sure sign that Ireland was a colony, a conquered land, no real part of Great Britain.[8] This is not to justify the indifference – one has obligations to colonies and to conquered peoples – but only to suggest that the Irish would have been better served by a government, virtually any government, of their own. Perhaps Burke came closest to describing the fundamental right that is at stake here when he wrote: 'Government is a contrivance of human wisdom to provide for human wants. Men have a right that these wants should be provided for by this wisdom.'[9] It only has to be said that the wisdom in question is the wisdom not of a ruling class, as Burke seems to have thought, but of the community as a whole. Only its culture, its character, its common understandings can define the 'wants' that are to be provided for. But culture, character, and common understandings are not givens; they don't operate automatically; at any particular moment, the citizens must argue about the extent of mutual provision.

They argue about the meaning of the social contract, the original and reiterated conception of the sphere of security and welfare. This is not a hypothetical or an ideal contract of the sort John Rawls has described. Rational men and women in the original position, deprived of all particular knowledge of their social standing and cultural understanding, would probably opt, as Rawls has argued, for an equal distribution of whatever goods they were told they needed.[10] But this formula doesn't help very much in determining what choices people will make, or what choices they should make, once they know who and where they are. In a world of particular cultures, competing conceptions of the good, scarce resources, elusive and expansive needs, there isn't going to be a single formula, universally applicable. There isn't going to be a single universally approved path that carries us from a notion like, say, 'fair shares' to a comprehensive list of the goods to which that notion applies. Fair shares of what?

Justice, tranquillity, defence, welfare, and liberty: that is the list provided by the United States Constitution. One could construe it as an exhaustive list, but the terms are vague; they provide at best a starting point for public debate. The standard appeal in that debate is to a larger idea: the Burkeian general right, which takes on determinate force only under determinate conditions and requires different sorts of provision in different times and places. The idea is simply that we have come together, shaped a community, in order to cope with difficulties and dangers that we could not cope with alone. And so whenever we find ourselves confronted with difficulties and dangers of that sort, we look for communal assistance. As the balance of individual and collective capacity changes, so the kinds of assistance that are looked for change, too.

The history of public health in the West might usefully be told in these terms. Some minimal provision is very old, as the Greek and Jewish examples suggest; the measures adopted were a function of the community's sense of danger and the extent of its medical knowledge. Over the years, living arrangements on a larger scale bred new dangers, and scientific advance generated a new sense of danger and a new awareness of the possibilities of coping. And then groups of citizens pressed for a wider programme of communal provision, exploiting the new science to reduce the risks of urban life. That, they might rightly say, is what the community is for. A similar argument can be made in the case of social security. The very success of general provision in the field of public health has greatly extended the span of a normal human life and then also the span of years during which men and women are unable to support themselves, during which they are physically but most often not socially, politically, or morally incapacitated. Once again, support for the disabled is one of the oldest and most common forms of particular provision. But now it is required on a much larger scale than ever before. Families are overwhelmed by the costs of old age and look for help to the political community. Exactly what ought to be done will be a matter of dispute. Words like *health, danger, science,* even *old age,* have very different meanings in different cultures; no external specification is possible. But this is not to say that it won't be clear enough to the people involved that something – some particular set of things – ought to be done.

Perhaps these examples are too easy. Disease is a general threat; old age, a general prospect. Not so unemployment and poverty, which probably lie beyond the ken of many well-to-do people. The poor can always be isolated, locked into ghettos, blamed and punished for their own misfortune. At this point, it might be said, provision can no longer be defended by invoking anything like the 'meaning' of the social contract. But let us look more closely at the easy cases; for, in fact, they involve all the difficulties of the difficult ones. Public health and social security invite us to think of the political community, in T. H. Marshall's phrase, as a 'mutual benefit club'.[11] All provision is reciprocal; the members take turns providing and being provided for, much as Aristotle's citizens take turns ruling and being ruled. This is a happy picture, and one that is really understandable in contractualist terms. It is not only the case that rational agents, knowing nothing of their specific situation, would agree to these two forms of provision; the real agents, the ordinary citizens, of every modern democracy have in fact agreed to them. The two are, or so it appears, equally in the interests of hypothetical and of actual people. Coercion is only necessary in practice because some minority of actual people don't understand, or don't consistently understand, their real interests. Only the reckless and the improvident need to be forced to contribute – and it can always be said of them that they joined in the social contract precisely in order to protect themselves against their own recklessness and improvidence. In fact, however, the reasons for coercion go much deeper than this; the political community is something more than a mutual benefit club; and the extent of communal provision in any given case – what it is and what it should be – is determined by conceptions of need that are more problematic than the argument thus far suggests.

Consider again the case of public health. No communal provision is possible here without the constraint of a wide range of activities profitable to individual members of the community but threatening to some larger number. Even something so simple, for example, as the provision of uncontaminated milk to large urban populations requires extensive public control; and control is a political achievement, the result (in the United States) of bitter struggles, over many years, in one city after another.[12] When the farmers or the middlemen of the dairy industry defended free enterprise, they were certainly acting rationally in their own interests. The same thing can be said of other entrepreneurs who defend themselves against the constraints of inspection, regulation, and enforcement. Public activities of these sorts may be of the highest value to the rest of us; they are not of the highest value to all of us. Though I have taken public health as an example of general provision, it is provided only at the expense of some members of the community. Moreover, it benefits most the most vulnerable of the others: thus, the special importance of the building code for those who live in crowded tenements, and of anti-pollution laws for those who live in the immediate vicinity of factory smokestacks or water drains. Social security, too, benefits the most vulnerable members, even if, for reasons I have already suggested, the actual payments are the same for everyone. For the well-to-do can, or many of them think they can, help themselves even in time of trouble and would much prefer not to be forced to help anyone else. The truth is that every serious effort at communal provision (insofar as the income of the community derives from the wealth of its members) is redistributive in character.[13] The benefits it provides are not, strictly speaking mutual.

Once again, rational agents ignorant of their own social standing would agree to such a redistribution. But they would agree too easily, and their agreement doesn't help us understand what sort of a redistribution is required: How much? For what purposes? In practice, redistribution is a political matter, and the coercion it involves is foreshadowed by the conflicts that rage over its character and extent. Every particular measure is pushed through by some coalition of particular interests. But the ultimate appeal in these conflicts is not to the particular interests, not even to a public interest conceived as their sum, but to collective values, shared understandings of membership, health, food and shelter, work and leisure. The conflicts themselves are often focused, at least overtly, on questions of fact; the understandings are assumed. Thus the entrepreneurs of the dairy industry denied as long as they could the connection between contaminated milk and tuberculosis. But once that connection was established, it was difficult for them to deny that milk should be inspected: *caveat emptor* was not, in such a case, a plausible doctrine. Similarly, in the debates over old-age pensions in Great Britain, politicians mostly agreed on the traditional British value of self-help but disagreed sharply about whether self-help was still possible through the established working-class friendly societies. These were real mutual-benefit clubs organized on a strictly voluntary basis, but they seemed about to be overwhelmed by the growing numbers of the aged. It became increasingly apparent that the members simply did not have the resources to protect themselves and one another from poverty in old age. And few British politicians were prepared to say that they should be left unprotected.[14]

Here, then, is a more precise account of the social contract: it is an agreement to redistribute the resources of the members in accordance with some shared understanding of their needs, subject to ongoing political determination in detail. The contract is a moral bond. It connects the strong and the weak, the lucky and the unlucky, the rich and the poor, creating a union that transcends all differences of interest, drawing its strength from history, culture, religion, language, and so on. Arguments about communal provision are, at the deepest level interpretations of that union. The closer and more inclusive it is, the wider the recognition of needs, the greater the number of social goods that are drawn into the sphere of security and welfare.[15] I don't doubt that many political communities have redistributed resources on very different principles, not in accordance with the needs of the members generally but in accordance with the power of the wellborn or the wealthy. But that, as Rousseau suggested in his *Discourse on Inequality*, makes a fraud of the social contract.[16] In any community, where resources are taken away from the poor and given to the rich, the rights of the poor are being violated. The wisdom of the community is not engaged in providing for their wants. Political debate about the nature of those wants will have to be repressed, else the fraud will quickly be exposed. When all the members share in the business of interpreting the social contract, the result will be a more or less extensive system of communal provision. If all states are in principle welfare states, democracies are most likely to be welfare states in practice. Even the imitation of democracy breeds welfarism, as in the 'people's democracies', where the state protects the people against every disaster except those that it inflicts on them itself.

So democratic citizens argue among themselves and opt for many different sorts of security and welfare, extending far beyond my 'easy' examples of public health and old-age pensions. The category of socially recognized needs is open-ended. For the people's sense of what they need encompasses not only life itself but also the good life, and the appropriate balance between these two is itself a matter of dispute. The Athenian drama and the Jewish academies were both financed with money that could have been spent on housing, say, or on medicine. But drama and education were taken by Greeks and Jews to be not merely enhancements of the common life but vital aspects of communal welfare. I want to stress again that these are not judgements that can easily be called incorrect.

AN AMERICAN WELFARE STATE

What sort of communal provision is appropriate in a society like our own? It's not my purpose here to anticipate the outcomes of democratic debate or to stipulate in detail the extent or the forms of provision. But it can be argued, I think, that the citizens of a modern industrial democracy owe a great deal to one another, and the argument will provide a useful opportunity to test the critical force of the principles I have defended up until now: that every political community must attend to the needs of its members as they collectively understand those needs; that the goods that are distributed must be distributed in proportion to need; and that the distribution must recognize and uphold the underlying equality of membership. These are very general principles; they are meant to apply to a wide range of communities – to any community, in fact, where the members are each other's equals (before God or the law), or where it can plausibly be said that, however they are treated in fact, they ought to be each other's equals. The principles probably don't apply to a community organized hierarchically, as in traditional India, where the fruits of the harvest are distributed not according to need but according to caste – or rather, as Louis Dumont has written, where 'the needs of each are conceived to be different, depending on [his] caste.' Everyone is guaranteed a share, so Dumont's Indian village is still a welfare state, 'a sort of co-operative where the main aim is to ensure the subsistence of everyone in accordance with his social function', but not a welfare state or a co-operative whose principles we can readily understand.[17] (But Dumont does not tell us how food is supposed to be distributed in time of scarcity. If the subsistence standard is the same for everyone, then we are back in a familiar world.)

Clearly, the three principles apply to the citizens of the United States; and they have considerable force here because of the affluence of the community and the expansive understanding of individual need. On the other hand the United States currently maintains one of the shabbier systems of communal provision in the Western world. This is so for a variety of reasons: the community of citizens is loosely organized; various ethnic and religious groups run welfare programmes of their own; the ideology of self-reliance and entrepreneurial opportunity is widely accepted; and the movements of the left, particularly the labour movement, are relatively weak.[18] Democratic decision-making reflects these realities, and there is nothing in principle wrong with that. Nevertheless, the established pattern of provision doesn't measure up to the internal requirements of the sphere of security and welfare, and the common understandings of the citizens point toward a more elaborate pattern. One might also argue that American citizens should work to build a stronger and more intensely experienced political community. But this argument, though it would have distributive consequences, is not, properly speaking, an argument about distributive justice. The question is, What do the citizens owe one another, given the community they actually inhabit?

Consider the example of criminal justice. The actual distribution of punishments is an issue I will take up in a later chapter. But the autonomy of punishment, the certainty that people are being punished for the right reasons (whatever those are), depends upon the distribution of resources within the legal system. If accused men and women are to receive their rightful share of justice, they must first have a rightful share of legal aid. Hence the institution of the public defender and the assigned counsel: just as the hungry must be fed, so the accused must be defended; and they must be defended in proportion to their needs. But no impartial observer of the American legal system today can doubt that the resources necessary to meet this standard are not generally available.[19] The rich and the poor are treated differently in American courts, though it is the public commitment of the courts to treat them the same. The argument for a more generous provision follows from that commitment. If justice is to be provided at all, it must be provided equally for all accused citizens without regard to their wealth (or their race, religion, political partisanship, and so on). I don't mean to underestimate the practical difficulties here; but this, again, is the inner logic of provision, and it makes for an illuminating example of complex equality. For the inner logic of reward and punishment is different, requiring, as I shall argue later, that distributions be proportional to desert and not to need. Punishment is a negative good that ought to be monopolized by those who have acted badly – and who have been found guilty of acting badly (after a resourceful defence).

Legal aid raises no theoretical problems because the institutional stuctures for providing it already exist, and what is at stake is only the readiness of the community to live up to the logic of its own institutions. I want to turn now to an area where American institutions are relatively underdeveloped, and where communal commitment is problematic, the subject of continuing political debate: the area of medical care. But here the argument for a more extensive provision must move more slowly. It isn't enough to summon up a 'right to treatment'. I shall have to recount something of the history of medical care as a social good.

The Case of Medical Care

Until recent times, the practice of medicine was mostly a matter of free enterprise. Doctors made their diagnosis, gave their advice, healed or didn't heal their patients, for a fee. Perhaps the private character of the economic relationship was connected to the intimate character of the professional relationship. More likely, I think, it had to do with the relative marginality of medicine itself. Doctors could, in fact, do very little for their patients; and the common attitude in the face of disease (as in the face of poverty) was a stoical fatalism. Or, popular remedies were developed that were not much less effective, sometimes more effective, than those prescribed by established physicians. Folk medicine sometimes produced a kind of communal provision at the local level, but it was equally likely to generate new practitioners, charging fees in their turn. Faith healing followed a similar pattern.

Leaving these two aside, we can say that the distribution of medical care has historically rested in the hands of the medical profession, a guild of physicians that dates at least from the time of Hippocrates in the fifth century BC. The guild has functioned to exclude unconventional practitioners and to regulate the number of physicians in any given community. A genuinely free market has never been in the interest of its members. But it is in the interest of the members to sell their services to individual patients; and thus, by and large, the well-to-do have been well cared for (in accordance with the current understanding of good care) and the poor hardly cared for at all. In a few urban communities – in the medieval Jewish communities, for example – medical services were more widely available. But they were virtually unknown for most people most of the time. Doctors were the servants of the rich, often attached to noble houses and royal courts. With regard to this practical outcome, however, the profession has always had a collective bad conscience. For the distributive logic of the practice of medicine seems to be this: that care should be proportionate to illness and not to wealth. Hence, there have always been doctors, like those honoured in ancient Greece, who served the poor on the side, as it were, even while they earned their living from paying patients. Most doctors, present in an emergency, still feel bound to help the victim without regard to his material status. It is a matter of professional Good Samaritanism that the call 'Is there a doctor in the house?' should not go unanswered if there is a doctor to answer it. In ordinary times, however, there was little call for medical help, largely because there was little faith in its actual helpfulness. And so the bad conscience of the profession was not echoed by any political demand for the replacement of free enterprise by communal provision.

In Europe during the Middle Ages, the cure of souls was public, the cure of bodies private. Today, in most European countries, the situation is reversed. The reversal is best explained in terms of a major shift in the common understanding of souls and bodies: we have lost confidence in the cure of souls, and we have come increasingly to believe, even to be obsessed with, the cure of bodies. Descartes's famous declaration that the 'preservation of health' was the 'chief of all goods' may be taken to symbolize the shift – or to herald it, for in the history of popular attitudes, Descartes's *Discourse on Method* came very early.[20] Then, as eternity receded in the popular consciousness, longevity moved to the fore. Among medieval Christians, eternity was a socially recognized need; and every effort was made to see that it was widely and equally distributed, that every Christian had an equal chance at salvation and eternal life: hence, a church in every parish, regular services, catechism for the young, compulsory communion, and so on. Among modern citizens, longevity is a socially recognized need; and increasingly every effort is made to see that it is widely and equally distributed, that every citizen has an equal chance at a long and healthy life: hence doctors and hospitals in every district, regular check-ups, health education for the young, compulsory vaccination, and so on.

Parallel to the shift in attitudes, and following naturally from it, was a shift in institutions: from the church to the clinic and the hospital. But the shift has been gradual: a slow development of communal interest in medical care, a slow erosion of interest in religious care. The first major form of medical provision came in the area of prevention, not of treatment, probably because the former involved no interference with the prerogatives of the guild of physicians. But the beginnings of provision in the area of treatment were roughly simultaneous with the great public health campaigns of the late nineteenth century, and the two undoubtedly reflect the same sensitivity to questions of physical survival. The licensing of physicians, the establishment of state medical schools and urban clinics, the filtering of tax money into the great voluntary hospitals: these measures involved, perhaps, only marginal interference with the profession – some of them, in fact, reinforced its guildlike character; but they already represent an important public commitment.[21] Indeed, they represent a commitment that ultimately can be fulfilled only by turning physicians, or some substantial number of them, into public physicians (as a smaller number once turned themselves into court physicians) and by abolishing or constraining the market in medical care. But before I defend that transformation, I want to stress the unavoidability of the commitment from which it follows.

What has happened in the modern world is simply that disease itself, even when it is endemic rather than epidemic, has come to be seen as a plague. And since the plague can be dealt with, it *must* be dealt with. People will not endure what they no longer believe they have to endure. Dealing with tuberculosis, cancer, or heart failure, however, requires a common effort. Medical research is expensive, and the treatment of many particular diseases lies far beyond the resources of ordinary citizens. So the community must step in, and any democratic community will in fact step in, more or less vigorously, more or less effectively, depending on the outcome of particular political battles. Thus, the role of the American Government (or governments, for much of the activity is at the state and local levels): subsidizing research, training doctors, providing hospitals and equipment, regulating voluntary insurance schemes, underwriting the treatment of the very old. All this represents 'the contrivance of human wisdom to provide for human wants.' And all that is required to make it morally necessary is the development of a 'want' so widely and deeply felt that it can plausibly be said that it is the want not of this or that person alone but of the community generally – a 'human want' even though culturally shaped and stressed.*

But once communal provision begins, it is subject to further moral constraints: it must provide what is 'wanted' equally to all the members of the community; and it must do so in ways that respect their membership. Now, even the pattern of medical provision in the United States, though it stops far short of a national health service, is intended to provide minimally decent care to all who need it. Once public funds are committed, public officials can hardly intend anything less. At the same time, however, no political decision has yet been made to challenge directly the system of free enterprise in medical care. And so long as that system exists, wealth will be dominant in (this part of) the sphere of security and welfare; individuals will be cared for in proportion to their ability to pay and not to their need for care. In fact, the situation is more complex than that formula suggests, for communal provision already encroaches upon the free market, and the very sick and the very old sometimes receive exactly the treatment they should receive. But it is clear that poverty remains a significant bar to adequate and consistent treatment. Perhaps the most telling statistic about contemporary American medicine is the correlation of visits to doctors and hospitals with social class rather than with degree or incidence of illness. Middle- and upper-class Americans are considerably more likely to have a private physician and to see him often, and considerably less likely to be seriously ill, than are their poorer fellow citizens.[25] Were medical care a luxury, these

---

* Arguing against Bernard Williams's claim that the only proper criterion for the distribution of medical care is medical need,[22] Robert Nozick asks why it doesn't then follow 'that the only proper criterion for the distribution of barbering services is barbering need'?[23] Perhaps it does follow if one attends only to be the 'internal goal' of the activity, conceived in universal terms. But it doesn't follow if one attends to the social meaning of the activity, the place of the good it distributes in the life of a particular group of people. One can conceive of a society in which haircuts took on such central cultural significance that communal provision would be morally required, but it is something more than an interesting fact that no such society has ever existed. I have been helped in thinking about these issues by an article of Thomas Scanlon's; I adopt here his 'conventionalist' alternative.[24]

discrepancies would not matter much; but as soon as medical care becomes a socially recognized need, and as soon as the community invests in its provision, they matter a great deal. For then deprivation is a double loss – to one's health and to one's social standing. Doctors and hospitals have become such massively important features of contemporary life that to be cut off from the help they provide is not only dangerous but also degrading. But any fully developed system of medical provision will require the constraint of the guild of physicians. Indeed, this is more generally true: the provision of security and welfare requires the constraint of those men and women who had previously controlled the goods in question and sold them on the market (assuming, what is by no means always true, that the market predates communal provision). For what we do when we declare this or that good to be a needed good is to block or constrain its free exchange. We also block any other distributive procedure that doesn't attend to need – popular election, meritocratic competition, personal or familiar preference, and so on. But the market is, at least in the United States today, the chief rival of the sphere of security and welfare; and it is most importantly the market that is pre-empted by the welfare state. Needed goods cannot be left to the whim, or distributed in the interest, of some powerful group of owners or practitioners.

Most often, ownership is abolished, and practitioners are effectively conscripted or, at least, 'signed up' in the public service. They serve for the sake of the social need and not, or not simply, for their own sakes: thus, priests for the sake of eternal life, soldiers for the sake of national defence, public [state] school teachers for the sake of their pupils' education. Priests act wrongly if they sell salvation; soldiers, if they set up as mercenaries; teachers, if they cater to the children of the wealthy. Sometimes the conscription is only partial, as when lawyers are required to be officers of the court, serving the cause of justice even while they also serve their clients and themselves. Sometimes the conscription is occasional and temporary, as when lawyers are required to act as 'assigned counsels' for defendants unable to pay. In these cases, a special effort is made to respect the personal character of the lawyer-client relationship. I would look for a similar effort in any fully developed national health service. But I see no reason to respect the doctor's market freedom. Needed goods are not commodities. Or, more precisely, they can be bought and sold only insofar as they are available above and beyond whatever level of provision is fixed by democratic decision making (and only insofar as the buying and selling doesn't distort distributions below that level).

It might be argued, however, that the refusal thus far to finance a national health service constitutes a political decision by the American people about the level of communal care (and about the relative importance of other goods): a minimal standard for everyone – namely, the standard of the urban clinics; and free enterprise beyond that. That would seem to me an inadequate standard, but it would not necessarily be an unjust decision. It is not, however, the decision the American people have made. The common appreciation of the importance of medical care has carried them well beyond that. In fact, federal, state, and local governments now subsidize different levels of care for different classes of citizens. This might be all right, too, if the classification were connected to the purposes of the care – if, for example, soldiers and defence workers were given special treatment in time of war. But the poor, the middle class, and the rich make an indefensible triage. So long as communal funds are spent, as they currently are, to finance research, build hospitals, and pay the fees of doctors in private practice, the services that these expenditures underwrite must be equally available to all citizens.

This, then, is the argument for an expanded American welfare state. It follows from the three principles with which I began, and it suggests that the tendency of those principles is to free security and welfare from the prevailing patterns of dominance. Though a variety of institutional arrangements is possible, the three principles would seem to favour provision in kind; they suggest an important argument against current proposals to distribute money instead of education, legal aid, or medical care. The negative income tax, for example, is a plan to increase the purchasing power of the poor – a modified version of simple equality.[26] This plan would not, however, abolish the dominance of wealth in the sphere of need. Short of a radical equalization, men and women with greater purchasing power could still, and surely would, bid up the price of needed services. So the community would be investing, though now only indirectly, in individual welfare but without fitting provision to the shape of need. Even with equal incomes, health care delivered through the market would not be responsive to need; nor would the market provide adequately for medical research. This is not an argument against the negative income tax, however, for it may be the case that money itself, in a market economy, is one of the things that people need. And then it too, perhaps, should be provided in kind.

I want to stress again that no *a priori* stipulation of what needs ought to be recognized is possible; nor is there any *a priori* way of determining appropriate levels of provision. Our attitudes toward medical care have a history; they have been different; they will be different again. The forms of communal provision have changed in the past and will continue to change. But they don't change automatically as attitudes change. The old order has its clients; there is a lethargy in institutions as in individuals. Moreover, popular attitudes are rarely so clear as they are in the case of medical care. So change is always a matter of political argument, organization, and struggle. All that the philosopher can do is to describe the basic structure of the arguments and the constraints they entail. Hence the three principles, which can be summed up in a revised version of Marx's famous maxim: From each according to his ability (or his resources); to each according to his socially recognized needs. This, I think, is the deepest meaning of the social contract. It only remains to work out the details – but in everyday life, the details are everything.

NOTES

1 Jean-Jacques Rousseau, 'A Discourse on Political Economy', *The Social Contract and Discourses*, trans. G. D. H. Cole (New York, 1950), pp. 302–3.
2 Edmund Burke, *Reflections on the French Revolution* (London, 1910), p. 75.
3 Cf. David Hume, *A Treatise of Human Nature*, bk. iii, part ii, ch. 8.
4 The quotation is from the Greek geographer Pausanias, in George Rosen, *A History of Public Health* (New York, 1958), p. 41.
5 Simone Weil, *The Need for Roots*, trans. Arthur Wills (Boston, 1955), p. 21.
6 Charles Fried, *Right and Wrong* (Cambridge, Mass, 1978), p. 122.
7 Michael Walzer, 'Philosophy and Democracy', *Political Theory 9* (1981), pp. 379–99. See also the thoughtful discussion in Amy Gutmann, *Liberal Equality* (Cambridge, England, 1980) especially pp. 197–202.
8 For an account of the famine and the British response, see C. B. Woodham-Smith, *The Great Hunger: Ireland 1845–1849* (London, 1962).
9 Burke, *French Revolution* [2], p. 57.
10 John Rawls, *A Theory of Justice* (Cambridge, Mass, 1971), part i, chs. 2 and 3.
11 T. H. Marshall, *Class, Citizenship and Social Development* (Garden City, New York, 1965), p. 298.
12 See Judith Walzer Leavitt, *The Healthiest City: Milwaukee and the Politics of Health Reform* (Princeton, 1982), ch. 5.

[13] See the careful discussion in Harold L. Wilensky, *The Welfare State and Equality* (Berkeley, 1975), pp. 87–96.

[14] P. H. J. H. Gosden, *Self-Help: Voluntary Association in the Nineteenth Century* (London, 1973), ch. 9.

[15] See, for example, Harry Eckstein's discussion of conceptions of community and welfare policies in Norway: *Division and Cohesion in Democracry: A Study of Norway* (Princeton, 1966), pp. 85–7.

[16] Rousseau, *Social Contract* (1), pp. 250–2.

[17] Louis Dumont, *Humo Hierarchus: The Caste System and Its Implications* (revised English ed., Chicago, 1980), p. 105.

[18] Wilensky, *Welfare State* (32), chs. 2 and 3.

[19] See Whitney North Seymour, *Why Justice Fails* (New York, 1973), especially ch. 4.

[20] René Descartes, *Discourse on Method*, trans. Arthur Wollaston (Harmondsworth, England, 1960), p. 85.

[21] For a brief account of these developments, see Odin W. Anderson, *The Uneasy Equilibrium: Private and Public Financing of Health Services in the United States, 1875–1965* (New Haven, 1968).

[22] Bernard Williams, 'The Idea of Equality', in *Problems of the Self* (Cambridge, England, 1973), p. 240.

[23] See Robert Nozick, *Anarchy, State, and Utopia* (New York, 1974), pp. 233–5.

[24] Thomas Scanlon, 'Preference and Urgency', *Journal of Philosophy*, 57 (1975), pp. 655–70.

[25] Monroe Lerner, 'Social Differences in Physical Health', John B. McKinley, 'The Help-Seeking Behavior of the Poor', and Julius Roth, 'The Treatment of the Sick', in *Poverty and Health: A Sociological Analysis*, ed. John Kosa and Irving Kenneth Zola (Cambridge, Mass, 1969), summary statements at pp. 103, 265, adn 280–1.

[26] Also, supposedly, cheaper form of welfare: see Colin Clark, *Poverty before Politics: A Proposal for a Reverse Income Tax* (Hobart Paper 73, London, 1977).

11
Michael Oakeshott: Political Education*

I

The expression 'political education' has fallen on evil days; in the wilful and disingenuous corruption of language which is characteristic of our time it has acquired a sinister meaning. In places other than this, it is associated with that softening of the mind, by force, by alarm, or by the hypnotism of the endless repetition of what was scarcely worth saying once, by means of which whole populations have been reduced to submission. It is, therefore, an enterprise worth undertaking to consider again, in a quiet moment, how we should understand this expression, which joins together two laudable activities, and in doing so play a small part in rescuing it from abuse.

Politics I take to be the activity of attending to the general arrangements of a set of people whom chance or choice have brought together. In this sense, families, clubs, and learned societies have their 'politics'. But the communities in which this manner of activity is pre-eminent are the hereditary co-operative groups, many of them of ancient lineage, all of them aware of a past, a present, and a future, which we call 'states'. For most people, political activity is a secondary activity – that is to say, they have something else to do besides attending to these arrangements. But, as we have come to understand it, the activity is one in which every member of the group who is neither a child nor a lunatic has some part and some responsibility. With us it is, at one level or another, a universal activity.

I speak of this activity as 'attending to arrangements', rather than as 'making arrangements', because in these hereditary co-operative

*© 1977 Permission granted by Rowman and Littlefield Publishers, Inc.

groups the activity is never offered the blank sheet of infinite possibility. In any generation, even the most revolutionary, the arrangements which are enjoyed always far exceed those which are recognized to stand in need of attention, and those which are being prepared for enjoyment are few in comparison with those which receive amendment: the new is an insignificant proportion of the whole. There are some people, of course, who allow themselves to speak

As if arrangements were intended
For nothing else but to be mended

but, for most of us, our determination to improve our conduct does not prevent us from recognizing that the greater part of what we have is not a burden to be carried or an incubus to be thrown off, but an inheritance to be enjoyed. And a certain degree of shabbiness is joined with every real convenience.

Now, attending to the arrangements of a society is an activity which, like every other, has to be learned. Politics make a call upon knowledge. Consequently, it is not irrelevant to enquire into the kind of knowledge which is involved, and to investigate the nature of political education. I do not, however, propose to ask what information we should equip ourselves with before we begin to be politically active, or what we need to know in order to be successful politicians, but to enquire into the kind of knowledge we unavoidably call upon whenever we are engaged in political activity and to get from this an understanding of the nature of political education.

Our thoughts on political education, then, might be supposed to spring from our understanding of political activity and the kind of knowledge it involves. And it would appear that what is wanted at this point is a definition of political activity from which to draw some conclusions. But this, I think, would be a mistaken way of going about our business. What we require is not so much a definition of politics from which to deduce the character of political education, as an understanding of political activity which includes a recognition of the sort of education it involves. For, to understand an activity is to know it as a concrete whole; it is to recognize the activity as having the source of its movement within itself. An understanding which leaves the activity in debt to something outside itself is, for that reason, an inadequate understanding. And if political activity is impossible without a certain kind of knowledge and a certain sort of education, then this knowledge and education are not mere appendages to the activity but are part of the activity itself and must be incorporated in our understanding of it. We should not, therefore, seek a definition of politics in order to deduce from it the character of political knowledge and education, but rather observe the kind of knowledge and education which is inherent in any understanding of political activity, and use this observation as a means of improving our understanding of politics.

My proposal, then, is to consider the adequacy of two current understandings of politics, together with the sort of knowledge and kind of education they imply, and by improving upon them to reach what may perhaps be a more adequate understanding at once of political activity itself and the knowledge and education which belongs to it.

In the understanding of some people, politics are what may be called an empirical activity. Attending to the arrangements of a society is waking up each morning and considering, 'What would I like to do?' or 'What would somebody else (whom I desire to please) like to see done?', and doing it. This understanding of political activity may be called politics without a policy. On the briefest inspection it will appear a concept of politics difficult to substantiate; it does not look like a possible manner of activity at all. But a near approach to it is, perhaps, to be detected in the politics of the proverbial oriental despot, or in the politics of the wall-scribbler and the vote-catcher. And the result may be supposed to be chaos modified by whatever consistency is allowed to creep into caprice. They are the politics attributed to the first Lord Liverpool, of whom Acton said, 'The secret of his policy was that he had none', and of whom a Frenchman remarked that if he had been present at the creation of the world he would have said, '*Mon Dieu, conservons le chaos*'. It seems, then, that a concrete activity, which may be described as an approximation to empirical politics, is possible. But it is clear that, although knowledge of a sort belongs to this style of political activity (knowledge, as the French say, not of ourselves but only of our appetites), the only kind of education appropriate to it would be an education in lunacy – learning to be ruled solely by passing desires. And this reveals the important point; namely, that to understand politics as a purely empirical activity is to misunderstand it, because empiricism by itself is not a concrete manner of activity at all, and can become a partner in a concrete manner of activity only when it is joined with something else – in science, for example, when it is joined with hypothesis. What is significant about this understanding of politics is not that some sort of approach to it can appear, but that it mistakes for a concrete, self-moved manner of activity what is never more than an abstract moment in any manner of being active. Of course, politics are the pursuit of what is desired and of what is desired at the moment; but precisely because they are this, they can never be the pursuit of merely what recommends itself from moment to moment. The activity of desiring does not take this course; caprice is never absolute. From a practical point of view, then, we may decry the *style* of politics which approximates to pure empiricism because we can observe in it an approach to lunacy. But from a theoretical point of view, purely empirical politics are not something difficult to achieve or proper to be avoided, they are merely impossible; the product of a misunderstanding.

The understanding of politics as an empirical activity is, then, inadequate because it fails to reveal a concrete manner of activity at all. And it has the incidental defect of seeming to encourage the thoughtless to pursue a *style* of attending to the arrangements of their society which is likely to have unfortunate results; to try to do something which is inherently impossible is always a corrupting enterprise. We must, if we can, improve upon it. And the impulse to improve may be given a direction by asking, 'What is it that this understanding of politics has neglected to observe?' What (to put it crudely) has it left out which, if added in, would compose an understanding in which politics are revealed as a self-moved (or concrete) manner of activity? And the answer to the question is, or seems to be, available as soon as the question is formulated. It would appear that what this understanding of politics lacks is something to set empiricism to work, something to correspond with specific hypothesis in science, an end to be pursued more extensive than a merely instant desire. And this, it should be observed, is not merely a good companion for empiricism; it is something without which empiricism in action is impossible. Let us explore this suggestion, and in order to bring it to a point I will state it in the form of a proposition: that politics appear as a self-moved manner of activity when empiricism is preceded and guided by an ideological activity. I am not concerned with the so-called ideological *style* of politics as a desirable or undesirable manner of attending to the arrangements of a society; I am concerned only with the contention that when to the ineluctable element of empiricism (doing what one wants to do) is added a political ideology, a self-moved manner of activity appears, and that consequently this may be regarded in principle as an adequate understanding of political activity.

As I understand it, a political ideology purports to be an abstract principle, or set of related abstract principles, which has been independently premeditated. It supplies in advance of the activity of attending to the arrangements of a society a formulated end to be pursued, and in so doing it provides a means of distinguishing between those desires which ought to be encouraged and those which ought to be suppressed or redirected.

The simplest sort of political ideology is a single abstract idea, such as Freedom, Equality, Maximum Productivity, Racial Purity, or Happiness. And in that case political activity is understood as the enterprise of seeing that the arrangements of a society conform to or reflect the chosen abstract idea. It is usual, however, to recognize the need for a complex scheme of related ideas, rather than a single idea, and the examples pointed to will be such systems of ideas as: 'the principles of 1789', 'Liberalism', 'Democracy', 'Marxism', or the Atlantic Charter. These principles need not be considered absolute or immune from change (though they are frequently so considered), but their value lies in their having been premeditated. They compose an understanding of *what* is to be pursued independent of *how* it is to be pursued. A political ideology purports to supply in advance knowledge of what 'Freedom' or 'Democracy' or 'Justice' is, and in this manner sets empiricism to work. Such a set of principles is, of course, capable of being argued about and reflected upon; it is something that men compose for themselves, and they may later remember it or write it down. But the condition upon which it can perform the service assigned to it is that it owes nothing to the activity it controls. 'To know the true good of the community is what constitutes the science of legislation,' said Bentham; 'the art consists in finding the means to realize that good.' The contention we have before us, then, is that empiricism can be set to work (and a concrete, self-moved manner of activity appear) when there is added to it a guide of this sort: desire and something not generated by desire.

Now, there is no doubt about the sort of knowledge which political activity, understood in this manner, calls upon. What is required, in the first place, is knowledge of the chosen political ideology – a knowledge of the ends to be pursued, a knowledge of what we want to do. Of course, if we are to be successful in pursuing these ends we shall need knowledge of another sort also – a knowledge, shall we say, of economics and psychology. But the common characteristic of all the kinds of knowledge required is that they may be, and should be, gathered in advance of the activity of attending to the arrangements of a society. Moreover, the appropriate sort of education will be an education in which the chosen political ideology is taught and learned, in which the techniques necessary for success are acquired, and (if we are so unfortunate as to find ourselves empty-handed in the matter of an ideology) an education in the skill of abstract thought and premeditation necessary to compose one for ourselves. The education we shall need is one which enables us to expound, defend, implement, and possibly invent a political ideology.

In casting around for some convincing demonstration that this understanding of politics reveals a self-moved manner of activity, we should no doubt consider ourselves rewarded if we could find an example of politics being conducted precisely in this manner. This at least would constitute a sign that we were on the right track. The defect, it will be remembered, of the understanding of politics as a purely empirical activity was that it revealed, not a manner of activity at all, but an abstraction; and this defect made itself manifest in our inability to find a *style* of politics which was anything more than an approximation to it. How does the understanding of politics as empiricism joined with an ideology fare in this respect? And without being over-confident, we may perhaps think that this is where we wade ashore. For we would appear to be in no difficulty whatever in finding an example of political activity which corresponds to this understanding of it: half the world, at a conservative estimate, seems to conduct its affairs in precisely this manner. And further, is it not so manifestly a possible style of politics that, even if we disagree with a particular ideology, we find nothing technically absurd in the writings of those who urge it upon us as an admirable style of politics? At least its advocates seem to know what they are talking about: they understand not only the manner of the activity but also the sort of knowledge and the kind of education it involves. 'Every schoolboy in Russia', wrote Sir Norman Angel, 'is familiar with the doctrine of Marx and can recite its catechism. How many British schoolboys have any corresponding knowledge of the principles enunciated by Mill in his incomparable essay on Liberty?' 'Few people', says Mr E. H. Carr, 'any longer contest the thesis that the child should be educated *in* the official ideology of his country.' In short, if we are looking for a sign to indicate that the understanding of politics as empirical activity preceded by ideological activity is an adequate understanding, we can scarcely be mistaken in supposing that we have it to hand.

And yet there is perhaps room for doubt: doubt first of all whether in principle this understanding of politics reveals a self-moved manner of activity; and doubt, consequentially, whether what have been identified as examples of a *style* of politics corresponding exactly to this understanding have been properly indentified.

The contention we are investigating is that attending to the arrangements of a society can begin with a premeditated ideology, can begin with independently acquired knowledge of the ends to be pursued.[1] It is supposed that a political ideology is the product of intellectual premeditation and that, because it is a body of principles not itself in debt to the activity of attending to the arrangements of a society, it is able to determine and guide the direction of that activity. If, however, we consider more closely the character of a political ideology, we find at once that this supposition is falsified. So far from a political ideology being the quasi-divine parent of political activity, it turns out to be its earthly stepchild. Instead of an independently premeditated scheme of ends to be pursued, it is a system of ideas abstracted from the manner in which people have been accustomed to go about the business of attending to the arrangements of their societies. The pedigree of every political ideology shows it to be the creature, not of premeditation in advance of political activity, but of meditation upon a manner of politics. In short, political activity comes first and a political ideology follows after; and the understanding of politics we are investigating has the disadvantage of being, in the strict sense, preposterous.

Let us consider the matter first in relation to scientific hypothesis, which I have taken to play a role in scientific activity in some respects similar to that of an ideology in politics. If a scientific hypothesis were a self-generated bright idea which owed nothing to scientific activity, then empiricism governed by hypothesis could be considered to compose a self-contained manner of activity; but this certainly is not its character. The truth is that only a man who is already a scientist can formulate a scientific hypothesis; that is, an hypothesis is not an independent invention capable of guiding scientific enquiry, but a dependent supposition which arises as an abstraction from within already existing scientific activity. Moreover, even when the specific hypothesis has in this manner been formulated, it is inoperative as a guide to research without constant reference to the traditions of scientific enquiry from which it was abstracted. The concrete situation does not appear until the specific hypothesis, which is the occasion of empiricism being set to work, is recognized as itself the creature of knowing how to conduct a scientific enquiry.

Or consider the example of cookery. It might be supposed that an ignorant man, some edible materials, and a cookery book compose together the necessities of a self-moved (or concrete) activity called cooking. But nothing is further from the truth. The cookery book is not an independently generated beginning from which cooking can spring; it is nothing more than an abstract of somebody's knowledge of how to cook: it is the stepchild, not the parent of the activity. The book, in its turn, may help to set a man on to dressing a dinner, but if it were his sole guide he could never, in fact, begin: the book speaks only to those who know already the kind of thing to expect from it and consequently how to interpret it.

Now, just as a cookery book presupposes somebody who knows how to cook, and its use presupposes somebody who already knows how to use it, and just as a scientific hypothesis springs from a knowledge of how to conduct a scientific investigation and separated from that knowledge is powerless to set empiricism profitably to work, so a political ideology must be understood, not as an independently premeditated beginning for political activity, but as knowledge (abstract and generalized) of a concrete manner of attending to the arrangements of a society. The catechism which sets out the purposes to be pursued merely abridges a concrete manner of behaviour in which those purposes are already hidden. It does not exist in advance of political activity, and by itself it is always an insufficient guide. Political enterprises, the ends to be pursued, the arrangements to be established (all the normal ingredients of a political ideology), cannot be premeditated in advance of a manner of attending to the arrangements of a society; *what* we do, and moreover what we want to do, is the creature of *how* we are accustomed to conduct our affairs. Indeed, it often reflects no more than a discovered ability to do something which is then translated into an authority to do it.

On 4 August 1789, for the complex and bankrupt social and political system of France was substituted the Rights of Man. Reading this document we come to the conclusion that somebody has done some thinking. Here, displayed in a few sentences, is a political ideology: a system of rights and duties, a scheme of ends – justice, freedom, equality, security, property, and the rest – ready and waiting to be put into practice for the first time. 'For the first time?' Not a bit of it. This ideology no more existed in advance of political practice than a cookery book exists in advance of knowing how to cook. Certainly it was the product of somebody's reflection, but it was not the product of reflection in advance of political activity. For here, in fact, are disclosed, abstracted and abridged, the common law rights of Englishmen, the gift not of independent premeditation or divine munificence, but of centuries of the day-to-day attending to the arrangements of an historic society. Or consider Locke's *Second Treatise of Civil Government*, read in America and in France in the eighteenth century as a statement of abstract principles to be put into practice, regarded there as a preface to political activity. But so far from being a preface, it has all the marks of a postscript, and its power to guide derived from its roots in actual political experience. Here, set down in abstract terms, is a brief conspectus of the manner in which Englishmen were accustomed to go about the business of attending to their arrangements – a brilliant abridgment of the political habits of Englishmen. Or consider this passage from a contemporary continental writer: 'Freedom keeps Europeans in unrest and movement. They wish to have freedom, and at the same time they know they have not got it. They know also that freedom belongs to man as a human right.' And having established the end to be pursued, political activity is represented as the realization of this end. But the 'freedom' which can be pursued is not an independently premeditated 'ideal' or a dream; like scientific hypothesis, it is something which is already intimated in a concrete manner of behaving. Freedom, like a recipe for game pie, is not a bright idea; it is not a 'human right' to be deduced from some speculative concept of human nature. The freedom which we enjoy is nothing more than arrangements, procedures of a certain kind: the freedom of an Englishman is not something exemplified in the procedure of *habeas corpus*, it *is*, at that point, the availability of that procedure. And the freedom which we wish to enjoy is not an 'ideal' which we premeditate independently of our political experience, it is what is already intimated in that experience.[2]

On this reading, then, the systems of abstract ideas we call 'ideologies' are abstracts of some kind of concrete activity. Most political ideologies, and certainly the most useful of them (because they unquestionably have their use), are abstracts of the political traditions of some society. But it sometimes happens that an ideology is offered as a guide to politics which is an abstract, not of political experience, but of some other manner of activity – war, religion, or the conduct of industry, for example. And here the model we are shown is not only abstract, but is also inappropriate on account of the irrelevance of the activity from which it has been abstracted. This, I think, is one of the defects of the model provided by the Marxist ideology. But the important point is that, at most, an ideology is an abbreviation of some manner of concrete activity.

We are now, perhaps, in a position to perceive more accurately the character of what may be called the ideological *style* of politics, and to observe that its existence offers no ground for supposing that the understanding of political activity as empiricism guided solely by an ideology is an adequate understanding. The ideological style of politics is a confused style. Properly speaking, it is a traditional manner of attending to the arrangements of a society which has been abridged into a doctrine of ends to be pursued, the abridgment (together with the necessary technical knowledge) being erroneously regarded as the sole guide relied upon. In certain circumstances an abridgment of this kind may be valuable; it gives sharpness of outline and precision to a political tradition which the occasion may make seem appropriate. When a manner of attending to arrangements is to be transplanted from the society in which it has grown up into another society (always a questionable enterprise), the simplification of an ideology may appear as an asset. If, for example, the English manner of politics is to be planted elsewhere in the world, it is perhaps appropriate that it should first be abridged into something called 'democracy' before it is packed up and shipped abroad. There is, of course, an alternative method: the method by which what is exported is the detail and not the abridgment of the tradition and the workmen travel with the tools – the method which made the British Empire. But it is a slow and costly method. And, particularly with men in a hurry, *l'homme à programme* with his abridgment wins every time; his slogans enchant, while the resident magistrate is seen only as a sign of servility. But whatever the apparent appropriateness on occasion of the ideological style of politics, the defect of the explanation of political activity connected with it becomes apparent when we consider the sort of knowledge and the kind of education it encourages us to believe is sufficient for understanding the activity of attending to the arrangements of a society. For it suggests that a knowledge of the chosen political ideology can take the place of understanding a tradition of political behaviour. The wand and the book come to be regarded as themselves potent, and not merely the symbols of potency. The arrangements of a society are made to appear, not as manners of behaviour, but as pieces of machinery to be transported about the world indiscriminately. The complexities of the tradition which have been squeezed out in the process of abridgment are taken to be unimportant: the 'rights of man' are understood to exist insulated from a manner of attending to arrangements. And because, in practice, the abridgment is never by itself a sufficient guide, we are encouraged to fill it out, not with our suspect political experience, but with experience drawn from other (often irrelevant) concretely understood activities, such as war, the conduct of industry, or trade union negotiation.

The understanding of politics as the activity of attending to the arrangements of a society under the guidance of an independently premeditated ideology is, then, no less a misunderstanding than the understanding of it as a purely empirical activity. Wherever else politics may begin, they cannot begin in ideological activity. And in an attempt to improve upon this understanding of politics, we have already observed in principle what needs to be recognized in order to have an intelligent concept. Just as scientific hypothesis cannot appear, and is impossible to operate, except within an already existing tradition of scientific investigation, so a scheme of ends for political activity appears within, and can be evaluated only when it is related to, an already existing tradition of how to attend to our arrangements. In politics, the only concrete manner of activity detectable is one in which empiricism and the ends to be pursued are recognized as dependent, alike for their existence and their operation, upon a traditional manner of behaviour.

Politics is the activity of attending to the general arrangements of a collection of people who, in respect of their common recognition of a manner of attending to its arrangements, compose a single community. To suppose a collection of people without recognized traditions of behaviour, or one which enjoyed arrangements which intimated no direction for change and needed no attention,[3] is to suppose a people incapable of politics. This activity, then, springs neither from instant desires, nor from general principles, but from the existing traditions of behaviour themselves. And the form it takes, because it can take no other, is the amendment of existing arrangements by exploring and pursuing what is intimated in them. The arrangements which constitute a society capable of political activity, whether they are customs or institutions or laws or diplomatic decisions, are at once coherent and incoherent; they compose a pattern and at the same time they intimate a sympathy for what does not fully appear. Political activity is the exploration of that sympathy; and consequently, relevant political reasoning will be the convincing exposure of a sympathy, present but not yet followed up, and the convincing demonstration that now is the appropriate moment for recognizing it. For example, the legal status of women in our society was for a long time (and perhaps still is) in comparative confusion, because the rights and duties which composed it intimated rights and duties which were nevertheless not recognized. And, on the view of things I am suggesting, the only cogent reason to be advanced for the technical 'enfranchisement' of women was that in all or most other important respects they had already been enfranchised. Arguments drawn from abstract natural right, from 'justice', or from some general concept of feminine personality, must be regarded as either irrelevant, or as unfortunately disguised forms of the one valid argument; namely, that there was an incoherence in the arrangements of the society which pressed convincingly for remedy. In politics, then, every enterprise is a consequential enterprise, the pursuit, not of a dream, or of a general principle, but of an intimation. What we have to do with is something less imposing than logical implications or necessary consequences: but if the intimations of a tradition of behaviour are less dignified or more elusive than these, they are not on that account less important. Of course, there is no piece of mistake-proof apparatus by means of which we can elicit the intimation most worthwhile pursuing; and not only do we often make gross errors of judgement in this matter, but also the total effect of a desire satisfied is so little to be forecast, that our activity of amendment is often found to lead us where we would not go. Moreover, the whole enterprise is liable at any moment to be perverted by the incursion of an approximation to empiricism in the pursuit of power. These are features which can never be eliminated; they belong to the character of political activity. But it may be believed that our mistakes of understanding will be less frequent and less disastrous if we escape the illusion that politics is ever anything more than the pursuit of intimations; a conversion, not an argument.

Now, every society which is intellectually alive is liable, from time to time, to abridge its tradition of behaviour into a scheme of abstract ideas; and on occasion political discussion will be concerned, not (like the debates in the *Iliad*) with isolated transactions, nor (like the speeches in Thucydides) with policies and traditions of activity, but with general principles. And in this there is no harm; perhaps even some positive benefit. It is possible that the distorting mirror of an ideology will reveal important hidden passages in the tradition, as a caricature reveals the potentialities of a face; and if this is so, the intellectual enterprise of seeing what a tradition looks like when it is reduced to an ideology will be a useful part of political education. But to make use of abridgment as a technique for exploring the intimations of a political tradition, to use it, that is, as a scientist uses hypothesis, is one thing; it is something different, and something inappropriate, to understand political activity itself as the activity of amending the arrangements of a

society so as to make them agree with the provisions of an ideology.
For then a character has been attributed to an ideology which it is
unable to sustain, and we may find ourselves, in practice, directed
by a false and a misleading guide: false, because in the abridgment,
however skilfully it has been performed, a single intimation is apt to
be exaggerated and proposed for unconditional pursuit and the
benefit to be had from observing what the distortion reveals is lost
when the distortion itself is given the office of a criterion;
misleading, because the abridgment itself never, in fact, provides
the whole of the knowledge used in political activity.

There will be some people who, though in general agreement
with this understanding of political activity, will suspect that it
confuses what is, perhaps, normal with what is necessary, and that
important exceptions (of great contemporary relevance) have been
lost in a hazy generality. It is all very well, it may be said, to observe
in politics the activity of exploring and pursuing the intimations of
a tradition of behaviour, but what light does this throw upon a
political crisis such as the Norman Conquest of England, or the
establishment of the Soviet *régime* in Russia? It would be foolish, of
course, to deny the possibility of serious political crisis. But if we
exclude (as we must) a genuine cataclysm which for the time being
made an end of politics by altogether obliterating a current
tradition of behaviour (which is *not* what happened in Anglo-
Saxon England or in Russia),[4] there is little to support the view that
even the most serious political upheaval carries us outside this
understanding of politics. A tradition of behaviour is not a fixed
and inflexible manner of doing things; it is a flow of sympathy. It
may be temporarily disrupted by the incursion of a foreign
influence, it may be diverted, restricted, arrested, or become dried-
up, and it may reveal so deep-seated an incoherence that (even
without foreign assistance) a crisis appears. And if, in order to meet
these crises, there were some steady, unchanging, independent
guide to which a society might resort, it would no doubt be well
advised to do so. But no such guide exists; we have no resources
outside the fragments, the vestiges, the relics of its own tradition of
behaviour which the crisis has left untouched. For even the help we
may get from the traditions of another society (or from a tradition
of a vaguer sort which is shared by a number of societies) is
conditional upon our being able to assimilate them to our own
arrangements. The hungry and helpless man is mistaken if he
supposes that he overcomes the crisis by means of a tin-opener:
what saves him is somebody else's knowledge of how to cook,
which he can make use of only because he is not himself entirely

ignorant. In short, political crisis (even when it seems to be imposed upon a society by changes beyond its control) always appears *within* a tradition of political activity; and 'salvation' comes from the unimpaired resources of the tradition itself. Those societies which retain, in changing circumstances, a lively sense of their own identity and continuity (which are without that hatred of their own experience which makes them desire to efface it) are to be counted fortunate, not because they possess what others lack, but because they have already mobilized what none is without and all, in fact, rely upon.

In political activity, then, men sail a boundless and bottomless sea; there is neither harbour for shelter nor floor for anchorage, neither starting-place nor appointed destination. The enterprise is to keep afloat on an even keel; the sea is both friend and enemy; and the seamanship consists in using the resources of a traditional manner of behaviour in order to make a friend of every hostile occasion.[5]

A depressing doctrine, it will be said – even by those who do not make the mistake of adding in an element of crude determinism which, in fact, it has no place for. A tradition of behaviour is not a groove within which we are destined to grind out our helpless and unsatisfying lives: *Spartam nactus es; hanc exorna*. But in the main the depression springs from the exclusion of hopes that were false and the discovery that guides, reputed to be of superhuman wisdom and skill, are, in fact, of a somewhat different character. If the doctrine deprives us of a model laid up in heaven to which we should approximate our behaviour, at least it does not lead us into a morass where every choice is equally good or equally to be deplored. And if it suggests that politics are *nur für die Schwindelfreie*, that should depress only those who have lost their nerve.

The sin of the academic is that he takes so long in coming to the point. Nevertheless, there is some virtue in his dilatoriness; what he has to offer may, in the end, be no great matter, but at least it is not unripe fruit, and to pluck it is the work of a moment. We set out to consider the kind of knowledge involved in political activity and the appropriate sort of education. And if the understanding of politics I have recommended is not a misunderstanding, there is little doubt about the kind of knowledge and the sort of education which belongs to it. It is knowledge, as profound as we can make it, of our tradition of political behaviour. Other knowledge, certainly, is desirable in addition; but this is the knowledge without which we cannot make use of whatever else we may have learned.

Now, a tradition of behaviour is a tricky thing to get to know. Indeed, it may even appear to be essentially unintelligible. It is neither fixed nor finished; it has no changeless centre to which understanding can anchor itself; there is no sovereign purpose to be perceived or invariable direction to be detected; there is no model to be copied, idea to be realized, or rule to be followed. Some parts of it may change more slowly than others, but none is immune from change. Everything is temporary. Nevertheless, though a tradition of behaviour is flimsy and elusive; it is not without identity, and what makes it a possible object of knowledge is the fact that all its parts do not change at the same time and that the changes it undergoes are potential within it. Its principle is a principle of *continuity*: authority is diffused between past, present, and future; between the old, the new, and what is to come. It is steady because, though it moves, it is never wholly in motion; and though it is tranquil, it is never wholly at rest.[6] Nothing that ever belonged to it is completely lost; we are always swerving back to recover and make something topical out of even its remotest moments: and nothing for long remains unmodified. Everything is temporary, but nothing is arbitrary. Everything figures by comparison, not with what stands next to it, but with the whole. And since a tradition of behaviour is not susceptible of the distinction between essence and accident, knowledge of it is unavoidably knowledge of its detail: to know only the gist is to know nothing. What has to be learned is not an abstract idea, or a set of tricks, not even a ritual, but a concrete, coherent manner of living in all its intricateness.

It is clear, then, that we must not entertain the hope of acquiring this difficult understanding by easy methods. Though the knowledge we see is municipal, not universal, there is no short cut to it. Moreover, political education is not merely a matter of coming to understand a tradition, it is learning how to participate in a conversation: it is at once initiation into an inheritance in which we have a life interest, and the exploration of its intimations. There will always remain something of a mystery about how a tradition of political behaviour is learned, and perhaps the only certainty is that there is no point at which learning it can properly be said to begin. The politics of a community are not less individual (and not more so) than its language, and they are learned and practised in the same manner. We do not begin to learn our native language by learning the alphabet, or by learning its grammar; we do not begin by learning words, but words in use; we do not begin (as we begin in reading) with what is easy and go on to what is more difficult; we do not begin at school, but in the cradle; and what we say springs always from our manner of speaking. And this is true also of our political education; it begins in the enjoyment of a tradition, in the observation and imitation of the behaviour of our elders, and there is little or nothing in the world which comes before us as we open our eyes which does not contribute to it. We are aware of a past and a future as soon as we are aware of a present. Long before we are of an age to take interest in a book about our politics we are acquiring that complex and intricate knowledge of our political tradition without which we could not make sense of a book when we come to open it. And the projects we entertain are the creatures of our tradition. The greater part, then – perhaps the most important part – of our political education we acquire haphazard in finding our way about the natural–artificial world into which we are born, and there is no other way of acquiring it. There will, of course, be more to acquire, and it will be more readily acquired, if we have the good fortune to be born into a rich and lively political tradition and among those who are well educated politically; the lineaments of *political* activity will earlier become distinct: but even the most needy society and the most cramped surroundings have some political education to offer, and we take what we can get.

But if this is the manner of our beginning, there are deeper recesses to explore. Politics are a proper subject for academic study; there is something to think about and it is important that we should think about the appropriate things. Here also, and everywhere, the governing consideration is that what we are learning to understand is a political tradition, a concrete manner of behaviour. And for this reason it is proper that, at the academic level, the study of politics should be an historical study – not, in the first place, because it is proper to be concerned with the past, but because we need to be concerned with the detail of the concrete. It is true that nothing appears on the present surface of a tradition of political activity which has not its roots deep in the past, and that not to observe it coming into being is often to be denied the clue to its significance; and for this reason genuine historical study is an indispensable part of a political education. But what is equally important is not what happened, here or there, but what people have thought and said about what happened: the history, not of political ideas, but of the manner of our political thinking. Every society, by the underlinings it makes in the book of its history, constructs a legend of its own fortunes which it keeps up to date and in which is hidden its own understanding of politics; and the historical investigation of this legend – not to expose its errors but to understand its prejudices – must be a pre-eminent part of a political education. It is, then, in the study of genuine history, and of this quasi-history which reveals in its backward glances the tendencies which are afoot, that we may hope to escape one of the most insidious current misunderstandings of political activity – the misunderstanding in which institutions and procedures appear as pieces of machinery designed to achieve a purpose settled in advance, instead of as manners of behaviour which are meaningless when separated from their context: the misunderstanding, for example, in which Mill convinced himself that something called 'Representative Government' was a 'form' of politics which could be regarded as proper to any society which had reached a certain level of what he called 'civilization'; in short, the misunderstanding in which we regard our arrangements and institutions as something more significant than the footprints of thinkers and statesmen who knew which way to turn their feet without knowing anything about a final destination.

Nevertheless, to be concerned only with one's own tradition of political activity is not enough. A political education worth the name must embrace, also, knowledge of the politics of other contemporary societies. It must do this because some at least of our political activity is related to that of other people's, and not to know how they go about attending to their own arrangements is not to know the course they will pursue and not to know what resources to call upon in our own tradition; and because to know only one's own tradition is not to know even that. But here again two observations must be made. We did not begin yesterday to have relations with our neighbours; and we do not require constantly to be hunting outside the tradition of our politics to find some special formula or some merely *ad hoc* expedient to direct those relations. It is only when wilfully or negligently we forget the resources of understanding and initiative which belongs to our tradition that, like actors who have forgotten their part, we are obliged to gag. And secondly, the only knowledge worth having about the politics of another society is the same kind of knowledge as we seek of our own tradition. Here also, *la verité reste dans les nuances*; and a comparative study of institutions, for example, which obscured this would provide only an illusory sense of having understood what nevertheless remains a secret. The study of another people's politics, like the study of our own, should be an oecological study of a tradition of behaviour, not an anatomical study of mechanical devices or the investigation of an ideology. And only when our study is of this sort shall we find ourselves in the way of being stimulated, but not intoxicated, by the manners of others. To range the world in order to select the 'best' of the practices and purposes of others (as the eclectic Zeuxis is said to have tried to compose a figure more beautiful than Helen's by putting together features each notable for its perfection) is a corrupting enterprise and one of the surest ways of losing one's political balance; but to investigate the concrete manner in which another people goes about the business of attending to its arrangements may reveal significant passages in our own tradition which might otherwise remain hidden.

There is a third department in the academic study of politics which must be considered – what, for want of a better name, I shall call a philosophical study. Reflection on political activity may take place at various levels: we may consider what resources our political tradition offers for dealing with a certain situation, or we may abridge our political experience into a doctrine, which may be used, as a scientist uses hypothesis, to explore its intimations. But beyond these, and other manners of political thinking, there is a range of reflection the object of which is to consider the place of political activity itself on the map of our total experience. Reflection of this sort has gone on in every society which, is politically conscious and intellectually alive; and so far as European societies are concerned, the enquiry has uncovered a variety of intellectual problems which each generation has formulated in its own way and has tackled with the technical resources at its disposal. And because political philosophy is not what may be called a 'progressive' science, accumulating solid results and reaching conclusions upon which further investigation may be based with confidence, its history is specially important: indeed, in a sense, it has nothing but a history, which is a history of the incoherences philosophers have detected in common ways of thinking and the manner of solution they have proposed, rather than a history of doctrines and systems. The study of this history may be supposed to have a considerable place in a political education, and the enterprise of understanding the turn which contemporary reflection has given to it, an even more considerable place. Political philosophy cannot be expected to increase our ability to be successful in political activity. It will not help us to distinguish between good and bad political projects; it has no power to guide or to direct us in the enterprise of pursuing the intimations of our tradition. But the patient analysis of the general ideas which have come to be connected with political activity – ideas such as nature, artifice, reason, will, law, authority, obligation, etc. – in so far as it succeeds in removing some of the crookedness from our thinking and leads to a more economical use of concepts, is an activity neither to be overrated nor despised. But it must be understood as an explanatory, not a practical, activity, and if we pursue it, we may hope only to be less often cheated by ambiguous statement and irrelevant argument. *Abeunt studia in mores.* The fruits of a political education will appear in the manner in which we think and speak about politics and perhaps in the manner in which we conduct our political activity. To select items from this prospective harvest must always be hazardous, and opinions will differ about what is most important. But for myself I should hope for two things. The more profound our understanding of political activity, the less we shall be at the mercy of plausible but mistaken analogy, the less we shall be tempted by a false or irrelevant model. And the more thoroughly we understand our own political tradition, the more readily its whole resources are available to us, the less likely we shall be to embrace the illusions which wait for the ignorant and the unwary: the illusion that in politics we can get on without a tradition of behaviour, the illusion that the abridgement of a tradition is itself a sufficient guide, and the illusion that in politics there is anywhere a safe harbour, a destination to be reached or even a detectable strand of progress. 'The world is the best of all possible worlds, and *everything* in it is a necessary evil.'

NOTES

[1] This is the case, for example, with Natural Law; whether it is taken to be an explanation of political activity or (improperly) as a guide to political conduct.

[2] Cf. 'Substantive law has the first look of being gradually secreted in the interstices of procedure.' Maine, *Early Law and Customs*, p. 389.

[3] E.g. a society in which law was believed to be a divine gift.

[4] The Russian Revolution (what actually happened in Russia) was not the implementation of an abstract design worked out by Lenin and others in Switzerland: it was a modification of *Russian* circumstances. And the French Revolution was far more closely connected with the *ancien régime* than with Locke or America.

[5] To those who seem to themselves to have a clear view of an immediate destination (that is, of a condition of human circumstance to be achieved), and who are confident that this condition is proper to be imposed upon everybody, this will seem an unduly sceptical understanding of political activity; but they may be asked where they have got it from, and whether they imagine that 'political activity' will come to an end with the achievement of this condition? And if they agree that some more distant destination may then be expected to disclose itself, does not

this situation entail an understanding of politics as an open-ended activity such as I have described? Or do they understand politics as making the necessary arrangements for a set of castaways who have always in reserve the thought that they are going to be 'rescued?'

6 The critic who found 'some mystical qualities' in this passage leaves me puzzled: it seems to me an exceedingly matter-of-fact description of the characteristics of any tradition – the Common Law of England, for example, the so-called British Constitution, the Christian religion, modern physics, the game of cricket, shipbuilding.

12

Hannah Arendt: The Revolutionary Tradition and its Lost Treasure*

I

... 'As Cato concluded every speech with the words, *Carthago delenda est*, so do I every opinion, with the injunction, "divide the counties into wards."'[1] Thus Jefferson once summed up an exposition of his most cherished political idea, which, alas, turned out to be as incomprehensible to posterity as it had been to his contemporaries. The reference to Cato was no idle slip of a tongue used to Latin quotations; it was meant to emphasize that Jefferson thought the absence of such a subdivision of the country constituted a vital threat to the very existence of the republic. Just as Rome, according to Cato, could not be safe so long as Carthage existed, so the republic, according to Jefferson, would not be secure in its very foundations without the ward system. 'Could I once see this I should consider it was as the dawn of the salvation of the republic, and say with old Simeon, "Nunc dimittis Domine."'[2]

Had Jefferson's plan of 'elementary republics' been carried out, it would have exceeded by far the feeble germs of a new form of government which we are able to detect in the sections of the Parisian Commune and the popular societies during the French Revolution. However, if Jefferson's political imagination surpassed them in insight and in scope, his thoughts were still travelling in the same direction. Both Jefferson's plan and the French *sociétés révolutionnaires* anticipated with an almost weird precision those councils, *soviets* and *Räte*, which were to make their appearance in every genuine revolution throughout the nineteenth and twentieth centuries. Each time they appeared, they sprang up as the spon-

*From *On Revolution* by Hannah Arendt. Copyright © 1963, 1965 by Hannah Arendt. Reprinted by permission of Viking Penguin Inc. Also in Great Britain by permission of Faber and Faber Ltd.

taneous organs of the people, not only outside of all revolutionary parties but entirely unexpected by them and their leaders. Like Jefferson's proposals, they were utterly neglected by statesmen, historians, political theorists, and, most importantly, by the revolutionary tradition itself. Even those historians whose sympathies were clearly on the side of revolution and who could not help writing the emergence of popular councils into the record of their story regarded them as nothing more than essentially temporary organs in the revolutionary struggle for liberation; that is to say, they failed to understand to what an extent the council system confronted them with an entirely new form of government, with a new public space for freedom which was constituted and organized during the course of the revolution itself.

This statement must be qualified. There are two relevant exceptions to it, namely a few remarks by Marx at the occasion of the revival of the Parisian Commune during the short-lived revolution of 1871, and some reflections by Lenin based not on the text by Marx, but on the actual course of the Revolution of 1905 in Russia. But before we turn our attention to these matters, we had better try to understand what Jefferson had in mind when he said with utmost self-assurance, 'The wit of man cannot devise a more solid basis for a free, durable, and well-administered republic.'[3]

It is perhaps noteworthy that we find no mention of the ward system in any of Jefferson's formal works, and it may be even more important that the few letters in which he wrote of it with such emphatic insistence all date from the last period of his life. It is true, at one time he hoped that Virginia, because it was 'the first of the nations of the earth which assembled its wise men peaceably together to form a fundamental constitution', would also be the first 'to adopt the subdivision of our counties into wards',[4] but the point of the matter is that the whole idea seems to have occurred to him only at a time when he himself was retired from public life and when he had withdrawn from the affairs of state. He who had been so explicit in his criticism of the Constitution because it had not incorporated a Bill of Rights, never touched on its failure to incorporate the townships which so obviously were the original models of his 'elementary republics' where 'the voice of the whole people would be fairly, fully, and peaceably expressed, discussed, and decided by the common reason' of all citizens.[5] In terms of his own role in the affairs of his country and the outcome of the Revolution, the idea of the ward system clearly was an afterthought; and, in terms of his own biographical development, the repeated insistence on the 'peaceable' character of these wards demonstrates that this system was to him the only possible non-violent alternative to his earlier notions about the desirability of recurring revolutions. At any event, we find the only detailed descriptions of what he had in mind in letters written in the year 1816, and these letters repeat rather than supplement one another. Jefferson himself knew well enough that what he proposed as the 'salvation of the republic' actually was the salvation of the revolutionary spirit through the republic. His expositions of the ward system always began with a reminder of how 'the vigor given to our revolution in its commencement' was due to the 'little republics', how they had 'thrown the whole nation into energetic action', and how, at a later occasion, he had felt 'the foundations of the government shaken under [his] feet by the New England townships', 'the energy of this organization' being so great that 'there was not an individual in their States whose body was not thrown with all its momentum into action.' Hence, he expected the wards to permit the citizens to continue to do what they had been able to do during the years of revolution, namely, to act on their own and thus to participate in public business as it was being transacted from day to day. By virtue of the Constitution, the public business of the nation as a whole had been transferred to Washington and was being transacted by the federal government, of which Jefferson still thought as 'the foreign branch' of the republic, whose domestic affairs were taken care of by the state governments.[6] But state government and even the administrative machinery of the county were by far too large and unwieldy to permit immediate participation; in all these institutions, it was the delegates of the people rather than the people themselves who constituted the public realm, whereas those who delegated them and who, theoretically, were the source and the seat of power remained forever outside its doors. This order of things should have sufficed if Jefferson had actually believed (as he sometimes professed) that the happiness of the people lay exclusively in their private welfare; for because of the way the government of the union was constituted — with its division and separation of powers, with controls, checks and balances, built into its very centre — it was highly unlikely, though of course not impossible, that a tyranny could arise out of it. What could happen, and what indeed has happened over and over again since, was that 'the representative organs should become corrupt and perverted',[7] but such corruption was not likely to be due (and hardly ever has been due) to a conspiracy of the representative organs against the people whom they represented. Corruption in this kind of government is much more likely to spring from the midst of society, that is, from the people themselves.

Corruption and perversion are more pernicious, and at the same time more likely to occur, in an egalitarian republic than in any other form of government. Schematically speaking, they come to pass when private interests invade the public domain, that is, they spring from below and not from above. It is precisely because the republic excluded on principle the old dichotomy of ruler and ruled that corruption of the body politic did not leave the people untouched, as in other forms of government, where only the rulers or the ruling classes needed to be affected, and where therefore an 'innocent' people might indeed first suffer and then, one day, effect a dreadful but necessary insurrection. Corruption of the people themselves – as distinguished from corruption of their representatives or a ruling class – is possible only under a government that has granted them a share in public power and has taught them how to manipulate it. Where the rift between ruler and ruled has been closed, it is always possible that the dividing line between public and private may become blurred and, eventually, obliterated. Prior to the modern age and the rise of society, this danger, inherent in republican government, used to arise from the public realm, from the tendency of public power to expand and to trespass upon private interests. The age-old remedy against this danger was respect for private property, that is, the framing of a system of laws through which the rights of privacy were publicly guaranteed and the dividing line between public and private legally protected. The Bill of Rights in the American Constitution forms the last, and the most exhaustive, legal bulwark for the private realm against public power, and Jefferson's preoccupation with the dangers of public power and this remedy against them is sufficiently well known. However, under conditions, not of prosperity as such, but of a rapid and constant economic growth, that is, of a constantly increasing expansion of the private realm – and these were of course the conditions of the modern age – the dangers of corruption and perversion were much more likely to arise from private interests than from public power. And it speaks for the high calibre of Jefferson's statesmanship that he was able to perceive this danger despite his preoccupation with the older and better-known threats of corruption in bodies politic.

The only remedies against the misuse of public power by private individuals lie in the public realm itself, in the light which exhibits each deed enacted within its boundaries, in the very visibility to which it exposes all those who enter it. Jefferson, though the secret vote was still unknown at the time, had at least a foreboding of how dangerous it might be to allow the people a share in public power without providing them at the same time with more public space than the ballot box and with more opportunity to make their voices heard in public than election day. What he perceived to be the mortal danger to the republic was that the Constitution had given all power to the citizens, without giving them the opportunity of *being* republicans and of *acting* as citizens. In other words, the danger was that all power had been given to the people in their private capacity, and that there was no space established for them in their capacity of being citizens. When, at the end of his life, he summed up what to him clearly was the gist of private and public morality, 'Love your neighbor as yourself, and your country more than yourself',[8] he knew that this maxim remained an empty exhortation unless the 'country' could be made as present to the 'love' of its citizens as the 'neighbor' was to the love of his fellow men. For just as there could not be much substance to neighbourly love if one's neighbour should make a brief apparition once every two years, so there could not be much substance to the admonition to love one's country more than oneself unless the country was a living presence in the midst of its citizens.

Hence, according to Jefferson, it was the very principle of republican government to demand 'the subdivision of the counties into wards', namely, the creation of 'small republics' through which 'every man in the State' could become 'an acting member of the Common government, transacting in person a great portion of its rights and duties, subordinate indeed, yet important, and entirely within his competence.'[9] It was 'these little republics [that] would be the main strength of the great one';[10] for inasmuch as the republican government of the Union was based on the assumption that the seat of power was in the people, the very condition for its proper functioning lay in a scheme 'to divide [government] among the many, distributing to every one exactly the functions he [was] competent to.' Without this, the very principle of republican government could never be actualized, and the government of the United States would be republican in name only.

Thinking in terms of the safety of the republic, the question was how to prevent 'the degeneracy of our government', and Jefferson called every government degenerate in which all powers were concentrated 'in the hands of the one, the few, the well-born or the many.' Hence, the ward system was not meant to strengthen the power of the many but the power of 'every one' within the limits of his competence; and only by breaking up 'the many' into assemblies where every one could count and be counted upon 'shall we be as republican as a large society can be.' In terms of the safety of the citizens of the republic, the question was how to make everybody feel

> that he is a participator in the government of affairs, not merely at an election one day in the year, but every day; when there shall not be a man in the State who will not be a member of some one of its councils, great or small, he will let the heart be torn out of his body sooner than his power wrested from him by a Caesar or a Bonaparte.

Finally, as to the question of how to integrate these smallest organs, designed for everyone, into the governmental structure of the Union, designed for all, his answer was: 'The elementary republics of the wards, the county republics, the State republics, and the republic of the Union would form a gradation of authorities, standing each on the basis of law, holding every one its delegated share of powers, and constituting truly a system of fundamental balances and checks for the government.' On one point, however, Jefferson remained curiously silent, and that is the question of what the specific functions of the elementary republics should be. He mentioned occasionally as 'one of the advantages of the ward divisions I have proposed' that they would offer a better way to collect the voice of the people than the mechanics of representative government; but in the main, he was convinced that if one would 'begin them only for a single purpose' they would 'soon show for what others they [were] the best instruments'.[11]

This vagueness of purpose, far from being due to a lack of clarity, indicates perhaps more tellingly than any other single aspect of Jefferson's proposal that the afterthought in which he clarified and gave substance to his most cherished recollections from the Revolution in fact concerned a new form of government rather than a mere reform of it or a mere supplement to the existing institutions. If the ultimate end of revolution was freedom and the constitution of a public space where freedom could appear, the *constitutio libertatis*, then the elementary republics of the wards, the only tangible place where everyone could be free, actually were the end of the great republic whose chief purpose in domestic affairs should have been to provide the people with such places of freedom and to protect them. The basic assumption of the ward system, whether Jefferson knew it or not, was that no one could be called happy without his share in public happiness, that no one could be called free without his experience in public freedom, and that no one could be called either happy or free without participating, and having a share, in public power.

II

It is a strange and sad story that remains to be told and remembered. It is not the story of revolution on whose thread the historian might string the history of the nineteenth century in Europe,[12] whose origins could be traced back into the Middle Ages, whose progress had been irresistible 'for centuries in spite of every obstacle', according to Tocqueville, and which Marx, generalizing the experiences of several generations, called 'the locomotive of all history'.[13] I do not doubt that revolution was the hidden *leitmotif* of the century preceding ours, although I doubt both Tocqueville's and Marx's generalizations, especially their conviction that revolution had been the result of an irresistible force rather than the outcome of specific deeds and events. What seems to be beyond doubt and belief is that no historian will ever be able to tell the tale of our century without stringing it 'on the thread of revolutions'; but this tale, since its end still lies hidden in the mists of the future, is not yet fit to be told.

The same, to an extent, is true for the particular aspect of revolution with which we now must concern ourselves. This aspect is the regular emergence, during the course of revolution, of a new form of government that resembled in an amazing fashion Jefferson's ward system and seemed to repeat, under no matter what circumstances, the revolutionary societies and municipal councils which had spread all over France after 1789. Among the reasons that recommended this aspect to our attention must first be mentioned that we deal here with the phenomenon that impressed most the two greatest revolutionists of the whole period, Marx and Lenin, when they were witnessing its spontaneous rise, the former during the Parisian Commune of 1871 and the latter in 1905, during the first Russian Revolution. What struck them was not only the fact that they themselves were entirely unprepared for these events, but also that they knew they were confronted with a repetition unaccounted for by any conscious imitation or even mere remembrance of the past. To be sure, they had hardly any knowledge of Jefferson's ward system, but they knew well enough the revolutionary role the sections of the first Parisian Commune had played in the French Revolution, except that they had never thought of them as possible germs for a new form of government but had regarded them as mere instruments to be dispensed with once the revolution came to an end. Now, however, they were confronted with popular organs – the communes, the councils, the *Räte*, the *soviets* – which clearly intended to survive the revolution. This contradicted all their theories and, even more importantly, was in flagrant conflict with those assumptions about the nature of power and violence which they shared, albeit unconsciously, with the rulers of the doomed or defunct regimes. Firmly anchored in the tradition of the nation-state, they conceived of revolution as a means to seize power, and they identified power with the monopoly of the means of violence. What actually happened, however, was a swift disintegration of the old power, the sudden loss of control over the means of violence, and, at the same time, the amazing formation of a new power structure which owed its existence to nothing but the organizational impulses of the people themselves. In other words, when the moment of revolution had come, it turned out that there was no power left to seize, so that the revolutionists found themselves before the rather uncomfortable alternative of either putting their own pre-revolutionary 'power', that is, the organization of the party apparatus, into the vacated power centre of the defunct government, or simply joining the new revolutionary power centres which had sprung up without their help.

For a brief moment, while he was the mere witness of something he never had expected, Marx understood that the *Kommunalverfassung* of the Parisian Commune in 1871, because it was supposed to become 'the political form of even the smallest village,' might well be 'the political form, finally discovered, for the economic liberation of labor.' But he soon became aware to what an extent this political form contradicted all notions of a 'dictatorship of the proletariat' by means of a socialist or communist party whose monopoly of power and violence was modelled upon the highly centralized governments of nation-states, and he concluded that the communal councils were, after all, only temporary organs of the revolution.[14] It is almost the same sequence of attitudes which, one generation later, we find in Lenin, who twice in his life, in 1905 and in 1917, came under the direct impact of the events themselves, that is to say, was temporarily liberated from the pernicious influence of a revolutionary ideology. Thus he could extol with great sincerity in 1905 'the revolutionary creativity of the people,' who spontaneously had begun to establish an entirely new power structure in the midst of revolution,[15] just as, twelve years later, he could let loose and win the October Revolution with the slogan: 'All power to the *soviets*.' But during the years that separated the two revolutions he had done nothing to reorient his thought and to incorporate the new organs into any of the many party programmes, with the result that the same spontaneous development in 1917 found him and his party no less unprepared than they had been in 1905. When, finally, during the Kronstadt rebellion, the *soviets* revolted against the party dictatorship and the incompatibility of the new councils with the party system became manifest, he decided almost at once to crush the councils, since they threatened the power monopoly of the Bolshevik party. The name 'Soviet Union' for post-revolutionary Russia has been a lie ever since, but this lie has also contained, ever since, the grudging admission of the overwhelming popularity, not of the Bolshevik party, but of the *soviet* system which the party reduced to impotence.[16] Put before the alternative of either adjusting their thoughts and deeds to the new and the unexpected or going to the extreme of tyranny and suppression, they hardly hesitated in their decision for the latter; with the exceptions of a few moments without consequence, their behaviour from beginning to end was dictated by considerations of party strife, which played no role in the councils but which indeed had been of paramount importance in the pre-revolutionary parliaments. When the Communists decided, in 1919, 'to espouse only the cause of a *soviet* republic in which the *soviets* possess a Communist majority',[17] they actually behaved like ordinary party politicians. So great is the fear of men, even of the most radical and least conventional among them, of things never seen, of thoughts never thought, of institutions never tried before.

The failure of the revolutionary tradition to give any serious thought to the only new form of government born out of revolution can partly be explained by Marx's obsession with the social question and his unwillingness to pay serious attention to questions of state and government. But this explanation is weak and, to an extent, even question-begging, because it takes for granted the overtowering influence of Marx on the revolutionary movement and tradition, an influence which itself still stands in need of explanation. It was, after all, not only the Marxists among the revolutionists who proved to be utterly unprepared for the actualities of revolutionary events. And this unpreparedness is all the more noteworthy as it surely cannot be blamed upon lack of thought or interest in revolution. It is well known that the French Revolution had given rise to an entirely new figure on the political scene, the professional revolutionist, and his life was spent not in revolutionary agitation, for which there existed but few opportunities, but in study and thought, in theory and debate, whose sole object was revolution. In fact, no history of the European leisure classes would be complete without a history of the professional revolutionists of the nineteenth and twentieth centuries, who, together with the modern artists and writers, have become the true heirs of the *hommes de lettres* in the seventeenth and eighteenth centuries. The artists and writers joined the revolutionists because 'the very word bourgeois came to have a hated significance no less aesthetic than political';[18] together they established Bohemia, that island of blessed leisure in the midst of the busy and overbusy century of the Industrial Revolution. Even among the members of this new leisure class, the professional revolutionist enjoyed special privileges since his way of life demanded no specific work whatsoever. If there was a thing he had no reason to complain of, it was lack of time to think, whereby it makes little difference if such an essentially theoretical way of life was spent in the famous libraries of London and Paris, or in the coffee houses of Vienna and Zurich, or in the relatively comfortable and undisturbed jails of the various *anciens régimes*.

The role the professional revolutionists played in all modern revolutions is great and significant enough, but it did not consist in the preparation of revolutions. They watched and analysed the progressing disintegration in state and society; they hardly did, or were in a position to do, much to advance and direct it. Even the wave of strikes that spread over Russia in 1905 and led into the first revolution was entirely spontaneous, unsupported by any political or trade-union organizations, which, on the contrary, sprang up only in the course of the revolution.[19] The outbreak of most revolutions has surprised the revolutionist groups and parties no less than all others, and there exists hardly a revolution whose outbreak could be blamed upon their activities. It usually was the other way round: revolution broke out and liberated, as it were, the professional revolutionists from wherever they happened to be – from jail, or from the coffee house, or from the library. Not even Lenin's party of professional revolutionists would ever have been able to 'make' a revolution; the best they could do was to be around, or to hurry home, at the right moment, that is, at the moment of collapse. Tocqueville's observation in 1848, that the monarchy fell 'before rather than beneath the blows of the victors, who were as astonished at their triumph as were the vanquished at their defeat', has been verified over and over again.

The part of the professional revolutionists usually consists not in making a revolution but in rising to power after it has broken out, and their great advantage in this power struggle lies less in their theories and mental or organizational preparation than in the simple fact that their names are the only ones which are publicly known.[20] It certainly is not conspiracy that causes revolution, and secret societies – though they may succeed in committing a few spectacular crimes, usually with the help of the secret police[21] – are as a rule much too secret to be able to make their voices heard in public. The loss of authority in the powers-that-be, which indeed precedes all revolutions, is actually a secret to no one, since its manifestations are open and tangible, though not neccessarily spectacular; but its symptoms, general dissatisfaction, widespread malaise, and contempt for those in power, are difficult to pin down since their meaning is never unequivocal.[22] Nevertheless, contempt, hardly among the motives of the typical professional revolutionist, is certainly one of the most potent springs of revolution; there has hardly been a revolution for which Lamartine's remark about 1848, 'the revolution of contempt', would be altogether inappropriate.

However, while the part played by the professional revolutionist in the outbreak of revolution has usually been insignificant to the point of non-existence, his influence upon the actual course a revolution will take has proved to be very great. And since he spent his apprenticeship in the school of past revolutions, he will invariably exert this influence not in favour of the new and the unexpected, but in favour of some action which remains in accordance with the past. Since it is his very task to assure the continuity of revolution, he will be inclined to argue in terms of historical precedents, and the conscious and pernicious imitation of past events, which we mentioned earlier, lies, partially at least, in the very nature of his profession. Long before the professional revolutionists had found in Marxism their official guide to the interpretation and annotation of all history, past, present and future, Tocqueville, in 1848, could already note: 'The imitation [i.e. of 1789 by the revolutionary Assembly] was so manifest that it concealed the terrible originality of the facts; I continually had the impression they were engaged in play-acting the French Revolution far more than continuing it.'[23] And again, during the Parisian Commune of 1871, on which Marx and Marxists had no influence whatsoever, at least one of the new magazines, *Le Père Duchêne*, adopted the old revolutionary calendar's names for the months of the year. It is strange indeed that in this atmosphere, where every incident of past revolutions was mulled over as though it were part of sacred history, the only entirely new and entirely spontaneous institution in revolutionary history should have been neglected to the point of oblivion.

Armed with the wisdom of hindsight, one is tempted to qualify this statement. There are certain paragraphs in the writings of the Utopian Socialists, especially in Proudhon and Bakunin, into which it has been relatively easy to read an awareness of the council system. Yet the truth is that these essentially anarchist political thinkers were singularly unequipped to deal with a phenomenon which demonstrated so clearly how a revolution did not end with the abolition of state and government but, on the contrary, aimed at the foundation of a new state and the establishment of a new form of government. More recently, historians have pointed to the rather obvious similarities between the councils and the medieval townships, the Swiss cantons, the English seventeeth-century 'agitators' – or rather 'adjustators', as they were originally called – and the General Council of Cromwell's army, but the point of the matter is that none of them, with the possible exception of the medieval town,[24] had ever the slightest influence on the minds of the people who in the course of a revolution spontaneously organized themselves in councils.

Hence, no tradition, either revolutionary or pre-revolutionary, can be called to account for the regular emergence and re-emergence of the council system ever since the French Revolution. If we leave aside the February Revolution of 1848 in Paris, where a *commission pour les travailleurs*, set up by the government itself, was almost exclusively concerned with questions of social legislation, the main dates of appearance of these organs of action and germs of a new state are the following: the year 1870, when the French capital under siege by the Prussian army 'spontaneously reorganized itself into a miniature federal body', which then formed the nucleus for the Parisian Commune government in the spring of 1871;[25] the year 1905, when the wave of spontaneous strikes in Russia suddenly developed a political leadership of its own, outside all revolutionary parties and groups, and the workers in the factories organized themselves into councils, *soviets*, for the purpose of representative self-government; the February Revolution of 1917 in Russia, when 'despite different political tendencies among the Russian workers, the organization itself, that is the *soviet*, was not even subject to discussion';[26] the years 1918 and 1919 in Germany, when, after the defeat of the army, soldiers and workers in open rebellion constituted themselves into *Arbeiter- und Soldatenräte*, demanding, in Berlin, that this *Rätesystem* become the foundation stone of the new German constitution, and establishing, together with the Bohemians of the coffee houses, in Munich in the spring of 1919, the short-lived Bavarian *Räterepublik*;[27] the last date, finally, is the autumn of 1956, when the Hungarian Revolution from its very beginning produced the council system anew in Budapest, from which it spread all over the country 'with incredible rapidity.'[28]

The mere enumeration of these dates suggests a continuity that in fact never existed. It is precisely the absence of continuity, tradition, and organized influence that makes the sameness of the phenomenon so very striking. Outstanding among the councils' common characteristics is, of course, the spontaneity of their coming into being, because it clearly and flagrantly contradicts the theoretical 'twentieth-century model of revolution – planned, prepared, and executed almost to cold scientific exactness by the professional revolutionaries.'[29] It is true that wherever the revolution was not defeated and not followed by some sort of restoration, the one-party dictatorship, that is, the model of the professional revolutionary, eventually prevailed, but it prevailed only after a violent struggle with the organs and institutions of the revolution itself. The councils, moreover, were always organs of order as much as organs of action, and it was indeed their aspiration to lay down the new order that brought them into conflict with the groups of professional revolutionaries, who wished to degrade them to mere executive organs of revolutionary activity. It is true enough that the members of the councils were not content to discuss and 'enlighten themselves' about measures that were taken by parties or assemblies; they consciously and explicitly desired the direct participation of every citizen in the public affairs of the country,[30] and as long as they lasted, there is no doubt that 'every individual found his own sphere of action and could behold, as it were, with his own eyes his own contribution to the events of the day.'[31] Witnesses of their functioning were often agreed on the extent to which the revolution had given birth to a 'direct regeneration of democracy', whereby the implication was that all such regenerations, alas, were foredoomed since, obviously, a direct handling of public business through the people was impossible under modern conditions. They looked upon the councils as though they were a romantic dream, some sort of fantastic utopia come true for a fleeting moment to show, as it were, the hopelessly romantic yearnings of the people, who apparently did not yet know the true facts of life. These realists took their own bearings from the party system, assuming as a matter of course that there existed no other alternative for representative government and forgetting conveniently that the downfall of the old regime had been due, among other things, precisely to this system.

For the remarkable thing about the councils was of course not only that they crossed all party lines, that members of the various parties sat in them together, but that such party membership played no role whatsoever. They were in fact the only political organs for people who belonged to no party. Hence, they invariably came into conflict with all assemblies, with the old parliaments as well as with the new 'constituent assemblies', for the simple reason that the latter, even in their most extreme wings, were still the children of the party system. At this stage of events, that is, in the midst of revolution, it was the party programmes more than anything else that separated the councils from the parties; for these programmes, no matter how revolutionary, were all 'ready-made formulas' which demanded not action but execution – 'to be carried out energetically in practice', as Rosa Luxemburg pointed out with such amazing clearsightedness about the issues at stake.[32] Today we know how quickly the theoretical formula disappeared in practical execution, but if the formula had survived its execution, and even if it had proved to be the panacea for all evils, social and political, the councils were bound to rebel against any such policy since the very cleavage between the party experts who 'knew' and the mass of the people who were supposed to apply this knowledge left out of account the average citizen's capacity to act and to form his own opinion. The councils, in other words, were bound to become superfluous if the spirit of the revolutionary party prevailed. Wherever knowing and doing have parted company, the space of freedom is lost.

The councils, obviously, were spaces of freedom. As such, they invariably refused to regard themselves as temporary organs of revolution and, on the contrary, made all attempts at establishing themselves as permanent organs of government. Far from wishing to make the revolution permanent, their explicitly expressed goal was 'to lay the foundations of a republic acclaimed in all its consequences, the only government which will close forever the era of invasions and civil wars'; no paradise on earth, no classless society, no dream of socialist or communist fraternity, but the establishment of 'the true Republic' was the 'reward' hoped for as the end of the struggle.[33] And what had been true in Paris in 1871 remained true for Russia in 1905, when the 'not merely destructive but constructive' intentions of the first *soviets* were so manifest that contemporary witnesses 'could sense the emergence and the formation of a force which one day might be able to effect the transformation of the State.'[34]

It was nothing more or less than this hope for a transformation of the state, for a new form of government that would permit every member of the modern egalitarian society to become a 'participator' in public affairs, that was buried in the disasters of twentieth-century revolutions. Their causes were manifold and, of course, varied from country to country, but the forces of what is commonly called reaction and counter-revolution are not prominent among them. Recalling the record of revolution in our century, it is the weakness rather than the strength of these forces which is impressive, the frequency of their defeat, the ease of revolution, and – last, not least – the extraordinary instability and lack of authority of most European governments restored after the downfall of Hitler's Europe. At any rate, the role played by the professional revolutionaries and the revolutionary parties in these disasters was important enough, and in our context it is the decisive one. Without Lenin's slogan, 'All power to the *soviets*', there would never have been an October Revolution in Russia, but whether or not Lenin was sincere in proclaiming the Soviet Republic, the fact of the matter was even then that his slogan was in conspicuous contradiction to the openly proclaimed revolutionary goals of the Bolshevik party to 'seize power', that is, to replace the state machinery with the party apparatus. Had Lenin really wanted to give all power to the *soviets*, he would have condemned the Bolshevik party to the same impotence which now is the outstanding characteristic of the Soviet parliament, whose party and non-party deputies are nominated by the party and, in the absence of any rival list, are not even chosen, but only acclaimed by the voters. But while the conflict between party and councils was greatly sharpened because of a conflicting claim to be the only 'true' representative of the Revolution and the people, the issue at stake is of a much more far-reaching significance.

What the councils challenged was the party system as such, in all its forms, and this conflict was emphasized whenever the councils, born of revolution, turned against the party or parties whose sole aim had always been the revolution. Seen from the vanguard point of a true Soviet Republic, the Bolshevik party was merely more dangerous but no less reactionary than all the other parties of the defunct regime. As far as the form of government is concerned – and the councils everywhere, in contradistinction to the revolutionary parties, were infinitely more interested in the political than in the social aspect of revolution[35] – the one-party dictatorship is only the last stage in the development of the nation-state in general and of the multi-party system in particular. This may sound like a truism in the midst of the twentieth century when the multi-party democracies in Europe have declined to the point where in every French or Italian election 'the very foundations of the state and the nature of the regime' are at stake.[36] It is therefore enlightening to see that in principle the same conflict existed even in 1871, during the Parisian Commune, when Odysse Barrot formulated with rare precision the chief difference in terms of French history between the new form of government, aimed at the Commune, and the old regime which soon was to be restored in a different, non-monarchical disguise:

> En tant que révolution sociale, 1871 procède directement de 1793, qu'il continue et qu'il doit achever . . . En tant que révolution politique, au contraire, 1871 est réaction contre 1793 et un retour à 1789. . . . *Il a effacé du programme les mots 'une et indivisible'* et rejetté l'idée autoritaire qui est une idée toute monarchique . . . *pour se rallier à l'idée fédérative, qui est par excellence l'idée libérale et républicaine*[37] (my italics).

These words are surprising because they were written at a time when there existed hardly any evidence – at any rate not for people unacquainted with the course of the American Revolution – about the intimate connection between the spirit of revolution and the principle of federation. In order to prove what Odysse Barrot felt to be true, we must turn to the February Revolution of 1917 in Russia and to the Hungarian Revolution of 1956, both of which lasted just long enough to show in bare outlines what a government would look like and how a republic was likely to function if they were founded upon the principles of the council system. In both instances councils or *soviets* had sprung up everywhere, completely independent of one another, workers', soldiers', and peasants' councils in the case of Russia, the most disparate kinds of councils in the case of Hungary: neighbourhood councils that emerged in all residential districts, so-called revolutionary councils that grew out of fighting together in the streets, councils of writers and artists, born in the coffee houses of Budapest, students' and youths' councils at the universities, workers' councils in the factories, councils in the army, among the civil servants, and so on. The formation of a council in each of these disparate groups turned a more or less accidental proximity into a political institution. The most striking aspect of these spontaneous developments is that in both instances it took these independent and highly disparate organs no more than a few weeks, in the case of Russia, or a few days, in the case of Hungary, to begin a process of co-ordination and integration through the formation of higher councils of a regional or provincial character, from which finally the delegates to an assembly representing the whole country could be chosen.[38] As in the case of the early covenants, 'cosociations', and confederations in the colonial history of North America, we see here how the federal principle, the principle of league and alliance among separate units, arises out of the elementary conditions of action itself, uninfluenced by any theoretical speculations about the possibilities of republican government in large territories and not even threatened into coherence by a common enemy. The common object was the foundation of a new body politic, a new type of republican government which would rest on 'elementary republics' in such a way that its own central power did not deprive the constituent bodies of their original power to constitute. The councils, in other words, jealous of their capacity to act and to form opinion, were bound to discover the divisibility of power as well as its most important consequence, the necessary separation of powers in government . . .

Freedom, wherever it existed as a tangible reality, has always been spatially limited. This is especially clear for the greatest and most elementary of all negative liberties, the freedom of movement; the borders of national territory or the walls of the city-state comprehended and protected a space in which men could move freely. Treaties and international guarantees provide an extension of this territorially bound freedom for citizens outside their own country, but even under these modern conditions the elementary coincidence of freedom and a limited space remains manifest. What is true for freedom of movement is, to a large extent, valid for freedom in general. Freedom in a positive sense is possible only among equals, and equality itself is by no means a universally valid principle but, again, applicable only with limitations and even within spatial limits. If we equate these spaces of freedom – which, following the gist, though not the terminology, of John Adams, we could also call spaces of appearances – with the political realm itself, we shall be inclined to think of them as islands in a sea or as oases in a desert. This image, I believe, is suggested to us not merely by the consistency of a metaphor but by the record of history as well.

The phenomenon I am concerned with here is usually called the 'élite', and my quarrel with this term is not that I doubt that the political way of life has never been and will never be the way of life of the many, even though political business, by definition, concerns more than the many, namely strictly speaking, the sum total of all citizens. Political passions – courage, the pursuit of public happiness, the taste of public freedom, an ambition that strives for excellence regardless not only of social status and administrative office but even of achievement and congratulation – are perhaps not as rare as we are inclined to think, living in a society which has perverted all virtues into social values; but they certainly are out of the ordinary under all circumstances. My quarrel with the 'élite' is that the term implies an oligarchic form of government, the domination of the many by the rule of a few. From this, one can only conclude – as indeed our whole tradition of political thought has concluded – that the essence of politics is rulership and that the dominant political passion is the passion to rule or to govern. This, I propose, is profoundly untrue. The fact that political 'élites' have always determined the political destinies of the many and have, in most instances, exerted a domination over them, indicates, on the one hand, the bitter need of the few to protect themselves against the many, or rather to protect the island of freedom they have come to inhabit against the surrounding sea of necessity; and it indicates, on the other hand, the responsibility that falls automatically upon those who care for the fate of those who do not. But neither this need nor this responsibility touches upon the essence, the very substance of their lives, which is freedom; both are incidental and secondary with respect to what actually goes on within the limited space of the island itself. Put into terms of present-day institutions, it would be in parliament and in congress, where he moves among his peers, that the political life of a member of representative government is actualized, no matter how much of his time may be spent in campaigning, in trying to get the vote and in listening to the voter. The point of the matter is not merely the obvious phoniness of his dialogue in modern party government, where the voter can only consent or refuse to ratify a choice which (with the exception of the American primaries) is made without him, and it does not even concern conspicuous abuses such as the introduction into politics of Madison Avenue methods, through which the relationship between representative and elector is transformed into that of seller and buyer. Even if there is communication between representative and voter, between the nation and parliament – and the existence of such communication marks the outstanding difference between the governments of the British and the Americans, on one side, and those of Western Europe, on the other – this communication is never between equals but between those who aspire to govern and those who consent to be governed. It is indeed in the very nature of the party system to replace 'the formula "government of the people by the people" by this formula: "government of the people *by an élite sprung from the people*" '.[39]

It has been said that 'the deepest significance of political parties' must be seen in their providing 'the necessary framework enabling the masses to recruit from among themselves their own élites',[40] and it is true enough that it was primarily the parties which opened political careers to members of the lower classes. No doubt the party as the outstanding institution of democratic government corresponds to one of the major trends of the modern age, the constantly and universally increasing equalization of society; but this by no means implies that it corresponds to the deepest significance of revolution in the modern age as well. The 'élite sprung from the people' has replaced the pre-modern élites of birth and wealth; it has nowhere enabled the people *qua* people to make their entrance into political life and to become participators in public affairs. The relationship between a ruling élite and the people, between the few, who among themselves constitute a public space, and the many, who spend their lives outside it and in obscurity, has remained unchanged. From the viewpoint of revolution and the survival of the revolutionary spirit, the trouble does not lie in the factual rise of a new élite; it is not the revolutionary spirit but the democratic mentality of an egalitarian society that tends to deny the obvious inability and conspicuous lack of interest of large parts of the population in political matters as such. The trouble lies in the lack of public spaces to which the people at large would have entrance and from which an élite could be selected, or rather, where it could select itself. The trouble, in other words, is that politics has become a profession and a career, and that the 'élite' therefore is being chosen according to standards and criteria which are themselves profoundly unpolitical. It is in the nature of all party systems that the authentically political talents can assert themselves only in rare cases, and it is even rarer that the specifically political qualifications survive the petty manoeuvres of party politics with its demands for plain salesmanship. Of course the men who sat in the councils were also an élite, they were even the only political élite, of the people and sprung from the people, the modern world has ever seen, but they were not nominated from above and not supported from below. With respect to the elementary councils that sprung up wherever people lived or worked together, one is tempted to say that they had selected themselves; those who organized themselves were those who cared and those who took the initiative; they were the political élite of the people brought into the open by the revolution. From these 'elementary republics', the councilmen then chose their deputies for the next higher council, and these deputies, again, were selected by their peers, they were not subject to any pressure either from above or from below. Their title rested on nothing but the confidence of their equals, and this equality was not natural but political, it was nothing they had been born with; it was the equality of those who had committed themselves to, and now were engaged in, a joint enterprise. Once elected and sent into the next higher council, the deputy found himself again among his peers, for the deputies on any given level in this system were those who had received a special trust. No doubt this form of government, if fully developed, would have assumed again the shape of a pyramid, which, of course, is the shape of an essentially authoritarian government. But while, in all authoritarian government we know of, authority is filtered down from above, in this case authority would have been generated neither at the top nor at the bottom, but on each of the pyramid's layers; and this obviously could constitute the solution to one of the most serious problems of all modern politics, which is not how to reconcile freedom and equality but how to reconcile equality and authority.

(To avoid misunderstanding: The principles for the selection of the best as suggested in the council system, the principle of self-selection in the grass-roots political organs, and the principle of personal trust in their development into a federal form of government are not universally valid; they are applicable only within the political realm. The cultural, literary, and artistic, the scientific and professional and even the social élites of a country are subject to very different criteria among which the criterion of equality is conspicuously absent. But so is the principle of authority. The rank of a poet, for instance, is decided neither by a vote of confidence of his fellow poets nor by fiat coming from the recognized master, but, on the contrary, by those who only love poetry and are incapable of ever writing a line. The rank of a scientist, on the other hand, is indeed determined by his fellow scientists, but not on the basis of highly personal qualities and qualifications; the criteria in this instance are objective and beyond argument or persuasion. Social élites, finally, at least in an egalitarian society where neither birth nor wealth count, come into being through processes of discrimination.)

It would be tempting to spin out further the potentialities of the councils, but it certainly is wiser to say with Jefferson, 'Begin them only for a single purpose; they will soon show for what others they are the best instruments' – the best instruments, for example, for breaking up the modern mass society, with its dangerous tendency toward the formation of pseudo-political mass movements, or rather, the best, the most natural way for interspersing it at the grass roots with an 'élite' that is chosen by no one but constitutes itself. The joys of public happiness and the responsibilities for public business would then become the share of those few from all walks of life who have a taste for public freedom and cannot be 'happy' without it. Politically, they are the best, and it is the task of good government and the sign of a well-ordered republic to assure them of their rightful place in the public realm. To be sure, such an 'aristocratic' form of government would spell the end of general suffrage as we understand it today; for only those who as voluntary members of an 'elementary republic' have demonstrated that they care for more than their private happiness and are concerned about the state of the world would have the right to be heard in the conduct of the business of the republic. However, this exclusion from politics should not be derogatory, since a political élite is by no means identical with a social or cultural or professional élite. The exclusion, moreover, would not depend upon an outside body; if those who belong are self-chosen, those who do not belong are self-excluded. And such self-exclusion, far from being arbitrary discrimination, would in fact give substance and reality to one of the most important negative liberties we have enjoyed since the end of the ancient world, namely, freedom from politics, which was unknown to Rome or Athens and which is politically perhaps the most relevant part of our Christian heritage.

This, and probably much more, was lost when the spirit of revolution – a new spirit and the spirit of beginning something new – failed to find its appropriate institution. There is nothing that could compensate for this failure or prevent it from becoming final, except memory and recollection. And since the storehouse of memory is kept and watched over by the poets, whose business it is to find and make the words we live by, it may be wise to turn in conclusion to two of them (one modern, the other ancient) in order to find an approximate articulation of the actual content of our lost treasure. The modern poet is René Char, perhaps the most articulate of the many French writers and artists who joined the Resistance during the Second World War. His book of aphorisms was written during the last year of the war in a frankly apprehensive anticipation of liberation; for he knew that as far as they were concerned, there would be not only the welcome liberation from German occupation but liberation from the 'burden' of public business as well. Back they would have to go to the *épaisseur triste* of their private lives and pursuits, to the 'sterile depression' of the pre-war years, when it was as though a curse hung over everything they did: 'If I survive, I know that I shall have to break with the aroma of these essential years, silently reject (not repress) my treasure.' The treasure, he thought, was that he had '*found* himself', that he no longer suspected himself of 'insincerity', that he needed no mask and no make-believe to appear, that wherever he went he appeared as he was to others and to himself, that he could afford 'to go naked'.[41] These reflections are significant enough as they testify to the involuntary self-disclosure, to the joys of appearing in word and deed without equivocation and without self-reflection that are inherent in action. And yet they are perhaps too 'modern', too self-centred to hit in pure precision the centre of that 'inheritance which was left to us by no testament'.

Sophocles in *Oedipus at Colonus*, the play of his old age, wrote the famous and frightening lines:

Μὴ Φῦναι τὸν ἅπαντα νι-
κᾷ λόγον. τὸ δ' ἐπεὶ Φανῇ,
βῆναι κεῖσ' ὁπόθεν περ ἥ-
κει πολὺ δεύτερον ὡς τάχιστα.

'Not to be born prevails over all meaning·uttered in words; by far the second-best for life, once it has appeared, is to go as swiftly as possible whence it came.' There he also let us know, through the mouth of Theseus, the legendary founder of Athens and hence her spokesman, what it was that enabled ordinary men, young and old, to bear life's burden: it was the polis, the space of men's free deeds and living words, which could endow life with splendour – τὸν βίον λαμπρὸν ποιεῖσθαι.

NOTES

[1] In the letter to John Cartwright, 5 June 1824.

[2] This quotation is from a slightly earlier period when Jefferson proposed to divide the counties 'into hundreds'. (See letter to John Tyler, 26 May 1810.) Clearly, the wards he had in mind were to consist of about a hundred men.

[3] Letter to Cartwright, quoted previously.

[4] Ibid.

[5] Letter to Samuel Kercheval, 12 July 1816.

[6] The citations are drawn from the letters just quoted.

[7] Letter to Samuel Kercheval, 5 Sept. 1816.

[8] Letter to Thomas Jefferson Smith, 21 Feb. 1825.

[9] Letter to Cartwright, quoted previously.

[10] Letter to John Tyler, quote previously.

[11] The citations are drawn from the letter to Joseph C. Cabell of 2 Feb. 1816, and from the two letters to Samuel Kercheval already quoted.

[12] George Soule, *The Coming American revolution*, New York, 1934, p. 53.

[13] For Tocqueville, see author's Introduction to *Democracy in America*; for Marx, *Die Klassenkämpfe in Frankreich, 1840–1850* (1850), Berlin, 1951, p. 124.

[14] In 1871 Marx called the Commune *die endlich entdeckte politische Form, unter der die ökonomische Befreiung der Arbeit sich vollziehen könnte*, and called this its 'true secret'. (See *Der Bürgerkrieg in Frankreich* (1871), Berlin, 1952, pp. 71, 76.) Only two years later, however, he wrote: 'Die Arbeiter müssen ... auf die entschiedenste Zentralisation der Gewalt in die Hände der Staatsmacht hinwirken. Sie dürfen sich durch das demokratische Gerede von Freiheit der Gemeinden, von Selbstregierung usw, nicht irre machen lassen' (in *Enthüllungen über den Kommunistenprozess zu Köln* (Sozialdemokratische Bibliothek Bd. IV), Hattingen Zürich, 1885, p. 81). Hence, Oskar Anweiler, to whose important study of the council system, *Die Rätebewegung in Russland 1905–1921*, Leiden, 1958, I am much indebted, is quite right when he maintains: 'Die revolutionären Gemeinderäte sind für Marx nichts weiter als zeitweilige politische Kampforgane, die die Revolution vorwärtstreiben sollen, er sieht in ihnen nicht die Keimzellen für eine grundlegende Umgestaltung der Gesellschaft, die vielmehr von oben, durch die proletarische zentralistische Staatsgewalt, erfolgen soll' (p. 19).

[15] I am following Anweiler, p. 101.

[16] The enormous popularity of the councils in all twentieth-century revolutions is sufficiently well known. During the German revolution of 1918 and 1919, even the Conservative party had to come to terms with the *Räte* in its election campaigns.

17 In the words of Leviné, a prominent professional revolutionist, during the revolution in Bavaria: 'Die Kommunisten treten nur für eine Räterepublik ein, in der die Räte eine kommunistische Mehrheit haben.' See Helmut Neubauer, 'München und Moskau 1918–1919: Zur Geschichte der Rätebewegung in Bayern', *Jahrbücher für Geschichte Osteuropas*, Beiheft 4, 1958.

18 See the excellent study of *The Paris Commune of 1871*, London, 1937, by Frank Jellinek, p. 27.

19 See Anweiler, *Die Rätebewegung*, p. 45.

20 Maurice Duverger – whose book on *Political Parties. Their Organization and Activity in the Modern State* (French edition, 1951), New York, 1961, supersedes and by far excels all former studies on the subject – mentions an interesting example. At the elections to the National Assembly in 1871, the suffrage in France had become free, but since there existed no parties the new voters tended to vote for the only candidates they knew at all, with the result that the new republic became the 'Republic of Dukes.'

21 The record of the secret police in fostering rather than preventing revolutionary activities is especially striking in France during the Second Empire and in Tsarist Russia after 1880. It seems, for example, that there was not a single anti-government action under Louis Napoleon which had not been inspired by the police; and the more important terrorist attacks in Russia prior to war and revolution seem all to have been police jobs.

22 Thus, the conspicuous unrest in the Second Empire, for instance, was easily contradicted by the overwhelmingly favourable outcome of Napoleon III's plebiscites, these predecessors of our public-opinion polls. The last of these, in 1869, was again a great victory for the Emperor; what nobody noticed at the time and what turned out to be decisive a year later was that nearly 15 per cent of the armed forces had voted against the Emperor.

23 Quoted from Jellinek, *The Paris Commune*, p. 194.

24 One of the official pronouncements of the Parisian Commune stressed this relation as follows: 'C'est cette idée communale poursuivie depuis le douzième siècle, affirmée par la morale, le droit et la science qui vient de triompher le 18 mars 1871.' See Heinrich Koechlin, *Die Pariser Commune von 1871 im Bewusstsein ihrer Anhänger*, Basel, 1950, p. 66.

25 Jellinek, *The Paris Commune*, p. 71.

26 Anweiler, *Die Rätebewegung*, p. 127, quotes this sentence by Trotsky.

27 For the latter, see Helmut Neubauer, 'München und Moskau'.

28 See Oskar Anweiler, 'Die Räte in der ungarischen Revolution', in *Osteuropa*, vol. VIII, 1958.

29 Sigmund Neumann, 'The Structure and Strategy of Revolution: 1848 and 1948', in *The Journal of Politics*, Aug. 1949.

30 Anweiler, *Die Rätebewegung*, p. 6, enumerates the following general characteristics: '(1) Die Gebundenheit an eine bestimmte abhängige oder unterdrückte soziale Schicht, (2) die radikale Demokratie als Form,

(3) die revolutionäre Art der Entstehung', and then comes to the
conclusion: 'Die diesen Räten zugrundeliegende Tendenz, die man als
'Rätegedanken' bezeichnen kann, ist das Streben nach einer möglichst
unmittelbaren, weitgehenden und unbeschränkten Teilnahme des Ein-
zelnen am öffentlichen Leben . . .'

31 In the words of the Austrian socialist Max Adler, in the pamphlet
Demokratie und Rätesystem, Wien, 1919. The booklet, written in the
midst of the revolution, is of some interest because Adler, although he
saw quite clearly why the councils were so immensely popular,
nevertheless immediately went on to repeat the old Marxist formula
according to which the councils could not be anything more than merely
'eine revolutionäre Uebergangsform', at best, 'eine neue Kampfform des
sozialistischen Klassenkampfes'.

32 Rosa Luxemburg's pamphlet on *The Russian Revolution*, translated by
Bertram D. Wolfe, 1940, from which I quote, was written more than
four decades ago. Its criticism of the 'Lenin-Trotsky theory of dictatorship' has lost nothing of its pertinence and actuality. To be sure, she
could not foresee the horrors of Stalin's totalitarian regime, but her
prophetic words of warning against the suppression of political freedom
and with it of public life read today like a realistic description of the
Soviet Union under Khrushchev: 'Without general elections, without
unrestricted freedom of press and assembly, without a free struggle of
opinion, life dies out in every public institution, becomes a mere
semblance of life, in which only the bureaucracy remains the active
element. Public life gradually falls asleep, a few dozen party leaders of
inexhaustible energy and boundless experience direct and rule. Among
them, in reality only a dozen outstanding heads do the leading and an
élite of the working class is invited from time to time to . . . applaud the
speeches of the leaders, and to approve proposed resolutions unani-
mously — at bottom, then, a clique affair. . . .'

33 See Jellinek, *The Paris Commune*, pp. 129 ff.

34 See Anweiler, *Die Rätebewegung* p. 110.

35 It is quite characteristic that in its justification of the dissolution of the
workers' councils in December 1956, the Hungarian government
complained: 'The members of the workers' council at Budapest wanted
to concern themselves exclusively with political matters.' See Oskar
Anweiler's article quoted previously.

36 Thus Duverger, *Political Parties*, p. 419.

37 Quoted from Heinrich Koechlin, *Die Pariser Commune*, p. 224.

38 For details of this process in Russia, see Anweiler's book, *Die
Rätebewegung*, pp. 155–8, and also the same author's article on
Hungary.

39 Duverger, *Political Parties*, p. 425.

40 Ibid., p. 426.

41 René Char, *Feuillets d'Hypnos*, Paris, 1946. For the English translation,
see *Hypnos Waking: Poems and Prose*, New York, 1956.

Index

POLS 2120

DATE DUE

7